Growing in the Prophetic is a ~~viduals~~ and congregations who d ~~ministry.~~ Through Mike Bickle's of knowledge and experience, many will find encouragement to exercise the spiritual gift of prophecy in balance and power.

—Francis Frangipane
Pastor and Author

Mike's journey in the Lord has been quite amazing. In the beginning, he was a young conservative, anti-charismatic, evangelical pastor. Now he is an intimate, passionate worshiper, moving in the supernatural and leading others into a powerful place in the Spirit.

He has moved a million miles in his heart and experience of God. It is this authenticity that stands out in the man. He is not afraid to explore, to quest, and to pioneer. This book is a journey into the territory of prophecy, the prophetic ministry, and the role of prophets.

Developing prophetic people is not easy. Pastoring a prophetic community is not for the fainthearted. Cultivating a safe place of relational accountability for prophets is a tough job. Only a leader who has been led into divine encounters with the Lord can undertake such a transitional process.

Mike's book is real, pragmatic, and rich in experience and wisdom. To love the gift of prophecy as a church is a good thing. To develop a prophetic community who can hear and act on the voice of the Lord is an altogether different proposition. *Growing in the Prophetic* is an important book to read and study. It will teach you transitional process. That alone is worth the investment.

I loved the initial book of this same title. If Mike has found a way to upgrade and expand its wisdom, then I am definitely first in line to read it!

—Graham Cooke
Brilliant Book House

Gentle but firm. Compassionate yet incisive. Abounding in under-standing.

—Colin Dye
Senior Pastor, Kensington Temple
London, England

Mike Bickle's practical wisdom will serve the body of Christ well.

—Terry Virgo
Leader of Pioneer International
London, England

A man of transparent integrity shows us the way forward into areas where angels have feared to tread.

—R. T. Kendall
Author, *Total Forgiveness*

Mike Bickle is a man with a remarkable teaching gift, quick to acknowledge past mistakes that he has clearly learned from. This is a book every charismatic should read if we are going to increase our ability to hear from God, speak to Him, and remain committed to Christ, to Scripture, and to one another.

—Gerald Coates
Leader of Pioneer International
London, England

At a time when the Spirit is speaking strongly to the churches about the gift of prophecy and the office of prophet, *Growing in the Prophetic* is an extremely important book. Mike Bickle brings an enviable combination of maturity and transparency to his exposition of biblical principles molding the prophetic along with valuable lessons learned, both positive and negative, through his ministry to the "Kansas City prophets."

—C. Peter Wagner
Professor of Church Growth
Fuller Theological Seminary, Pasadena, California

GROWING
IN THE
PROPHETIC

MIKE
BICKLE

CHARISMA
HOUSE

Most CHARISMA HOUSE BOOK GROUP products are available at special quantity discounts for bulk purchase for sales promotions, premiums, fundraising, and educational needs. For details, write Charisma House Book Group, 600 Rinehart Road, Lake Mary, Florida 32746, or telephone (407) 333-0600.

GROWING IN THE PROPHETIC by Mike Bickle
Published by Charisma House
Charisma Media/Charisma House Book Group
600 Rinehart Road
Lake Mary, FL 32746
www.charismahouse.com

Design Director: Bill Johnson
Cover design by Jerry Pomales

Library of Congress Cataloging-in-Publication Data

Bickle, Mike.
  Growing in the prophetic / Mike Bickle.
     p. cm.
  Includes bibliographical references.
  ISBN 978-1-59979-312-2
  1. Prophecy--Christianity. I. Title.

  BR115.P8B53 2008
  234'.13--dc22

2008030850

E-Book ISBN: 978-159979-989-6

This publication is translated in Spanish under the title *Creciendo en el ministerio profético*, copyright © 1998 by Mike Bickle, published by Casa Creación, a Charisma Media company. All rights reserved.

11 12 13 14 15 — 11 10 9 8 7
Printed in the United States of America

CONTENTS

PREFACE

W HY ANOTHER BOOK on the prophetic ministry? I've read many books on the prophetic over the years. Some focus on the various biblical categories of prophets and the supernatural manifestations that occur through them. Others focus on how to prophesy and then what to do with prophetic words.

This book touches on those subjects, but it also frankly discusses the joy and the pain of prophetic people in a local church context. I relate the perils, perplexities, and tensions involved in nurturing prophetic people among nonprophetic people. When Holy Spirit activity happens among weak people like us, the clash between selfish ambition and lack of wisdom is inevitable. Many tensions arise. Plus, we encounter Holy Spirit experiences that are foreign to us. All this makes for a challenging experience in our church life.

I pastored in a local church context for twenty-three years until I began the International House of Prayer missions base in Kansas City in 1999. On September 19, 1999, we began a ministry of worship with intercession that continues nonstop, twenty-four hours a day. Our staff members view themselves as "intercessory missionaries" because they do the work of the ministry and outreach from a place of night and day prayer. Our staff raises their own financial support as missionaries in a way similar to other mission organizations like Youth With A Mission and Campus Crusade for Christ. Currently, God has graciously joined about fifteen hundred people to us full-time. About five hundred people are our ministry staff, and another one thousand serve full-time as students or interns. They each are involved about fifty hours a week.

In addition to these, approximately two thousand people join with us in our Sunday celebration services. Thus, about four thousand people make up what I refer to as the "IHOP Missions Base family." We cry out daily for the release of the spirit of prophetic wisdom and revelation from Ephesians 1:17. The Lord has given us glorious answers. Many have had prophetic dreams, visions, and supernatural experiences.

We have hundreds of people actively involved on our prophetic teams. These teams give prophetic words to thousands of people each year. It is important from the start of this book to say that we only receive prophetic experiences that glorify Jesus, honor the Scriptures, and promote holiness and love for one another. This is the safeguard for subjective prophetic experiences.

My journey in pastoring prophetic people began suddenly, in the spring of 1983. I admit that I have made many mistakes in this journey, but I have learned some valuable lessons. I will share some of what I have learned in the last twenty-five years of being deeply involved with prophetic people and movements.

The future of the church is sure to be filled with people who operate in the prophetic anointing. In the generation in which the Lord returns, the whole church will receive dreams, visions, and prophetic experiences (Acts 2:17–21). This will be exciting as well as challenging. New dimensions of the Holy Spirit's ministry will certainly emerge that will demand faithfulness to the Scriptures as well as deep humility as learners (1 Cor. 3:18). This is not a good time in history for a "know-it-all," but rather it's the proper time for the virtue of humility expressed in a teachable spirit as we go to greater depths in the prophetic.

CHAPTER 1

"THERE'S BEEN A TERRIBLE MISTAKE"

J OHN WIMBER HAD set it all up. It was July 1989 when four thousand
people gathered to a prophetic conference hosted by the Vineyard Christian Fellowship in Anaheim, California.

John had spoken a couple of times at the conference, then introduced me
and others who were going to bring messages on the prophetic ministry.
I taught on the nurturing and administration of the prophetic ministry in
the local church and offered some practical advice on how to encourage
people who were just beginning to receive prophetic impressions, visions,
and dreams. I told stories about how we had experienced God's use of
dreams, visions, angels, and His audible voice to accomplish His purposes
in our church life. I shared a few stories about how God confirmed some
of these prophetic revelations with signs in nature—comets, earthquakes,
droughts, and floods occurring at precisely predicted times.

I guess I should have been clearer about the fact that seldom do any of
these supernatural experiences ever happen through me directly. I had been
mostly a spectator of the prophetic ministry and, initially, a reluctant one at
that. Yes, I was the pastor of a church that had about ten people who traveled full-time with a focus on prophetic ministry, but I had only had a few
prophetic experiences myself. Mostly, I told what happened in their experiences, not mine.

In my early days of ministry in the middle 1970s, I was a conservative evangelical doing youth ministry, hoping one day to attend Dallas Theological Seminary. I was anti-charismatic and proud of it. However, by 1983, I found myself surrounded by a group of unusual people whom some referred to as prophets. I had no experience with the prophetic ministry; however, I became the leader of these ten to fifteen prophetic people. "Why me, Lord?" I asked many times in the years that followed.

The Vineyard conference where I spoke in July 1989 was mainly attended by conservative evangelical church leaders who had been blessed by John Wimber's teaching on healing, but who for the most part had not been exposed to prophetic ministry. They represented a rapidly growing number of believers in Jesus who have a great longing to hear more directly from God in a supernatural and personal way.

I had finished my morning session and was leading the ministry time when John Wimber came up on the platform and whispered in my ear, "Would you pray and ask the Holy Spirit to release the gift of prophecy to people?"

For those of you who have had the privilege of being around John Wimber before his death in November 1997, you know that there was not an ounce of hype or showmanship in him. He would invite the Holy Spirit to move over an audience and touch thousands of people in the same tone of voice that he gave the announcements. It was in that matter-of-fact way that he asked me to pray for the people to receive what I had just been describing.

With four thousand spiritually hungry people watching us, I whispered back to John, "Can I do that since I'm not prophetically gifted myself?"

John responded, "Just go ahead and pray for the release, and let the Lord touch whomever He touches."

"Why am *I* praying for these people?" I thought. I looked around for help from one of the well-known prophetic ministers who were also speaking at the conference. They should have been the ones praying for the people to receive more grace for prophetic ministry. None of them were in the auditorium at that moment, so I was obviously on my own.

"Well, OK, John, if you want me to," I said. It would be a harmless prayer.

John announced that I was going to ask the Holy Spirit to release the gift of prophecy in people's lives. So I prayed. I noticed one of the leaders from my church in Kansas City, at the back of the conference auditorium, pointing at me and quietly laughing. He knew I was not a prophet, and he also knew that I was in deep waters over my head in leading this ministry time that was "supposed" to release the prophetic anointing to others.

As soon as the meeting was over, a long line of people formed, anxiously waiting to talk with me. Some wanted me to pray personally for the prophetic gift to be imparted to them. Others wanted me to give them a "word from the Lord," that is, to prophesy what God wanted to say about them and His plan for their lives.

I had recently introduced prophetic ministers to the conference, those who for years had operated in prophetic ministry in ways that had amazed me. However, some attending the conference had mistakenly determined that I was an anointed prophet and certainly the man to see if they wanted the prophetic gift released in them.

Over and over I explained to the people lined up to see me, "No, I don't have a word for you. No, I can't impart prophetic gifts. No, I'm not prophetically gifted."

I looked around for John but could not find him. After spending some time explaining this individually to about twenty-five people in the line, I stood up on the stage and made an announcement on the microphone: *"There's been a terrible mistake!* I am not a prophet. I don't have a prophetic ministry. I do not have any prophetic words to give you!" Then I left the meeting.

Richard Foster, author of *Celebration of Discipline*, had been waiting for me to finish praying for people so that we could go to lunch. Heading for the car, I was stopped by several people in the parking lot who wanted me to prophesy to them. Of course, I had no prophetic words for them either.

Finally, we made our escape and found a restaurant about ten miles from the meeting place. But to my surprise, while I was standing at the salad bar with a plate of food in my hand, I was asked by two different people who were attending the conference to prophesy to them. I wished that I had made it clearer during my session that I was not a prophet, nor was I the son of a prophet.

Those either excited or desperate to hear from God are seldom restrained and polite. I was getting impatient and exasperated with people's persistence. The fact that I was with Richard Foster, whom I had wanted to meet for a long time, increased my irritation. It was also a bit embarrassing. Richard laughed when I said to him, "I'm not a prophetic person! A terrible mistake has been made today."

Yet, the stir that day was insignificant compared to the uproar that was to come a few years later related to the prophetic ministry that I was related to. It seemed to me that God had picked the wrong man to pastor a team of prophetic people.

A RELUCTANT INTRODUCTION TO PROPHETIC MINISTRY

Many people know about God only in the context of things far away and long ago. They are hungry to know that God is involved with their lives in an intimate way in the present. When that knowledge is dramatically awakened for the first time, people often overreact for a short season and often become overly zealous. There is a great hunger in God's people to hear directly from Him in a supernatural way. I see this hunger increasing even more as the years go by.

Many people involved with prophetic ministries have been brought into it kicking and screaming because they had been taught that the gift of prophecy had passed away. A good example of this is my close friend Dr. Jack Deere. He was formerly a professor at Dallas Theological Seminary and a committed cessationist before he met John Wimber and experienced the demonstrations of God's power. (A cessationist believes the supernatural gifts of the Holy Spirit ceased after the Book of Acts.) He also went through a difficult, soul-searching journey as he came to embrace the prophetic ministry. Being a brilliant Bible teacher, he had to make sure that it all was 100 percent scriptural.

We value seeing ministry of the gifts of the Holy Spirit operate in relation to the written Word of God. This is a nonnegotiable aspect of the IHOP Missions Base quest to grow in the prophetic. Eight leaders of our missions base have master's degrees, plus another four have doctorates—mostly from conservative evangelical, non-charismatic seminaries. Another five men earned law degrees before joining our missions base staff. The personality profiles of these men and women are usually in strong contrast to those who are focused on flowing in prophetic ministry, but the diversity is essential. We all need each other.

The Lord has helped us to establish an academically challenging, full-time Bible school called the Forerunner School of Ministry. The scholarly types and the prophetic ministers teach side by side as one ministry team. It is essential to combine the gifts of the Spirit with a responsible scholarship in the Scriptures.

Like many people in the IHOP Missions Base family, most of these seminary-educated staff members are not highly prophetic. They are pastors and teachers who have felt a strong calling to be a part of a ministry that embraces, among other things, the prophetic ministry.

It may surprise you that many of the leaders in our midst with prophetic giftings were actually raised up in a church that was not pursuing the spiritual gifts.

So many times God's calling cuts directly across the grain of our natural strengths and previous doctrinal training. God wants to integrate strong evangelical training in the Scriptures with supernatural manifestations of the Holy Spirit. It is common for God to call people to something for which they are not naturally acclimated. For example, Peter, the uneducated fisherman, was called as an apostle to the educated Jews. Paul, the self-righteous Pharisee, was called as an apostle to the pagan Gentiles.

I started off as a skeptic when I was first encountered the prophetic ministry. No one would have ever suspected from my early religious training and affiliations that I would ever have become involved in a prophetic ministry. God must have a sense of humor.

BECOMING ANTI-CHARISMATIC

In February 1972, at the age of sixteen, I was touched by the Holy Spirit's power. At an Assembly of God church in Kansas City named Evangel Temple, the Holy Spirit seemed to engulf me, and I spoke in tongues for the first time. Before that experience, I had never heard of the gift of tongues. I had no idea what had happened to me. I asked the people who prayed for me to help me understand what happened. They said I spoke in tongues. I asked, "What is that?" They told me to read 1 Corinthians 14 and then to come back to the next meeting to learn more about it.

Though I had a powerful encounter with God, I was immediately convinced by my Presbyterian youth leaders that the experience was a demonic counterfeit. I concluded that I had been deceived and thus considered my experience of speaking in tongues as a counterfeit experience. Immediately, I renounced it and committed to resist anything charismatic. I reasoned that anything that seemed so real could deceive other unsuspecting people unless they were warned. So, I set out to warn other "innocent" believers to beware of "counterfeit" experiences such as speaking in tongues.

For the next five years it became my personal mission to debunk charismatic theology and rescue from deception those who also had been led astray by "counterfeit" experiences.

I didn't like charismatic people any more than I liked charismatic theology. The ones I had met seemed to boast of *having it all*. I felt they were arrogant as well as spiritually shallow. In my estimation, they were lacking in many things, especially in passion for the Scriptures and personal holiness. As a young Christian, I was a committed student of evangelical greats, absorbing myself in the writings of J. I. Packer, John Stott, Jonathan Edwards, Dr. Martyn Lloyd-Jones, A. W. Tozer, and others like them. I took my zeal for evangelical orthodoxy and my crusade against supernatural gifts of the Spirit with me everywhere I ministered God's Word when I spoke at various college campus ministries throughout the Midwest. My goal was to get charismatics to denounce their experiences as being unscriptural counterfeits.

ANOTHER TERRIBLE MISTAKE

In April 1976, at the age of twenty, I was invited to a small rural town to give a sermon for a little Lutheran home group of twenty-five people. The small town was Rosebud, Missouri, and was a one-hour drive from St. Louis. The home group attendees were searching for a pastor to start a new church for them. I did not know that they were involved in the Charismatic Renewal that was sweeping through the Lutheran church at that time. I accepted their invitation and taught on the baptism of the Holy Spirit from an anti-charismatic position. This was a sermon that I had taught many times on college campuses. I took it from John Stott's little book on the baptism of the Holy Spirit. I wanted to make it clear to this home group that I didn't want anything to do with charismatic heresies.

Though these people obviously loved Jesus, they were not aware of all the theological arguments against tongues. Thus, the doctrinal implications of my anti-charismatic sermon went right over their heads. Most of them had only recently become involved in the Lutheran charismatic movement.

The couple who provided the main leadership to this home group were "experienced charismatics." They were out of town the weekend I spoke. When they got back, they heard that the young preacher named Mike Bickle had spoken on the "baptism of the Spirit." Well, that was good enough for them, so they hired me to be their pastor. They assumed I was in agreement with their *charismatic* theology because of the report that I spoke on the baptism of the Holy Spirit. Ironically, I assumed they all understood from that sermon that I was *anti-charismatic*. I was totally unsuspecting of what would happen in the following months as I was getting accustomed to my new role as pastor. The leading couple asked me to extend the altar call for salvation to also offer prayer for people to speak in tongues. "I don't believe in speaking in tongues," I quickly answered. It then became clear that they did not know when hiring me that I was anti-charismatic. I groaned, "Oh, there's been a terrible mistake!"

"I'm the pastor of a charismatic church!" I grimaced to myself. I wanted to immediately resign this little country church. I couldn't believe it. How could I have gotten myself into this mess? In retrospect, there was no doubt that God Himself got me into it. However, I had grown to really like these people. I trusted their genuineness, their love for the Scriptures, and their commitment to evangelism. How could such lovers of Jesus be deceived charismatics?

My experience with this church was God's way of breaking down some of my prejudices against charismatics. Because of the godliness and humility of the people in this small country church, I actually enjoyed relating to charismatics even though I was convinced they were theologically in error. Mike Bickle was now tolerating charismatics. That was OK for now because I had already made plans to move to Mexico to live as a missionary. I thought to myself, "I can endure anything for a short season." So I did not resign the church.

AMBUSHED BY GOD

A few months later, I encountered the first public prophetic word that was aimed at me; of course, I didn't believe it. This preacher called me out and said, "Young man at the back of the room, God's going to shift you from where you are, and you will begin to regularly teach hundreds of young adults—immediately."

"Not me," I thought to myself. I was not going to remain in America to run a youth ministry. I had already made arrangements to join a missionary organization in Mexico City. I set my heart on spending my life in Mexico and South America. I rejected this prophetic word and said to myself, "This cannot be." Then the preacher continued to prophesy by saying, "Even though you say in your heart this very moment, 'This cannot be,' God will do it immediately." People were clapping. I just wanted to get out of there.

The very next week I drove an hour to visit a friend in St. Louis and accidentally met the pastor of the largest charismatic church in the region. It has several thousand members. He looked at me and said, "I know we are strangers, but I have an unusual request for you. The Lord just spoke to me and said that you are supposed to teach our Saturday night service where over one thousand young adults gather each week." Before I could think about it, I heard myself say yes. I was shocked that I had so quickly agreed to teach in a charismatic church. It seemed like a compromise to accept this invitation. I was embarrassed. What would my friends think? They were also anti-charismatic.

I reluctantly went to the service, and after I finished teaching, the pastor came to the platform to end the service and asked if the young people wanted me to come back the next week. They applauded, so under the pressure of the moment, I agreed to be the speaker the next week. The same thing happened the following Saturday night. They were so receptive to me that I began to conclude that I was being sent there by God to change their wrong theology. I agreed to teach there for the next twelve Saturday nights in a row.

The next month, on my wedding day, the elders of my little country church had a private meeting with the pastor of this large charismatic church during the wedding reception. They agreed that I should be the next youth pastor at this large church. Without ever consulting me, they simply made this announcement at the end of the wedding reception. I was so excited to be married to Diane, that I simply responded, "Great, I'll work anywhere!"

During our honeymoon, I realized I was the youth pastor of a large charismatic church—I couldn't believe I did it. I asked myself, "How could I let this happen? This is a terrible mistake." It seemed I was constantly being ambushed by God to do things I had prejudices against.

My reluctant journey into the gifts of the Spirit was just beginning. The prophecy that I received from the Full Gospel Businessmen's Fellowship preacher saying that I would immediately begin to regularly teach hundreds of young people had been fulfilled within two months. I was now the youth pastor of this large church in St. Louis. However, I still didn't believe in the gift of tongues or the gift of prophecy, so I could have never imagined what would happen in the years ahead when I moved to Kansas City. Little did I realize that I, a conservative evangelical, was about to get involved with spiritual gifts, particularly the gift of prophecy, on a level that seemed very unusual, even to many charismatics.

In the spring of 1979, the leadership of this large church asked me to plant a new church on the other side of St. Louis as a part of their vision to reach out to the city. So, in September 1979, I planted a new church. The church was growing, and my wife, Diane, and I assumed that we would serve there for many years. I gave up the idea of being a missionary to Mexico. That God had a different plan for us wasn't so strange, but it was the way He communicated this plan to us that challenged my faith.

THE NEXT STEP OF FAITH

In June 1982, three years after the new church was founded in St. Louis, I met a man who claimed to have had prophetic encounters with God. His name was Augustine, and he had a traveling prophetic ministry before he died in August 1996. His prophecies helped me conclude that I was to move to Kansas City to plant a new church. Soon after I moved, I met Bob Jones in March 1983 in Kansas City. These men both talked about unusual experiences that included audible voices, angelic visitations, Technicolor visions, and signs in the heavens, to name a few of the more spectacular ones.

Some of their prophetic experiences had major implications for the direction of my ministry. If God was so interested in getting my attention, why didn't He just give me my own vision? Of course, I didn't have much faith in the validity of such experiences. By this time, I had accepted the idea of God healing the sick, but I wasn't prepared for prophetic experiences.

At first these men's claims seemed to be the stuff of vivid but misguided imaginations rather than genuine revelations from God. But soon, the Holy Spirit confirmed their genuineness. At the same time, my most trusted friends and co-workers also began believing these were true prophecies. Though all of this ran contrary to my long-term reservations about this kind of thing, I decided to take a step of faith and allow for the prophetic ministry in our church.

From 1983 to 1985, my experiences with prophetic ministry brought great blessing to the new church that I planted in Kansas City. Yes, if not handled properly, it can cause much confusion and division. Yes, I made many mistakes in my early days in administrating the prophetic ministry in this new church.

Initially, there were five to six people with prophetic ministries whom the Lord gathered to our young church within its first couple years. Then, after that, another seven to eight prophetic ministries joined us as well. We were in for very interesting times. I could never have imagined the dramatic unfolding of events that were to come. Stay with me as I tell you more.

CHAPTER 2

CONFIRMING PROPHECIES THROUGH THE ACTS OF GOD IN NATURE

THE CONFIRMATION OF prophetic words by the acts of God in nature is not a common topic in the church today. But undoubtedly in the End Times, signs in the heavens as well as the very forces of nature on Earth will serve as a dramatic testimony both to the church and to unbelievers.

In Kansas City, we have seen these kinds of things happen only a few times, and we know of a few instances in other ministries. It is, however, our assumption that the church in other parts of the world might be experiencing more of this than the Western church is.

When the prophetic ministry flourishes, it is often confirmed by signs and wonders. In his sermon on the Day of Pentecost, Peter quoted the Joel 2 promise for a last-days' revival. Of course, the last days began with the cross, the Resurrection, and the outpouring of the Holy Spirit on the Day of Pentecost. However, the complete fulfillment of the Joel 2 promises will be in the final decades of the last days—those years just prior to the second coming of Jesus, which I refer to as the "End Times."

The first half of the passage in Acts 2 speaks of the outpouring of the Spirit and the increase of prophetic revelation on the entire body of Christ:

And it shall come to pass in the last days, says God,
That I will pour out of My Spirit on all flesh;
Your sons and your daughters shall prophesy;
Your young men shall see visions,
Your old men shall dream dreams.
And on My menservants and on My maidservants
I will pour out My Spirit in those days;
And they shall prophesy.

—Acts 2:17–18

The second half of the passage focuses on the great increase of the acts of God in nature:

I will show wonders in heaven above
And signs in the earth beneath:
Blood and fire and vapor of smoke.
The sun shall be turned into darkness,
And the moon into blood,
Before the coming of the great and awesome day of the LORD.
And it shall come to pass
That whoever calls on the name of the LORD
Shall be saved.

—Acts 2:19–21

There is a specific order and sequence in the text: the outpouring of the Spirit, followed by the increase of prophetic dreams and visions, followed by the occurring of confirming signs in the sky and on the earth. We have witnessed a few supernatural confirmations in nature of significant prophetic words.

We believe that what we have seen is only a small token of what will happen in a far more dramatic way in many ministries throughout the nations. The End Times will be accompanied by a multiplication of all four elements of the Joel 2 prophecy:

1. The outpouring of the Spirit

2. Prophetic dreams and visions

3. Signs and wonders on Earth and in the heavens

4. A wholehearted calling out to Jesus—first for salvation, second for deliverance from calamity, and finally in wholeheartedness and extravagant love for God (Matt. 22:37)

This chapter is intended to encourage you about God's glory being released in an unprecedented way in the days to come. In the End Times, there will be a significant increase of prophetic visions and dreams with confirming signs and wonders in nature. These prophetic events will not take place simply within the confines of a few *prophetic-type* churches but before the eyes of all mankind—believers and unbelievers alike.

As we ponder the meaning of our own prophetic experiences, we conclude that there are several reasons the Lord gives confirmations of prophecies by supernatural acts of God in nature. The closer we get to the Lord's return, the more we will need to understand how to administrate prophetic revelations that are confirmed by an act of God in nature. Thus, one aim of this chapter is to share the few things that we have learned about this.

THE UNEXPECTED SNOWFALL

Augustine, the preacher whom God used prophetically in my move from St. Louis to Kansas City in 1982, warned me of a false prophet who would be present in the early days of our new church plant in Kansas City.

On March 7, 1983, not long after our arrival in Kansas City, an unusual man named Bob Jones came to my office and introduced himself to me. I was at first skeptical about him and thought he was the false prophet I had been warned about by Augustine. However, to my consternation, in my first meeting with Bob, he also warned me of a false prophet who would be in the midst of our new church plant. I wondered to myself, "Could Bob Jones be this false prophet himself and still give me a warning about a false prophet?" This thought was enough to keep me in turmoil for several days!

It seemed odd to me that Bob was wearing a winter coat that day. This was strange because the winter snow was long gone, and the temperature had been in the fifties, sixties, and seventies for the previous week or so in Kansas City. Why was he wearing a heavy winter coat?

In this first meeting, Bob prophesied that God was going to raise up worldwide a young adult prayer movement led by prophetic singers and musicians in Kansas City. During this meeting, he told me that the Lord would confirm this prophecy with a sign in nature; he said that it would be a sign that we would see in the sky as an unusual weather pattern (Acts 2:19). More specifically, he told me that on the first day of spring, an unexpected snow would come, and at that time he would sit around a table with me as I accepted his prophetic ministry. I didn't take the prophecy seriously since I assumed Bob was the false prophet I had been warned about by Augustine. I dismissed the matter, thinking that anyone who prophesied his own acceptance had to be a false prophet. I left perplexed by this odd man was who was wearing a heavy winter coat on a warm day.

Several weeks later, a well-known preacher named Art Katz was visiting our Sunday morning church service. I had heard of Art but had never met him. After the service, I saw Bob Jones talking privately with him. I expected Art to reject Bob as I had done. Instead, when I came up to greet him, the first thing he said was, "Mike, this man Bob Jones is a prophet of God. He just told me the secrets of my heart!" Art's testimony about Bob surprised me.

Art had intended to fly out Sunday after the church service, but his small private plane was grounded due to a sudden change in the weather. About 9:00 p.m. that night, Art insisted on seeing Bob again. We met at my house from 10:00 p.m. until 3:00 a.m. It was a very unusual and emotional evening. I was overwhelmed by the private things that God revealed to Bob about my personal life. In the emotion of the moment, I blurted out, "Bob, I believe you are a prophet." Bob smiled as he reminded me that on March 7, he prophesied that I would accept him on the first day of spring as the snow melted. I then realized that it was March 21, the first day of spring, and the snow that had come unexpectedly was melting that very moment. As we sat around the table, I had just accepted Bob Jones with my own mouth. All of it happened just as Bob had prophesied that it would two weeks earlier on March 7.

The unexpected snow on March 21 was precisely predicted by Bob to confirm the prophetic vision that God was raising up a prophetic young adult prayer movement of prophetic singers and musicians in Kansas City. The prediction of unexpected snow coming exactly on March 21, after several weeks of unseasonably warm weather[1] was a small yet significant sign in the heavens or sky that confirmed Bob's prophecy to us.

Incidentally, soon after my first meeting with Bob Jones, I met with one of the pastors of the church that Bob had attended for several years. I asked him what kind of man Bob Jones really was. This pastor told me that Bob was a godly man with a proven prophetic ministry that bore much good fruit. He also told me Bob had prophesied that a group of young people would come to south Kansas City in the spring of 1983 who would be used by God in a coming revival. Thus, the pastor blessed Bob's decision to join our new church.

THE UNEXPECTED COMET

Several weeks had passed since the snow incident on March 21. We continued to meet every night at 7:00 p.m. to pray for revival. It was at the Wednesday evening prayer meeting, on April 13, 1983, that I had another unusual prophetic experience with God. This was the second time that I had heard what I refer to as the "internal audible voice" of God through which the Holy Spirit spoke to me with unmistakable clarity. He told me to call believers from Kansas City to twenty-one days of fasting and prayer for revival (Dan. 10:3). The story of the angel Gabriel appearing to Daniel to reveal God's purpose in the End Times was emphasized to me (Dan. 9:20–27).

I had reservations about this. How was I, a new young pastor in the city, going to call the city to prayer and fasting? Who would listen to me? The other pastors would think I was full of pride to presume such a thing! The next morning, I called Bob Jones. It was only a month ago when I had first received his prophetic ministry. I had not needed his help until this day.

Over the telephone I explained, "Bob, last night I received a very unusual word from the Lord. I need prophetic confirmation of it. Can you help?" In his calm drawl Bob replied, "Yeah, I know all about it. God already told me what He told you last night."

This seemed a little bizarre to me, but strange and unusual things were becoming more common. How could Bob Jones already know what God had spoken to me last night? I immediately drove to his house with a couple of guys. On the way, I explained to them that God had spoken to me about calling a twenty-one-day fast for revival. The Scripture passage God spoke to me through was Daniel 9, in which the angel Gabriel spoke to Daniel about God's End Time purposes (Dan. 9:24, 27; 10:3).

Before we proceed, I want to define how I use two terms: "last days" and "End Times." The last days began on the Day of Pentecost and will continue through to the second coming of Jesus. I use the term "the End Times" to refer to the final decades of the last days. I also use "End Times" synonymous with "generation in which the Lord returns."

Getting back to the story, I arrived at Bob's house anxious to see if he had received the same message from God that I had received the night before. If I ever needed a prophetic word confirmed, it was then. I put Bob to the test by asking him to tell me what God had revealed to me. With a big smile on his face, he told us that the previous night in a dream the angel Gabriel had spoken to him about Daniel 9. We sat there in awe, listening as he told us the implications of what Gabriel said. Bob knew that, in this, God was calling us to gather to pray for revival according to Joel 2:12–17. He told us that there would be an unpredicted comet coming across the heavens that would confirm this sacred assembly of fasting and prayer for twenty-one days, which was to begin on May 7. I wondered where this new prophetic journey would lead us.

Three weeks later, on May 7, 1983, the day our twenty-one-day fast began, the newspaper reported:

> Scientists will have a rare chance next week to study a recently discovered comet that is coming within the extremely close range of 3 million miles.... Dr. Gerry Neugebauer, principal U.S. investigator on the international Infrared Astronomical Satellite Project (IRAS) said, "... It was sheer good luck we happened to be looking where the comet was passing."[2]

God had given me a prophetic revelation to call for twenty-one days of fasting and prayer for revival in Kansas City and America. He told Bob Jones that He would confirm this with an unexpected comet as a sign in the heavens on May 7. The newspaper testified to this on the very day that the fast began. Seven hundred people gathered together on the first evening of the fast. We were full of faith and excitement. We had no idea that things were going to turn out very different from what we were expecting.

It Shall Not Rain

May 28, 1983, the last day of the twenty-one days of fasting, had finally come. Bob Jones shocked us all when he stood up to give a most disappointing prophetic word. He said that God was going to withhold the revival on Kansas City and America that He promised because it was not yet His perfect timing to release it. He explained that currently there was a spiritual drought over America and that God had appointed a precise day that He would interrupt it by pouring out the rain of His Spirit on the nation.

He continued by prophesying that God would confirm this disappointing prophetic word by sending a natural drought for three months to Kansas City that would be interrupted by rain on the day of His choosing. Bob prophesied that we would see the rain come precisely on August 23, 1983. We all agreed that it was very bold to prophesy in front of hundreds of people the exact day that it would rain three months in advance. Bob explained that God was going to speak to us prophetically through the weather in Kansas City through the summer of 1983. In other words, as surely as the natural drought in Kansas City would be interrupted by natural rain precisely on the day of God's choosing (August 23), so also the spiritual drought in America would be interrupted by the rain of the Holy Spirit on precisely the day of God's choosing sometime in the future. We were stunned, confused, and even somewhat angry at this prophetic word. We had high expectations for the release of revival in Kansas City and America immediately, not at some "strategic date" far in the future.

Although prophesying that involves the withholding of rain is unusual, it is certainly not without biblical precedent. Elijah prophesied to King Ahab: "As the LORD God of Israel lives, before whom I stand, there shall not be dew nor rain these years, except at my word" (1 Kings 17:1).

How were we to respond to such an unexpected and even offensive prophetic word? We were to understand that God gave us these supernatural confirmations so we would have assurance that would help us sustain faithfulness in prayer while we were waiting on His precise timing for the full release of revival.

The three-month drought in Kansas City began near the end of June. Through July and the first three weeks of August there was almost no rain.

The credibility of Bob Jones's prophetic ministry in the eyes of the thousand people who participated in the twenty-one-day fast was on the line.

August 23 had finally come. At noon that day, I talked to one of the intercessors and said that it didn't look like rain was coming that day. He replied, "You better hope it rains, or you'll have to leave town." I was definitely feeling the pressure.

Our church gathered the evening of August 23 to cry out for rain. Just as the church service was preparing to begin, there came a downpour of rain. Everyone was shouting and praising God. God had supernaturally confirmed the validity of the twenty-one-day solemn assembly of prayer and fasting (May 7–28). We now knew that the spiritual drought over America was sure to break and revival would come on God's appointed day. We were all exuberant.

In a more personal way, we had no idea we were also laboring in prayer for the future birthing of the IHOP Missions Base, which would not start for another sixteen years.

I want to note that the drought continued the next day and lasted another five weeks—three months in all, as prophesied, with the exception of the notable rain on August 23 that interrupted it. In a one-hundred-year period, it was one of the driest summers on record in Kansas City.

CONVINCING POWER, IRREFUTABLE TRUTH

The purpose of the outpouring of the Spirit, the increase of the prophetic ministry, and, finally, the signs and wonders in nature is to awaken the church to passionate Christianity and to bring many people to salvation. The Joel 2 prophecy quoted by Peter makes this point by saying, "It shall come to pass that whoever calls on the name of the LORD shall be saved" (Acts 2:21).

Calling on the name of the Lord refers to unbelievers calling on His name for salvation, but it also includes believers wholeheartedly calling on the name of Jesus in their passion for God and in persistent intercession. Thus, the confirmation of prophetic words by acts of God in nature is meant to help us stay consistent in our faith and prayer.

Supernatural confirmation by acts of God in nature strengthens our faith as it provides irrefutable proof of the specific direction that God is speaking to us. This brings us great encouragement and perseverance so we do not lose heart in the time of waiting or even suffering.

Signs and wonders in nature are not to be taken lightly. They are not given for trivial reasons. Don't expect God to show a sign in the heavens concerning which car you are supposed to buy. He does not move stars or send earthquakes to entertain us or stir up our curiosity. The measure of His power in confirming a prophetic word is proportional to the significance of the purpose of the prophetic message being confirmed. God will display unprecedented signs and wonders in nature in the End Times because they will confirm the great ingathering of souls leading to the second coming of Jesus.

God has used many different ministries over the years to prophesy and intercede concerning the great revival that is coming to America and other nations. No ministry or denomination is more significant to God than the others. The comet on May 7 and the rain on August 23 were *not* merely to verify something in Kansas City. They had a much bigger purpose than that. It was to confirm God's plans to many others that He was surely going to visit our nation with full-scale revival.

The Book of Revelation gives insight into the signs in the heavens and on the earth that will confirm and announce God's End Times purposes. Compare the events that occur when the Lamb opens the sixth seal to the signs prophesied in Joel 2:28–32:

> I looked when He opened the sixth seal, and behold, there was a great earthquake; and the sun became black as sackcloth of hair, and the moon became like blood. And the stars of heaven fell to the earth, as a fig tree drops its late figs when it is shaken by a mighty wind. Then the sky receded as a scroll when it is rolled up, and every mountain and island was moved out of its place.
>
> —Revelation 6:12–14

In Revelation 11, John records seeing two witnesses and says of them:

> And I will give power to my two witnesses, and they will prophesy one thousand two hundred and sixty days in sackcloth. . . . These have power to shut heaven, so that no rain falls in the days of

their prophecy; and they have power over waters to turn them to blood, and to strike the earth with all plagues, as often as they desire.

—Revelation 11:3, 6

As we approach the End Times, there will be a great increase of the prophecies confirmed by the acts of God in nature. The greatest prophecy and the greatest sign that will ever be seen in the heavens is the last one—the actual appearing of Jesus.

Immediately after the tribulation of those days the sun will be darkened, and the moon will not give its light; the stars will fall from the heaven, and the powers of the heavens will be shaken. Then the sign of the Son of Man will appear in heaven, and then all the tribes of the earth will mourn, and they will see the Son of Man coming on the clouds of heaven with power and great glory.

—Matthew 24:29–30

PROPHETIC REVELATION AND TESTING

It is important to note the connection between the abundance of prophetic revelation and a higher degree of testing that goes with it. Paul's thorn in the flesh was given to keep him from exalting himself in light of the great prophetic revelations that he received.

And lest I should be exalted above measure *by the abundance of the revelations*, a thorn in the flesh was given to me, a messenger of Satan to buffet me, lest I be exalted above measure.

—2 Corinthians 12:7, emphasis added

Note that his thorn was given *because of* abundant prophetic revelation. My good friend Francis Frangipane says, "New levels bring new devils." In other words, new levels of power and revelation attract new devils in spiritual warfare to get us to back down from the higher purposes of God.

On the other hand, God also gives powerful revelation *because of* the difficulty that is yet to come. For example, Paul received a vision instructing him to take his missionary efforts into Macedonia (Acts 16:6–10). That decision resulted in Paul and Silas being severely beaten with rods and thrown into prison. The strength of their initial prophetic direction to go to Macedonia is what kept strengthening them with the knowledge that God was with them in their difficulty (Acts 16:22–24).

This "revelation-before-testing" principle is repeated many times in the Scriptures. For example, see the miracles of the Exodus before the wilderness testing, Joseph's dreams before being sold into slavery, David's supernatural military victories along with Samuel's prophetic words before the wilderness temptations in which David was pursued by jealous King Saul, and so on. Powerful prophetic revelations stabilize us for future difficulties.

In other words, prophetic revelation sometimes causes difficulty, and other times it prepares us to endure it. In the End Times, the awesome signs and wonders in the heavens and on Earth prophesied in Acts 2:17–21 will be much greater than anything ever before seen in history.

LEARNING FROM MISTAKES

At our church, many stood in amazement at the natural confirmations—the comet, the snow, and the drought. However, some put too much honor and attention on the prophets of the Lord instead of the Lord of the prophets and unfortunately got somewhat out of balance in the midst of the amazing prophetic activity that was occurring. No matter how great the power is that the Holy Spirit releases through a prophet, we are to focus our hearts and attention first on loving, worshiping, and obeying Jesus.

Our pride and lack of balance caused us to endure some painful but necessary corrections in the early 1990s. The Lord is jealous for His people. He will not allow us to exalt ourselves or to make weak prophets the focus of His kingdom. The Lord disciplined us for our pride and errors as well as allowed us to see great failures in the lives of some of those used most in the prophetic ministry in Kansas City. This caused us much pain and disappointment as our enemies mocked us for receiving from weak and fallen prophetic men. We learned to not put our trust in prophetic people but rather in the prophetic leadership of the Holy Spirit.

Some people may respond to this admission of our errors by saying, "Aha! That's the reason we shouldn't get involved in the prophetic. It will only get us off balance and get our eyes off Jesus." I argued with the Lord more than once, telling Him of the perils of embracing the prophetic ministry. I was tempted like many others to just back away from prophets. It seemed that things would be easier without all the difficulty that comes with the prophetic ministry. I have fully repented of such wrong thinking and am more resolved than ever to receive any prophetic ministry that the Lord would send me. I want all that He will give us, regardless how weak the prophetic vessels are or how immature the response of the people is to their ministry. I am resolved to embrace the Holy Spirit's ministry through prophetic people regardless of what it costs. I have made several conclusions.

First, I have reminded God many times that my involvement in prophetic ministry was never my idea. I have said, "God, You got me into this; now You must give me the direction and defend my reputation as I embrace prophetic ministry!" We must not expect the Lord to lead the church in a way so that nothing risky or troubling happens. A ministry that resists the prophetic dynamic of the Holy Spirit will inevitably end up in a spiritual rut that could have been avoided.

Second, the outpouring of the Spirit, the prophetic ministry, and the signs and wonders in nature are clearly a part of God's agenda for the End Times. God has ordained that the church needs the input of the prophetic ministry to stay properly encouraged and focused as well as to minimize unbelief that plagues so many ministries today. What we have experienced in Kansas City is only a drop in the bucket compared to the magnitude and the frequency of the prophetic ministry that is coming to the church worldwide. This will become more obvious as the Lord's return draws closer.

Third, one reason we must embrace the prophetic is simply because the Scripture teaches us to: "Pursue love, and desire spiritual gifts, but especially that you may prophesy" (1 Cor. 14:1); "Desire earnestly to prophesy" (1 Cor. 14:39); and "Do not despise prophecies" (1 Thess. 5:20). It is easy to despise prophecies, but we are commanded not to.

CHAPTER 3

PROPHETIC ADMINISTRATION: REVELATION, INTERPRETATION, AND APPLICATION

ANY ARE VERY excited about the prospect of receiving prophetic revelation from God. As glorious as it is to receive information from God, it is only the beginning of the process of what I refer to as administrating the prophetic ministry. I learned, the hard way, that failure to do this is what leads many who are initially zealous for the prophetic ministry to conclude that it is just too much work to mess with. I felt this way for a while. However, now I understand that, if I apply what the Bible teaches about providing pastor leadership in the process of administrating the prophetic ministry, the benefits far outweigh the difficulties. This is a threefold process that involves wisdom, understanding, and knowledge. There is great value when these three virtues work together in God's house.

> Through wisdom a house is built, and by understanding it is established; by knowledge the rooms are filled with all precious and pleasant riches.
>
> —Proverbs 24:3–4

Administrating prophecy or providing biblical leadership to this process involves three distinct things: revelation (knowledge), interpretation (understanding), and application (wisdom). First, we must receive the revelation or the divine information. Second, we must interpret it accurately. Third, we must apply it with wisdom. The interpretation answers the question, What does the revelation mean? The application answers the questions, When and how will this come to pass? and What should I do? Application is the action that should be taken based on the interpretation of the divine information that was received.

The gift of leadership or of "administrations" in the prophetic messengers is like a vital organ in the body of charismatic gifts (1 Cor. 12:28). In fact, the main purpose of Paul's writings of 1 Corinthians 12–14 had to do with necessity of leadership in walking out the tension of exercising and/or restraining charismatic activity in the Corinthian church. We desire to both encourage and nurture the prophetic as well as properly judge and restrain it so that maximum edification of the churches will result. Paul said, "Since you are zealous of spiritual gifts, seek to abound for the edification of the church" (1 Cor. 14:12, NAS).

Do not be confident that you have administrated prophecy until all three components have been properly unitized. The Lord often uses different people to accomplish this process. Do not be confident that you have administrated prophecy well until all three components have been discerned with wisdom. Also, the Lord will often use three different people to put these parts together. The challenge that I have faced most over the years is not the result of prophetic people receiving incorrect information. In most cases, the information they received was from the Lord and, therefore, was right. The problems begin when we interpret and apply the information incorrectly.

RECEIVING DIVINE INFORMATION

We use the term *revelation* to refer to the prophetic information that one receives from God. The Holy Spirit can give us the prophetic information in many different ways, including by prophetic impressions, dreams, open vision, mental visions, the audible voice of God, trances, experiences in the third heaven, and so forth. Prophetic information about a person or situation does not automatically come with the wisdom or power to bring a change to that person or situation. The release of God's power is often a separate operation of the Spirit. For instance, someone may prophetically discern an illness through a word of knowledge and yet not have the anointing to release the healing that the sick person needs. Rather, they may simply supply the knowledge that God knows and cares about the condition, thus inspiring faith in others to receive.

INTERPRETING DIVINE INFORMATION

The interpretation of prophetic information refers to properly understanding it. We must gain God's perspective on the revelatory information before it becomes most beneficial to us. Even with accurate revelation, it is common for people to wrongly interpret it. There are often symbolic and mysterious elements to prophetic visions and dreams. God told Aaron and Miriam that when He speaks prophetically, He usually does so by a vision or dream that has symbolic or dark sayings.

> Hear now My words: If there is a prophet among you, I, the LORD, make Myself known to him in a vision; I speak to him in a dream. Not so with My servant Moses....I speak with him face to face, even plainly, and not in dark sayings.
>
> —Numbers 12:6–8

There are often symbolic and mysterious elements to visions, dreams, spoken words, and so on. Revelation often comes in bits and pieces, and we also need understanding from the Lord to "make sense" of the revelation. Paul states in the context of supernatural knowledge and prophecy that we prophesy in part (1 Cor. 13:9).

Jesus often spoke in parables to hide truth so that only those hungry for God would gain understanding. He said, "I speak to them in parables, because seeing they do not see, and hearing they do not hear, nor do they understand" (Matt. 13:13).

In the same way, the Holy Spirit often speaks to us prophetically in dreams and visions using parables. Only those who are desperate to know God's heart will understand what He is saying.

Therefore, it is important that we be cautious and not overly confident and dogmatic in giving or receiving prophecy. Often we do not, and are not supposed to, fully understand the revelation until the circumstances unfold that actually bring its fulfillment. God purposely gives the information in a dark saying or parable. We must resist the temptation to manufacture the interpretation before it is clear. If we don't, we are setting ourselves up for disaster.

Many times the ones who are best at receiving a revelation seem worst at interpreting it. We cannot mold a true revelation around the interpretation we prefer. Revelation often comes in bits and pieces, and thus, we need to have enough humility and patience to know when more understanding is needed before we proceed.

When it comes to the fulfillment of a prophecy, we encourage people to have an attitude of "open expectancy."

In light of this, it is important for us to be cautious about being overly confident and dogmatic in the ministering of prophecy. Often we do not, and are not supposed to, understand the revelation until the circumstances unfold that actually bring its fulfillment. This helps us to know how to make a godly response to those circumstances when they are at hand.

The grace to receive revelation is not the same as the grace to discern the interpretation. We have people who interpret prophetic revelation with much greater clarity than the people who receive the revelation. The other distinct grace from God is the ability to apply what has been interpreted. We have a council of prophetic people who are regularly involved with this.

I have seen seasoned prophetic ministers receive words from the Lord that predicted events with great accuracy. Nevertheless, they rarely know when or how the events will actually take place.

Bob Jones has an amazing gift of prophecy, but he says that he tends to miss it on interpretation and application. One time Bob gave a person a word along with the phrase, "By the end of the year." Well, the end of the year came and the prophecy had not come to pass. I went back to Bob and questioned him about it. It turns out that "by the end of the year" was not a part of the revelation.

"Well," said Bob, "why would the Lord give it if it weren't going to happen by the end of the year?"

The prophetic information or the revelation itself does not help people much until it goes through the process of interpretation and application. The interpretation may be accurate, but if a person jumps the gun and gets ahead of God in the application, then hurt and confusion may result.

Consequently, there is as much a need for God's wisdom in the interpretation and application as there is in receiving the revelation itself.

The misinterpretation of revelation can either come from the one who received the prophetic information directly from God, or it can come with the people who accept it from the prophet. Let me give an example. In a public meeting, a member of our prophetic team spoke to a man whom he had never met, saying, "You have a music ministry. You're called to be a singer. Great increase is coming to you and your ministry. You will influence nations." What our prophetic team member actually saw in a vision were "musical notes around the man." So he concluded that the man was called to sing or play an instrument on a worship team; however, the man did not play or sing at all. He was the owner of a music store. He was a businessman with an international business, not a musician soon to have a worldwide ministry.

When debriefing after the meeting, our prophetic team member said, "Well, how was I supposed to know he owned a music store?" That is precisely the point—he wasn't supposed to know. It seemed obvious to him that the person would be in the music ministry as a performer. However, when he made an assumption about prophetic revelation based on what *seemed obvious*, he got it wrong. He could have said, "I see musical notes around you; does this mean anything to you?"

It is easy to receive a revelation or divine information and then, without even realizing it, cross over the line to the interpretation of that revelation. We must constantly remember to distinguish between the raw data (divine information) and the interpretation of its meaning.

Additionally, many people become disillusioned over the fact that they may not see the prophetic revelation come to pass. Often, the prophecy did not come to pass as they *assumed* or interpreted that it would. The problem was that they allowed revelation and interpretation to run together in their minds until they could no longer distinguish between what God had actually said and the wrong expectation they created by their wrong interpretation.

The exact way that God brings about a word in our lives is normally quite different than we envision when we first receive it. We are tempted to add our conclusions to the Lord's word to us, and the two become confused over time. The life within a seed and a plant are essentially the same, but the form of the seed must die for the form of the plant to be given birth (1 Cor. 15:36–38). So the "form" of a prophecy's fulfillment can be very different from the "form" of the expectation of its fulfillment we originally project, and yet the essence of the revelation remains true. This is why it's vital that we do not look to prophecy alone for guidance. It can be a vital part of the "machinery," but it must not be made out to be the whole of the "machine." We also encourage people to "hold," "sit on," or "shelve" revelations that do not have a clear interpretation.

If they are shared, they should be communicated with the qualification that the interpretation is not yet clear. It is often wise to write them down and share them with pastoral leaders or those recognized as gifted at interpretation of obscure revelations, but generally they are not for public consumption.

INTERPRETING PROPHETIC SCRIPTURES

The interpretation of revelation is often contrary to the obvious. The scribes and Pharisees were perfect examples of this in their approach to prophetic scriptures. The tradition of the elders was more than a collection of their customs; it was the theological interpretation of the Torah, the first five books of the Old Testament. As centuries passed, those traditions were written down in what became the Talmud.

To the scribes and Pharisees, Jesus was a lawbreaker because He did not keep the traditions of the elders. These religious leaders could no longer distinguish between revelation (the Torah) and interpretation (the Talmud). To them, the interpretations and applications were obvious and indisputable. This tendency to mix up revelation and interpretation shows up in every generation. The Pharisees misinterpreted the prophets' true revelations about the Messiah and thus missed the purpose of God for their generation by rejecting Jesus.

One of the characteristics of prophetic revelation is that it is sometimes parabolic or symbolic; thus, it is only fully understood *after* future events have taken place. From the Old Testament perspective, it was not altogether

Prophetic Administration: Revelation, Interpretation, and Application

clear what the Messiah would look like. The prophets foretold the coming of both a kingly Messiah and a suffering servant, but no one considered that both were the same person. Obviously, kingly messiahs aren't servants, and they don't suffer.

Even the disciples had a hard time with it. The Gospels show how baffled the disciples were. The messianic secret is a theme that runs throughout the Gospels. They had a difficult time figuring out who Jesus was and the nature of His eternal earthly kingdom.

The Gospel of John, which was probably written a few decades after the others (around A.D. 90), looks back at Jesus with greater hindsight. In John's Gospel, there is no mystery about Jesus's identity. Clear affirmations of His deity are found in the first verse and throughout the entire book.

For the disciples, and even for some of the Pharisees and scribes, the interpretation of events foretold in prophetic revelation was difficult while they were happening, but their meaning became crystal clear after the foretold events had taken place. We have to be careful about locking into precisely our interpretation of prophetic revelation before the events happen lest we miss what God is saying to us.

LESSONS LEARNED BY FAILING TO ACCURATELY INTERPRET PROPHECY

Prophetic revelation that is wrongly interpreted can cause chaos in someone's life. Over time we learned to administrate prophetic information. In that learning process, however, we naïvely allowed some unfortunate things to happen. One situation was the result of a wrong interpretation being applied to an authentic prophetic revelation, and it turned into a pastoral nightmare.

I happened to be out of town that morning, which is not to say that it wouldn't have occurred if I had been there. One of the members of the prophetic team received a word from the Lord for a man in our congregation. This man was horrified as the prophetic person publicly shared that he lacked integrity in his finances.

When I returned, I went to the person who gave that prophecy and asked him exactly what he had seen. He told me that he had seen a dark cloud over the area of the man's finances. He interpreted this to mean that the man was stealing money, but his interpretation was totally wrong!

Soon after this prophecy, the man's business partner embezzled a large sum of money from him. The prophetic word was a warning to the man to watch out for someone who might steal money from him, but it was mistakenly pronounced as a judgment against his character. The brother was humiliated publicly by the prophetic word, and he missed the warning that someone was stealing from him.

In this, we neglected to follow the scriptural protocol necessary in giving corrective prophecies. If the man was in fact guilty of financial sin, then he should have been approached privately as called for in Matthew 18:15–17.

If we had interpreted the prophetic word accurately as a gracious warning from God to help the man prevent someone stealing from him, then it would have been spoken differently. It would have been spoken something like, "The Lord is indicating there is a dark cloud over you in the financial arena. Let's pray that God will protect you from the enemy's attack." If we had properly distinguished between the revelation and the interpretation, perhaps the warning could have prevented the financial loss.

INTERPRETING PROPHECY THROUGH OUR PRIDE

When someone prophesies to us about our promotion, we must guard our hearts against believing everything that is prophesied to us simply because we *want it to be true*. It is easy to accept prophecies that are not based in truth because of our unperceived ambition that helps us to believe great things about our ministries whether or not the Lord confirms them in an authentic way. Prophetic words that promise us future promotion can stir up our pride just as gasoline stirs up a fire. Because we long for such words to be true in our lives, we do not always apply the same standards of truth to them as we would if we were helping a friend interpret prophecies over his or her life. In other words, some people will run with positive prophecies without really caring if they are truly from God.

I have received plenty of flattering prophetic words that simply were not true. I just push "delete" and move on and forget them. If we find our identity in Jesus, then we are not as prone to be a sucker for flattering words that are not based in truth. A man with an ambitious or insecure heart is more often seduced by an exaggerated or flattering prophetic word.

HOPE DEFERRED MAKES THE HEART SICK

One problem that comes from believing wrong information is that we have wrong expectations about the future. Prophecy is meant to stir up our hope or expectations. If what we hope for does not happen, then we are prone to be disappointed and hurt. Proverbs 13:12 says, "Hope deferred makes the heart sick." Deferred hope disappoints us so much that we can get into despair or even become angry with God or the prophetic ministry in general. There are Christians who are unaware of the fact that they are angry with God. They have become cynical, critical, and angry in their spirits toward all prophetic ministry. The problem is that they are heartsick over unfulfilled hopes and expectations. The answer is not to throw the baby out with the bathwater in totally rejecting what the Bible says about prophecy. They should go back over the prophetic words that they received to see where they misinterpreted them or where they simply believed a word that was wrong. If we do not take the time and care to interpret prophetic revelation accurately, we can end up heartsick. People who are disillusioned and offended with God lose their spiritual vigor. It doesn't happen overnight, but it does eventually happen. The enemy wants to drive a wedge between God and us, just as he tried to do with Job.

THE APPLICATION OF PROPHETIC REVELATION

The last step in our process of prophetic administration is application. The application refers to the wisdom of how to apply the information that we recently interpreted. Even if there is a true prophetic revelation with an accurate interpretation, the process of administrating prophecy has just begun. It must be properly applied, and therefore many different questions must be asked and answered. The application answers the questions: When? How? To whom does this revelation apply? What should I do? Application is the practical action that we are to take as we respond in faith to the revelation and its interpretation.

I recommend asking the following questions: Who is supposed to hear it? Who is supposed to share it? Whom do we tell—the leaders, only certain individuals or intercessors, or the whole church? How much of it is to be shared—30 percent or 100 percent? When should it be shared? Why? What is the desired impact? What mind-sets do we want to see changed, or what actions are to be taken? The overarching question that must be considered in all of these things is, What will bring about the maximum amount of edification related to the unity, purity, witness, and growth of God's people?

I repeat again that the grace to receive revelation and to discern its interpretation is not the same as the grace to apply it with wisdom. The biggest challenge for the prophetic council at the IHOP Missions Base is definitely in this area of application.

God rarely works on the timetable that we think He should. If we press for the application outside of God's timing, then we find ourselves trying to step through a door that is not yet opened.

Another aspect of the application involves who should be told the revelation and interpretation and when they should be told. The question we must answer when we receive prophetic revelation is if it is to be spoken to the entire congregation or only to the leadership.

Joseph learned the hard way that telling his brothers about his prophetic dreams could get him into trouble (Gen. 37). His brothers interpreted the dreams accurately and came up with their own application—get rid of Joseph! Like Joseph, many people have a hard time not revealing what they have heard from God. It's our nature to want others to know that *God* has a special plan for us.

The same thing is true of the person through whom prophetic revelation comes. The prophetic person often feels he should tell everything to everyone immediately. He wants everyone to know he was the one who received special revelation. Sometimes he is pressured by the desire to want credit for receiving an important revelation.

Prophetic people who unconsciously strive to get recognition for their prophecies often wind up getting corrected instead of credit. If we do not take the credit, then we do not have to take the blame. I understand the reasons for wanting to be recognized, but it's still selfish ambition, and it confuses the process of administrating prophetic revelation in a way that most honors Jesus and serves His people. The sign that a prophetic person has a wrong motivation is that he or she pushes to get recognition. I've learned to not promote those kind of prophetic people. They strive to make sure the people know that they are the one who received the important prophetic word. Our perspective on applying prophetic revelation is influenced by our need for others to know that we are the one hearing from God in a special way.

It is my opinion that the majority of the problems caused by prophetic ministry are caused, not by incorrect prophecies, but by inaccurate—even presumptuous—interpretations and applications.

We need to take the time to work through the process of administrating prophetic ministry and prophetic revelation because the benefits of prophetic revelation to the local church are too great and the consequences of shutting it out are too severe.

THE NEED FOR PROPHETIC CONFIRMATION

When we receive a prophetic word from someone, we must hold it at arm's length and not seek to interpret or apply it *until God Himself confirms it.* Paul taught that everything is to be established by God as He confirms His truth to us.

> By the mouth of two or three witnesses every word shall be established.
> —2 Corinthians 13:1

When people act on a new direction before receiving the confirmation, they get off track. For example, if you receive an accurate revelation from a prophetic person that God is calling you to have a new street ministry, do not go out immediately and start a new ministry. Wait for the Lord to confirm it to you in a clear way.

You may receive the prophetic word as a "notification" that God may communicate to you concerning a new ministry direction, but do not act on it until the Lord confirms it.

On other occasions, prophetic words confirm something you have already received from the Lord. The principle that I am emphasizing is that no one should act on a prophetic word until the Lord confirms it.

We require that all directional prophecies for our corporate ministry at the IHOP Missions Base be shared first with our leadership team before it is spoken publicly so that we may interpret first.

CHAPTER 4

OVERVIEW OF
THE PROPHETIC MINISTRY

P ROPHECY IS THE testimony of Jesus's heart for His people. An angel told the apostle John that the "testimony of Jesus is the spirit of prophecy" (Rev. 19:10). When the Holy Spirit reveals aspects of Jesus's heart and will to us in various supernatural ways, we often refer to it as receiving or operating in the spirit of prophecy.

It is important to make a clear distinction between the authority of Scripture and prophetic utterances that have varying degrees of accuracy. In this chapter I use some of Wayne Grudem's ideas. He is a well-respected theologian who loves the work of the Holy Spirit. He was formerly a professor at Trinity Evangelical Divinity School and wrote *The Gift of Prophecy*. This is a good book that provides a theological framework for prophecy from the Old and New Testaments. Grudem wrote, "Most prophecy is human words reporting something that God brings to mind."[1] The Spirit conveys to our mind thoughts we communicate in contemporary language. They are a mixture of God's words and man's words that combine divine inspiration with the human process. Although it is possible to speak 100 percent accurate words from God, yet most often prophecy is a mixture. In either case, we are called to "weigh what is said" by testing everything, yet holding fast to what is good without despising prophecy (1 Cor. 14:29; 1 Thess. 5:20–21).

CONTEMPORARY PROPHETIC MINISTRY GIFTS

I usually use the term *prophetic people* instead of the term *prophet*. We should only refer to someone as a *prophet* cautiously and sparingly. There are many different levels of prophetic gifting as well as experience, maturity, and credibility. One issue we must answer when investigating the validity of a prophecy is its authority. If the gift of prophecy is some kind of "divine utterance," why does it often sound so weak? Why aren't we taking everything that is prophesied as an infallible inspired utterance?

Grudem answers this as he explains that the Old Testament prophets were commissioned to speak "God's very words," which carried an absolute, divine authority. He argues that in the New Testament, only the twelve apostles had that same authority to speak and write "God's very words." All other prophecy was and is simply, "A very human—and sometimes partially mistaken—report of something the Holy Spirit brought to someone's mind."[2]

Grudem makes a helpful distinction between the divinely authoritative "very word of God" that became our Scriptures and the words of prophets in the early church, which must be judged and sifted and even at times not even spoken.

> Let two or three prophets speak, and let the others judge. But if anything is revealed to another who sits by, let the first keep silent.
>
> —1 Corinthians 14:29–30

He argues convincingly for a qualitative difference between the "very words of God" spoken only by those with apostolic authority (New Testament Scripture) and the inspired messages of the prophets in the early church.

However, I would like to suggest adding a dimension to Grudem's argument. While Paul and the other writers of the New Testament did at times write "God's very words," it must be acknowledged that they did not always speak "God's very words." While personally affirming the divine inspiration and infallibility of Scripture, I believe that Paul could have written additional letters that were not necessarily "God's very words."

What about other people? Can people today speak "God's very words" occasionally? Can prophecy be 100 percent accurate? Is all prophecy, as Grudem argues, only "human words reporting something God brings to mind," and therefore a mixed-up combination of divine inspiration and the human spirit?

While affirming the value of the "mixed lot," Grudem makes a helpful distinction between the authority of Scripture and the prophetic utterances in the early church. It is absolutely clear that contemporary prophetic words should not be treated in the way in which we treat Scripture. All the prophetic people I know wholeheartedly agree with this statement. As Grudem states, prophesy is reporting "in human words what God brings to mind." God conveys to our mind thoughts that we communicate in contemporary language. They are a mixture of God's words and man's words. Some "prophetic words" may be 10 percent God's words and 90 percent man's words, while others have a greater revelatory content. On occasion God speaks to His servants in an audible voice. These are His "very words" that may be reported with a high degree of accuracy. It is clear that some prophetic utterances "ring more true" than others. I have attempted to graph this phenomena of mixing our thoughts and ideas with God's words:

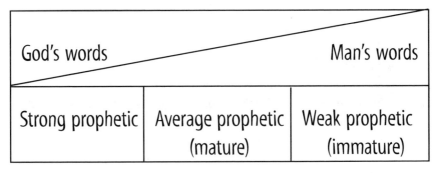

What I am trying to illustrate is that all prophecy today has a degree of mixture in it. Sometimes this yields a "mature" word that reflects more ideally what God would like to communicate, and sometimes it is communicated in a much-less-than-ideal fashion, yielding a "weak" word of lesser value, but still one that should not be despised.

Whatever the case, and however reputable the prophet may be, we are commanded by Scripture to weigh what is said (1 Cor. 14:29–30). Paul instructs the Thessalonian church: "Do not despise prophecies. Test all things; hold fast to what is good" (1 Thess. 5:20–21). If the prophetic utterance is from God, then the Holy Spirit will bring the words home to our hearts and give us an internal witness of the fact that it is indeed something God is saying to us. He will also confirm the word by other prophetic people (2 Cor. 13:1) or by other means, including acts of God in nature. (See chapter 2.)

WHO CAN PROPHESY?

The church, from its inception on the Day of Pentecost, was to be of a prophetic nature. It is clear that the spirit of prophecy is potentially available to all (Acts 2:17–18). "For you can all prophesy one by one, that all may learn…" (1 Cor. 14:31).

Paul urges the Corinthians to seek this gift (1 Cor. 14:1, 24, 39) while acknowledging that not all are prophets (1 Cor. 12:29). What is going on? Again, I find Grudem helpful but not adequate. His definition of *prophesy* is "speaking merely human words to report something God brings to mind." This definition allows for a type of prophetic utterance that is possible for every believer, and rightfully so. He also acknowledges that in the New Testament some people ministered more regularly in prophecy and were called "prophets" (Agabus in Acts 11, 21; Philip's daughters in Acts 21; Barnabas in Acts 13:1). Grudem does not acknowledge that there was an "office" of prophet. However, most Pentecostals and charismatics would disagree with him. Paul says that apostles and prophets will continue to function *TILL* or until the church is fully mature. Surely, all admit that the church has not yet reached this point of maturity. Therefore, *TILL* this occurs, we need apostles and prophets to equip the saints for the work of ministry.

> And He Himself gave some to be apostles, some prophets, some evangelists, and some pastors and teachers, for the equipping of the saints for the work of ministry…till we all come to the unity of the faith…to a perfect man, to the measure of the stature of the fullness of Christ.
> —Ephesians 4:11–13

John gives the report of all heaven rejoicing in Babylon's destruction along with the End Time apostles and prophets who were persecuted by Babylon:

"Rejoice over her, O heaven, and you holy apostles and prophets, for God has avenged you on her!" Then a mighty angel took up a stone like a great millstone and threw it into the sea, saying, "Thus with violence the great city Babylon shall be thrown down, and shall not be found anymore.... And in her was found the blood of prophets and saints, and of all who were slain on the earth."

—Revelation 18:20–24

Grudem argues that the term *prophet* is more of a description of function rather than an office or title.

> The distinction between function and office would be reflected in the greater and lesser degrees of prophetic ability, all ranged along a wide spectrum in any given congregation. Prophets would differ in ability among themselves, while they would also see changes in the extent of their own prophetic abilities over a period of time. Those with a high degree of prophetic ability would prophesy more frequently, at greater length, with more clear and forceful revelations, about more important subjects, and over a wider range of topics.[3]

Grudem points out that some people, like Agabus in the Book of Acts, ministered regularly in prophecy, and while we may not want to give him the *office* of prophet, he had an acknowledged and reputable ministry in prophecy. I would like to expand on this idea of a continuum and suggest that there are levels of prophetic ministry that distinguish the different levels or measures of prophetically gifted people.

1. Simple prophecy

A simple prophecy is given when any believer speaks an impression that God has brought to his or her mind. We all are to earnestly seek to prophesy (1 Cor. 14:1, 39). All men and women, old and young alike, are to speak forth words from God (Acts 2:17). Yet, not all are prophets (1 Cor. 12:29). Simple prophecy is usually within the scope of encouragement, comfort, and exhortation that is explained in 1 Corinthians 14:3, and it doesn't include correction, new direction, or predictive elements of prophetic words.

> But he who prophesies speaks edification and exhortation and comfort to men.... For you can all prophesy one by one, that all may learn and...be encouraged.
>
> —1 Corinthians 14:3, 31

These are often simple impressions that God brings to mind. These include words of knowledge (i.e., specific information regarding the physical, spiritual, or emotional status of someone). Occasionally, this includes receiving "visions" (mental pictures) or dreams. The person giving the prophecy speaks (mostly using his or her own words) an idea that God had brought to mind. These words are given in a small group setting or in the ministry line (not publicly on the mic). Small groups can afford opportunity for more people to experience and participate in this kind of prophesying. The inspirational prophetic words are edifying when given by prophetic singers. It's best to limit the number of prophecies used in a public service so that its overuse does not ruin its effectiveness.

2. Prophetic gifting

Believers who regularly receive impressions, dreams, visions, or other types of revelation have prophetic gifting. These can often be symbolic, being in the form of parables and riddles. This group receives more regular prophetic information than the first group yet lacks clarity in understanding what they receive. I have met many people at levels 1 and 2; these groups account for the vast majority of those who prophesy in charismatic-type churches.

3. Prophetic ministry

Believers whose gifting has been recognized, nurtured, and commissioned for regular ministry in the local church are in prophetic ministry. There is still a symbolic element in what they receive, but through the process of team ministry, it is possible to discern much of the interpretation and application of their revelation. Those in prophetic ministry will receive words and dreams on a regular basis and will have "open visions" on occasion (i.e., angelic visitations, audible voice). They will sometimes receive detailed information such as names, faces, dates, and future events. They occasionally operate in other sign gifts (healing, miracles, deliverance). They may, in private, expose unconfessed sin (2 Sam. 12:1–7). They give simple prophecies yet also give direction and correction. These people are "gifted" in that they receive an unusual amount of revelation, but they are still being trained (have maturity of character and wisdom of God's corporate purposes). They may receive words of correction and direction that they should write and submit to the leadership.

It is vital to distinguish between simple prophecy and prophecy that has "authority." Every believer is able to prophesy on a simple level. However, to prophesy with authority is much "weightier" and should not be done publicly without the confirmation of the leaders of the church, who are responsible before God to oversee the church's life.

4. Prophetic office

Believers whose ministry is somewhat like the prophets of the Old Testament occupy the office of the prophet. They give correction, direction, and bring new emphasis in the church body. They provide direction and correction to those in government in the church, marketplace, or political arenas. They often minister in signs and wonders and are known to regularly speak very accurate words from God as Samuel did.

> Samuel grew, and the LORD was with him and let none of his words fall to the ground. And all Israel from Dan to Beersheba knew that Samuel had been established as a prophet of the LORD.
>
> —1 Samuel 3:19–20

This doesn't mean that prophets are 100 percent infallible, but their words are to be taken seriously. Unlike the Old Testament ground rules for prophets, where 100 percent accuracy was required upon the penalty of death, the New Testament doesn't require the same standard of its prophets. Their credibility has been clearly established by their proven track record of accurate prophecies along with the godly lifestyle and their love and honor of Scripture. They predict future events with accuracy. They have a regular flow of divine revelation, including open visions and prediction of natural events (i.e., weather patterns, political developments). Their words may be confirmed through natural signs (i.e., earthquakes, storms, droughts). Their words carry much authority as they speak with much greater accuracy. They minister frequently in sign gifts. They must have a proven ministry (that may take years). All who exercise prophetic authority must be under authority. Some have experiences that indicate they have been sovereignly chosen by God (miraculous birth, angelic visitation, and the like). The stature necessary for the office of prophet includes *gifts* (accurate revelation), *fruit* (mature character), and *wisdom* (understanding of God's corporate purpose and ways).

Operating at a high level of supernatural activity also exposes those so gifted to a greater intensity of satanic assault, and ethical compromise can leave them unprotected targets in a very dangerous realm. Prophets need greater godliness, wisdom, faith, and nearness to Jesus to withstand the added attack of the enemy that comes because of their gifting.

What I have described as different levels of prophetic ministry is simply an attempt to provide labels for what most authors who have written on prophetic ministry believe.

There are really no clear-cut standards for deciding if a person is at Level I, II, III, or IV, or exactly what the distinctions are. These are not biblical distinctions; they are simply categories that help us to communicate with each other more effectively. It may become apparent that more levels are necessary, but I believe that the initial groupings will provide some framework for further research.

I know hundreds of people, many within the IHOP Missions Base family and others outside of it, who minister in Level I, simple prophecy, and many others who could be described by Level II—being used periodically to give a strong prophetic word.

I have known a few Level III prophetic ministers throughout the years. These are men and women who regularly receive dreams, visions, and supernatural encounters as a part of their lifestyle. They function in this way as a gift to the body of Christ. Some of these people may one day be recognized as being in the office of a New Testament prophet.

What I have called "the Level IV prophetic office" represents a maturity and power in prophetic ministry that parallel the Old Testament ministries of men like Samuel and Elijah. In my mind, recognizing a person as a Level IV New Testament prophet involves three issues:

1. The prophet has a level of supernatural giftedness that is evidenced by regularly receiving divine information from the Holy Spirit. The validity of this gift is proven over time.

2. The prophet has a godly character, which is an essential mark of a true prophet. Jesus said that you would know true and false prophets by their fruit (Matt. 7:15–20). The fruit Jesus refers to includes the impact of their ministry as well as the fruit of the Holy Spirit's sanctifying work operating in their character. True prophets consistently seek to walk in holiness with deep passion for Jesus.

3. The prophet has the matured wisdom of God that has come through experience and relationship with the Holy Spirit. This wisdom enables the person to be an instrument of the prophetic knowledge and power of God in a way that builds up the people of God and the purpose of God. This wisdom is foundational to using the prophetic in a manner that will build up the local church.

I have seen the Holy Spirit work in these three areas with the prophetic ministers I know. Some have grown more than others. However, I remain reluctant to refer to people publicly as being in the office of a New Testament prophet as measured by the maturity level of their gifting, character, and wisdom. I would rather err on the side of caution. Prophetically gifted people must be well proven in the context of long-term relationships in the local church, regardless of their level.

I think the church does itself harm when it allows people to quickly identify themselves as "apostles" or "prophets" simply because they consider themselves to be so or because it looks good on a brochure. By doing this, we trivialize the gifts and callings of God and hinder the emerging of God's genuine ministry gifts to the church. I feel that in the coming generation, there will be many Level III prophetic ministries and more than a few Level IV prophets. Pastors will need to learn how to nurture effectively these prophetic ministries and incorporate them into the ministering life of the church.

We believe that the prophecy at all four levels is progressively being restored to the church in our day. We have witnessed the Lord dramatically confirm major revelations in this way. Boundaries set by the Holy Spirit do not quench the Holy Spirit—they are charismatically designated boundaries on charismatic activity. A river without banks can be very destructive!

I firmly believe that the church will yet become the prophetic community that Peter described in Acts 2. Lord, help us.

BENEFITS OF PROPHECY

To convince pastors and leaders that it is worth it to expend time, energy, and patience to effectively administrate prophecy, they need to see its value and benefits. God regularly provides insight into His plans in the market-place, the local church, or its individual members by foretelling the location and timings of activities, buildings, or financial issues.

When we receive the Holy Spirit's direction on locations of buildings and the timing of major financial expenditures, we are far more confident in going forward.

At critical junctures and times of decision making, the Lord has provided direction and guidance on numerous occasions through prophetic revelation or happenings from two, three, or more unsolicited and mutually independent sources. Exact buildings, intersections, amounts of money, words that would be spoken to us, people whom we would encounter, and exact timings of several events have all been "seen" prophetically, confirmed, and then later fulfilled in our actual experience.

One significant benefit of prophetic ministry in my ministry over the years has been in receiving divine information about new leaders being sent by God to help our team. When new leaders are sent and established by prophetic words, then others have greater confidence that God is at work in steering the church or the business. For example, four of our leaders were specified by name through prophetic revelation without human knowledge of their existence. Both first and last names were given to two of them. Other leaders' families, giftings, circumstances, and the like were seen before-hand by revelation. This "prophetic backdrop" has provided a high level of confidence in the divine ordaining of our being joined in relationship and function rather than by ourselves or others. (Of course, many other things besides prophecy contributed to the addition of every leader.)

He gives us warnings of coming attacks by foretelling people's words and actions, circumstances, or the nature and area of the attack. "To be forewarned is to be forearmed."

The Holy Spirit warns us of satanic attack. On several occasions the Lord has given us prophetic warnings of direct and satanic assaults on our work. This insight has helped us brace ourselves and keep our poise and perspective in the battle. False corrections and the emotional drain they create have been avoided. People whom the enemy has sent to disrupt our ministry have been neutralized. A little "secret intelligence" helps in any war.

Prophetic words help us to sustain faith. Colossians 1:9 points out that we are strengthened by the knowledge of God's will:

> We...do not cease to pray for you, and to ask that you may be filled with the knowledge of His will in all wisdom and spiritual understanding.

The prophetic ministry sustains hope in us that strengthens us to know God's will with much greater certainty. Because God's will has been prophetically revealed and confirmed throughout our history, we have been strengthened in times of weakness, barrenness, heavenly silence, persecution, and lack of anointing. There is an overriding and undergirding corporate consciousness that God is with us despite the obstacles, difficulties, mistakes, and setbacks we encounter. It has often stimulated our repentance, motivation, sacrifice, sense of awe, and other like issues of the heart that are so often intangible.

> Attaining to all riches of the full assurance of understanding...
> —Colossians 2:2

All Can Prophesy

In Numbers 11:16–29, we see two very different mind-sets toward the spirit of prophesy. Joshua had a mind-set that was very different than that of Moses (Num. 11:16–17, 24–29). Moses's mind-set foreshadowed God's intentions in anointing many people in raising up a prophetic End Time church.

The Joshua mind-set was wrong and is seen when he complained to Moses that others besides Moses were prophesying, such as Eldad and Medad, who also missed the "anointed commissioning service." Joshua had an exclusive attitude, which wanted the Holy Spirit to rest only on Moses and not on any other people. This attitude brings an undue exaltation to a select group of highly anointed individuals.

The Moses mind-set understood the generosity of God, who ultimately wants all of His people to operate in the Spirit. Moses's insight foreshadowed the revelation that God will anoint all of His people with prophecy as seen in Joel 2:28–29. Instead of having the "man of the hour" mind-set, we see that God desires to raise up a family of children who can all operate in the power of the Spirit. Paul emphasized this when he declared that he wished that all would prophesy (1 Cor. 14:5, 31). A new wineskin is emerging that is calling forth friends who live as a prophetic community, where all can prophesy. This is the paradigm in which the prophetic anointing will reach its highest measure. A normative life of prayer and fasting with depth in the Word and giving will provide the context for this.

God wants to change our identity from just being "gifted servants" into being intimate friends with Him as Moses was. In the new covenant, God gave the Holy Spirit to all so we could all receive revelation about what is on His heart. He loves to share with us His thoughts and actions.

We must possess a tenacious pursuit for prophecy. We were all meant to hear, see, and operate in the Spirit. It is our inheritance to prophesy. One reason that people are weak in prophecy is because of lack of confidence that they can receive from God. We can receive the small whisper from His heart. The question that always arises is, "Was that God or not?" The risk of failure cripples some with fear that they will be rejected if they make mistakes. The enemy knows this, and so he strikes at our hearts with accusations to stir up our fears.

God wants us to pursue the things of the Spirit. He wants us to ask for more. The first step in doing this is found in believing that God really wants to give more to you. We give expression to this desire through prayer. We ask the Lord to open our eyes to "see." For those of us who haven't experienced this yet, we must ask for spiritual sight (Eph. 1:17). What does this mean exactly? It's the realm of seeing in dreams, having visions both internal and external, and also includes seeing angels and/or the demonic realm. We must ask the Lord to open our ears to hear His voice. It includes the external audible voice of the Lord or angelic realm, and the whisper or small faint voice of the Holy Spirit. We must ask the Lord to allow us to feel His presence. We may feel a variety of things such as external feelings of pressure on our bodies (like an energy), either cold or burning sensations, weightiness (which causes some to kneel), or a literal wind or breeze around us. Internally, emotions may go from sobbing to laughing or deep inner awareness of peace and solitude. The easiest and most basic way to stay "spiritually alert" is to regularly ask the question, "Lord, what are You saying or doing? Show me." Faint impressions are the most common manifestation we experience. However, if we don't ask what God is saying or doing, then we will miss out on many opportunities that help us grow in our ability to be sensitive to the Holy Spirit.

NURTURING THE PROPHETIC MINISTRY

People who long to grow in the prophetic must overcome their fear of judgment and rejection. The leadership team can help this by nurturing and making sure we judge fruit, not methods. We judge the prophetic by the fruit it bears, not the methods that it operates with (Matt. 7:15–20). The fruit we want in the prophetic people and those who receive from them is greater passion for Jesus and holy living as we honor the written Word.

We must create a safe atmosphere of encouragement with much mercy and patience for mistakes so that people can grow in confidence and stature in their prophetic gifting without fearing rebuke and rejection. One of the best places to grow in the prophetic is in more private small group settings. Groups give mercy to those with teachable spirits. However, we must avoid "unsanctified mercy" to those who refuse to cooperate with a stubborn spirit. Let the people know that they must take risks to grow, even if sometimes they make mistakes. Solomon taught us that the oxen brings great strength and increase to the farm; however, he makes a mess in the barn. The increase of strength is worth the mess that comes with it.

> Where no oxen are, the trough is clean; but much increase comes by the strength of an ox.
>
> —Proverbs 14:4

Allow for the risk, and accept the inevitable of being humbled as a congregation as you pursue more growth in the prophetic. Remember that the very oxen that bring strength to the farm also bring a mess to the stable. Some prefer to have a ministry that is like the clean stables, even if it means losing the strength and increase that the prophetic ministry brings.

CHAPTER 5

THE DIFFERENCE BETWEEN THE GIFT OF PROPHECY AND BEING A PROPHET

M Y STORY WITH the prophetic really took off when I planted a new church in Kansas City in December 1982. A few months after the church was started, I met people who claimed to have divine encounters with God. Further, they claimed that their encounters had major implications for the direction of my life and ministry. They referred to unusual claims. They were audible voices, angelic visitations, multiple "Technicolor" visions, literal signs in the heavens, and trances, just to name a few. They were dramatically confirmed. Little by little, my doubts and fears slowly gave way to believe that Jesus, the head of the church, was truly involved in these prophetic events. This was the beginning of my personal journey in learning the principles of administrating prophetic revelation. Prophecy can generate faith and clarity, but admittedly it can also cause much confusion, bring condemnation, and be counterproductive if it is not properly administrated. Over the next sixteen years that I pastored this church before the IHOP Missions Base started, we had many victories, along with some defeats and even painful disappointments. Some of the most prominent prophetic vessels from those early days caused some pain and confusion for a short season. One of the main issues that I had to settle was what the Scripture said about the difference between Old Testament prophets and New Testament prophets and then to reconcile how the spirit of prophecy was available to everyone without viewing them as being a prophet.

When people first hear of someone being called a prophet, they might think of a man with wild hair and fiery eyes crying out against sin and calling fire down from heaven. Others might think of someone pronouncing judgment and doom or predicting the end of the world. Though the image may be a little distorted, this is the picture many people have in their minds of prophets as they appear in the Old Testament. The character of New Testament prophets and prophecy is, however, somewhat different from that of the Old Testament. Some people have difficulty with the idea of modern-day prophets and prophecy because they are looking at them through Old Testament paradigm.

We live in a new era in our relationship with God under the new covenant. There are several key differences between Old Testament prophets and prophetic ministry in the New Testament. Every believer is called to earnestly desire to prophesy (1 Cor. 14:1). Luke describes the young church in Antioch as having prophets in it (Acts 13:1).

NEW TESTAMENT PROPHECY

In Old Testament times, there were usually only a few prophets in the whole earth at any one time. Yes, there were companies of prophets that are referred to occasionally. We do not have much detail about them. However, it is clear that the well-known Old Testament prophetic ministries usually operated alone or nearly alone. Sometimes prophets were contemporaries, like Haggai and Zechariah, or Ezekiel and Daniel, but usually they functioned as one of the lone mouthpieces of God in their generation. No prophet exemplifies this more than Elijah, who stood alone against King Ahab, the prophets of Baal, and the sins of rebellious Israel. John the Baptist fits that mold as well—the man of God coming out of the wilderness to proclaim repentance in preparing the way of the Lord.

In the New Testament, there may have been several prophets in every city where the church was established instead of merely a few real prophets (Level IV) for the whole world as in the Old Testament times. With the outpouring of the Spirit, the gift of prophecy was widely dispersed throughout the universal community of God's people. In the Old Testament, there were few prophets relative to the number of God's people. The fate of the whole nation could literally depend upon the accuracy of one prophet's revelation.

In the Old Testament there was "prophetic concentration," and in the New Testament there was "prophetic distribution." The fate of the church would never depend on the accuracy of one prophet. With potentially several or even a number of prophets in each geographic location, the same kind of accuracy of revelation is not needed because of the safeguard of other prophets' mandate to judge each other's words and even Spirit-anointed believers' ability to test, discern, confirm, or deny a claim of revelation (1 Cor. 14:29; 1 John 2:27).

The gift of prophecy, the prophetic ministry, and the word of the Lord are *diffused* and *distributed* throughout the entire body of Christ. Today, there are probably people with prophetic giftings residing in most nations of the earth. They may be immature, but they are probably present.

Under the new covenant we don't usually see prophets who live by themselves in the wilderness. The prophetic ministry is a vital part of the body of Christ in a city. Prophetic people are mandated by Scripture to be involved in the local church, not separated from it. Prophetic people serve within the church as one of the "joints that supply" the other parts of the church, enabling it to be the prophetic voice in the earth (Eph. 4:16).

In the New Testament, the prophetic ministry is directed less to national leaders and more to the church. In the Old Testament, prophets often— though not always—warned of coming judgment on the king and/or the nation and then restoration after they repented. Old Testament prophets focused on speaking to the nation's leaders. In the New Testament, some prophetic ministries have access to national leaders whereas most are called to focus on the body of Christ in their region.

There is another major difference between Old and New Testament prophets. Because Old Testament prophets received direct and unmistakable revelation, they were 100 percent accurate. They did not need to have the others "discern" the prophetic word they gave. The only way they missed it was by blatantly changing what God had said or deliberately making up a false prophecy. Consequently, the Old Testament judgment on false prophets was to stone them to death.

> But the prophet who presumes to speak a word in My name,
> which I have not commanded him to speak…that prophet shall
> die. And if you say in your heart, "How shall we know the word
> which the LORD has not spoken?"—when a prophet speaks in the
> name of the LORD, if the thing does not happen or come to pass,
> that is the thing which the LORD has not spoken.
>
> —Deuteronomy 18:20–22

The Old Testament requirement for prophets was 100 percent accuracy. This was required on the penalty of death. These prophets spoke with a clear and unmistakable "Thus saith the Lord!" They claimed repeatedly that their very words were the words that God had given them to deliver.

> I will be with your mouth and teach you what you shall say.
>
> —Exodus 4:12

> Behold, I have put My words in your mouth.
>
> —Jeremiah 1:9

The New Testament doesn't require the same standard of its prophets who prophesy by faith and often from subtle impressions of the Holy Spirit. The safeguard of New Testament prophecy is given in the mandate to judge each other's words. In the New Testament, Paul taught us specifically to "let two or three prophets speak, and let *the others judge*" (1 Cor. 14:29, emphasis added). The Revised Standard Version translates the passage this way: "…let the others weigh what is said."

We don't stone people if they miss it once, nor do we believe everything they say, even if they are accurate 99 percent of the time. We still judge their prophecies. Paul gives similar instructions to the church in Thessalonica, telling them to not despise prophecies but to test them:

> Do not despise prophecies. Test all things; hold fast what is good.
>
> —1 Thessalonians 5:20–21

This passage implies that some prophetic utterances will contain a measure of error—"Test all things; hold fast what is good" was written in reference to prophetic utterances. Nowhere in the New Testament is there the suggestion that a Christian should be executed, excommunicated, or even branded a "false prophet" for simply relaying an inaccurate prophecy, for such a word should be weeded out in the process of the church's proper response to prophecy.

We do not find in the Old Testament any instance in which the prophecy of a true prophet was "discerned" by other prophets so that the good might be sorted from the bad, the accurate from the inaccurate. Why? Because God was thought to be the speaker of all that a prophet spoke in His name, it was unthinkable that a true prophet should deliver some oracle that was a mixture of accurate and inaccurate information. There was no middle ground. They were true prophets who spoke the very word of God and should be obeyed as such, or they were false prophets and should be put to death.[1]

Today, we are commanded to "judge all prophecy" because in the New Testament we prophesy by faith often only having a subtle impression of the Holy Spirit, thus lacking full clarity. First Corinthians 13:9 says, "For we know in part and we prophesy in part."

In the Old Testament, prophets were the representatives of the Lord to the king—who had the power to punish them if they falsely prophesied. There was never a question about accurately discerning the genuine word from God. For the prophet, it was only a matter of whether he had the courage to deliver it.

The essence of Old Testament prophetic ministry was limited to those who received *direct revelation from God.* In the New Testament, we prophesy by faith, which involves speaking out the subtle impressions that the Holy Spirit gives us. We learn to prophesy according to the measure of our faith, thus we can mix up God's ideas with our words and thoughts. For as Romans 12:6 says, "Let us prophesy in proportion to our faith."

The Old Testament prophets did not struggle in their attempt to discern subtle impressions of the Spirit from their own thoughts. The message was clear and unmistakable. They did not need to be judged and discerned, because they only spoke as they received an open vision rather than a subtle impression.

Can you imagine Noah saying, "I feel the Lord is impressing upon my heart that He's going to destroy the world with a flood and that I should consider building an ark." Stepping out in faith for them was not a matter of proclaiming with confidence what they only remotely sensed. It was repeating what God clearly said regardless of the consequences.

It is difficult for some to accept the idea of prophesying by faith according to the subtle impressions of the Holy Spirit with the chance of missing it and giving a wrong prophetic word. The reason, of course, is that they have failed to understand the transition in prophetic ministry. While they clearly see other aspects of the Old Testament changing under the new covenant, their understanding of prophetic ministry is still based on an Old Testament model.

Many prophetic people I know express their prophetic impressions by asking questions of the person they are ministering to. For example, when they feel impressed by the Spirit that the person they are talking to may have a specific sickness, it is OK to ask them if they have the illness. The gifts of the Spirit can operate in the course of natural dialogue. I call it "being supernaturally natural." We don't have to roll our eyes back, speak in King James English, raise our voice like a Pentecostal preacher, and end with "saith the Lord." If we tone it down and even slow it, many will receive us more easily. In other words, it will still work! They are not more impressed or receptive to a "dialed up" style of delivery.

The Holy Spirit gives us prophetic impressions not so that we can be known as a prophet, but in order to help other people. Often if a prophetic person asks someone about his illness because of prophetic impression from the Holy Spirit, and the person acknowledges the illness, there is still the temptation for the prophet to add the comment: "Well, the Lord told me that..." Sometimes we are so desperate to make sure that people know we are special because we receive impressions from the Holy Spirit. It is better to not be so focused on getting the attention for receiving from the Spirit and be content just to see people get blessed and be thankful to the Lord. There's not as much personal glory associated with that more dialed-down, low-key ministry style, but then we don't stone prophetic people who make mistakes, either. Prophetic people need to understand that this is not about personal recognition and glory. The gift is diffused throughout the body of Christ in order that Jesus is exalted and the people are helped.

The "spiritual climates" surrounding Pentecostal/charismatic movements have often wittingly or unwittingly fostered an unhealthy pressure on people who wanted to be close and useful to God to directly act and speak on God's behalf with great assurance. When such bold activity is proven inaccurate, it's hard for people to admit, "It wasn't God." It's much more convenient to "sweep" the mess under their psychological and social "rugs"; however, in the long run, the integrity of their faith and relationships is undermined, and their intimacy with Jesus suffers tremendously.

As Christians launch out and learn to prophesy according to the measure of their faith, they are bound to get their "signals crossed" more than once by "going beyond their measure" and speaking out of their own mind or spirit. This is due to the inevitable immaturity through which we must all learn. This realization takes some of the pressure out of prophesying and helps people grow in their gifting in a loving atmosphere and receive correction and adjustment without totally "wiping them out." Those who regularly give inaccurate "prophecies" must not speak so often or so specifically. They should stay within the boundaries of simple prophecy.

Because the church has not generally been good at or wise in our administration of the prophetic, many with prophetic anointings have suffered in their development in personality and gifting.

In the atmosphere of being generous to one another, we must not neglect to discern and judge false prophets (Matt. 7:15–16). Yes, there are evil deceivers—false prophets—who creep into Christian congregations and maliciously entice and deceive unsuspecting and undiscerning believers through false prophecy. These should be purged from the church if they will not repent.

PRIESTS AND PROPHETS
UNDER THE NEW COVENANT

God has called His church to function as a kingdom of priests, who all have direct access to God (Heb. 4:16; 1 Pet. 2:5, 9; Rev. 1:5). In the new covenant, each believer has the ability to hear directly from God through the indwelling Holy Spirit:

I will make a new covenant with the house of Israel.... I will put My law in their minds, and write it on their hearts...for they all shall know Me, from the least of them to the greatest of them, says the LORD.

—Jeremiah 31:31–34

In the old covenant, priestly and prophetic ministries were reserved for a select few. They were put to death for failure to function in a proper way. Both prophets and priests were put to death for functioning presumptuously (Deut. 18:18–22; Lev. 10:1–3).

The new covenant is different. Peter emphasized that *all* our sons and daughters, old and young, would prophesy because of the outpouring of the Spirit (Acts 2:17–18). Instead of a limited few, everyone is a priest, and the spirit of prophecy is diffused throughout the entire body of Christ. Instead of only audible-voice-of-God revelations and open visions, much prophetic ministry is imparted by impressions of the Holy Spirit on our hearts. Instead of stoning prophets, we are instructed to judge and discern that which they speak to know if it is from God.

Over the fifteen hundred years that followed after the Day of Pentecost, many reverted back to the Old Testament understanding of the priesthood by elevating it to include only full-time clergy. Martin Luther, an Augustinian monk and a priest, was troubled by this Old Testament understanding of the priesthood. The priests were few and exclusive. Luther taught the doctrine that we know today as the *priesthood of the believer.* This New Testament understanding of priesthood is an accepted foundation of evangelical theology, but in his day it was radical enough to get him condemned to death.

Luther also taught the doctrine of *private judgment*, which is the principle that every person can hear God and interpret the Scriptures for himself. That was another radical idea for the sixteenth century. There are parallels in Luther's emphasis on the priesthood of all believers to the New Testament understanding of prophetic ministry. Every Christian can hear from God, exercise discernment, and be led by the Holy Spirit. Ministry that was exclusive in the Old Testament (prophet and priest) is now diffused and common in the New.

The New Testament doctrines of the priesthood of all believers and of private judgment (hearing God for oneself) open the door for much more Holy Spirit activity in the church. God's plan all along has been to have a kingdom of priests made up of His very own sons and daughters who can all prophesy. Imagine hundreds of millions of born-again believers worldwide who can prophesy by the power of the indwelling Spirit. With so many more people prophesying, more fruitfulness comes, along with more opportunities for error and mistakes. Though it can sometimes be messy, unpredictable, and hard to control, the glorious doctrine of the priesthood of all believers is here to stay. No evangelical will deny this. All of us agree that this is a truth worth defending.

New Testament prophetic ministry is an extension of this idea that we are all priests, and, therefore, we can all hear from God. The focus of most prophesying is on edification, exhortation, and comfort (1 Cor. 14:3). In fact, everyone who is born again is able to prophesy on this level (what I have referred to as Level I prophecy). This is often referred to as *inspirational prophecy* or *simple prophecy*.

However, prophetic ministry in the church is difficult for some fundamentalists and conservative evangelicals because they embrace an Old Testament understanding of the prophetic, in which only a few receive direct revelation that is 100 percent accurate—otherwise, they are put to death.

Although New Testament prophecy does at times come by way of dreams, visions, and the audible voice of God, much prophetic revelation can be more subtle. More common forms of revelation are impressions by the Holy Spirit—the *still small voice*, so to speak—as opposed to the always unmistakable, audible voice of God.

PACKAGING PROPHETIC MINISTRY

The spirit of prophecy operates in different packages because there are so many different personalities in the body of Christ. Usually people have no problem with the woman in the prayer group who senses the Holy Spirit is impressing her heart to pray a particular burden. This is in a package that many people understand and are comfortable with. However, if she speaks up during the Sunday morning service, interspersed with "Thus saith the Lord," she could get a significantly different response. If the same message with the very same words are used in a different setting, she may be received in a completely different way. Sometimes we are more concerned about the package and not concerned enough with the message.

It bothers me when prophetic people preface everything with "Thus saith the Lord." They may say this because they have heard others do it. Or perhaps it is an attempt to be more dramatic or to increase the chance of being heard. Sometimes it may come from an Old Testament understanding of the prophetic. Whatever the case, it is far easier to receive people who dial down the drama and mysticism when they proclaim what God has given them.

There are many different levels in which one may receive revelation in the body of Christ, from subtle impressions to audible voices to angelic visitations. Therefore, it is better if the one speaking is clearer about what he or she has received. Subtle impressions don't need to be punctuated in the same way as an open vision. A person may eventually find himself sounding like the boy who cried, "Wolf!" when he says, "But I *did* hear something this time. Thus saith the Lord—*really!*" And all the people yawn.

TEMPTATION COMES WITH POWER

If you could heal blind eyes in just one out of ten attempts, you would gather crowds of hundreds of thousands of people anywhere in the world on twenty-four-hour notice. If you could heal ten out of ten as Jesus did, you would be the most powerful person in the nation. Remember, they tried to make Jesus king because He healed the sick and multiplied the fish and the loaves. The release of supernatural ministry with overt demonstrations of power puts a lot of attention on the people God uses.

Because genuine miracles are so unique, when they are openly displayed, the nations will come to receive them. The rich, famous, and powerful people on Earth will do just about anything to be a part of genuine miracles from God. There are a lot of millionaires in the world, but how many people can raise the dead as the prophet Elijah did? A prophet of the stature similar to those in the Old Testament would face incredible temptations because so many rich and powerful people would seek their favor.

This is why it is important for those with a gift of prophecy to remain accountable to a body of believers who are mature and sensitive toward that gift and the unique temptations and attacks that come with it. Humility and teachability are key attributes prophetic people must have in order to be continuously in a place where all the glory and honor is directed to God. For it is God who extends them the grace to operate in His power.

CHAPTER 6

WOMEN OPERATING IN
PROPHETIC MINISTRY

T HE MINISTRY OF women in the church is a hotly debated topic in many circles today. Unfortunately, the effectiveness of the church throughout history has been diminished because the ministry of women has been so limited. The intransigent and sometimes chauvinistic position of some in the church is a result of long-held stereotypes about women, dysfunctional male-female relationships, and a truncated view of early church history.

My purpose here is neither to put forth a comprehensive theological framework for women in ministry nor to attempt an exegesis of the New Testament texts that relate to the role of women in the church.

My purpose is to cite some examples from church history and how women function in prophetic ministry at the IHOP Missions Base.

The church in the End Times will flourish as both men and women receive powerful dreams and visions that bring others to deep relationships with Jesus. In Acts 2:17–18, we can plainly see that God intends to pour out His Spirit on His sons *and* daughters, and *they* shall prophesy. We will never be fully effective if one-half of God's army is kept out of the battle against Satan's onslaught. We need men and women both to take their place boldly before God's throne and function together with confidence and security in the body of Christ. Together we can experience the passionate love of God for us and then use our authority in Jesus to plunder the kingdom of darkness in our generation.

WOMEN THROUGHOUT CHURCH HISTORY

The significant involvement of women in the ministry of Jesus is well documented. Women were witnesses of His crucifixion and resurrection when males were conspicuously absent. Luke declares that the women who had followed Jesus from Galilee still followed along as Christ was carried to the tomb (Luke 23:27–31). Matthew tells how they kept watch over the sepulcher after the men had fled (Matt. 27:61). John records that the group of people immediately beneath the cross consisted of three women and one man (John 19:25–27). Though it broke all kinds of social and religious traditions, Jesus made a point to include women in His ministry.

It is little wonder that the prominence of women continued in the development of the early church. A number of women served as leaders in the house churches that were a part of the larger church in the city of Rome. Some of those mentioned are Priscilla, Chloe, Lydia, Apphia, Nympha, the mother of John Mark, and possibly the "elect lady" of John's second epistle. Paul mentions Phoebe and refers to her as "a servant [literally, 'deaconess'] of the church in Cenchrea" (Rom. 16:1).

Paul also talks about Junia, referring to her as being "outstanding among the apostles" (v. 7, NAS). Some have debated the exact meaning of this verse. Until the Middle Ages, the identity of Junia as a female apostle was unquestioned. Later translators attempted to change the gender by changing the name to Junias.[1]

Women functioned as prophetic ministers. Philip, who was as one of the seven men appointed to the administration of feeding the poor (Acts 6), was head of the church in Caesarea. He had four virgin daughters who were recognized as prophetesses in the church (Acts 21:8–9). Some believe that these prophetesses became the standard and model for prophetic ministers in the early church.

When Pope Miltiades proclaimed that two female followers of Montanus were heretics, he contrasted them with Philip's daughters. Miltiades explained that their problem was not that they were women prophets (for this is what

Philip's daughters were), but rather that they were false prophets. Eusebius mentions one Quadratus, a man famous in the second century, who "shared with the daughters of Philip the distinction of a prophetic gift."[2]

The church quickly spread from its birthplace in Jerusalem into areas where the predominant culture was pagan, Greco-Roman, or both. In these settings, women commonly held high positions and influence in social, political, and religious circles. The idea of women having a leading influence in the church was therefore not thought of in negative terms.

About A.D. 112, the Roman governor Pliny the Younger wrote about his efforts to deal with the Christians in Bithynia. He found it necessary to interrogate the leaders of the church, two slave women called *ministrae,* or deaconesses.[3]

There are countless examples of women who served the church with complete and tireless devotion or who, without flinching, endured terrible tortures and martyrdom. A significant step in the process of Christianity's gaining political and social dominance in Rome was the large number of female converts among the upper class.

Men were less likely to become Christians because doing so would cause them to lose their status in society. The inordinate number of upper-class women is perhaps the reason that Celestas, bishop of Rome in A.D. 220, attempted to give women of the senatorial class an ecclesiastical sanction to marry slaves of freedmen.

These highborn women seized the opportunity to become students of the Word. One of these was a fourth-century woman named Marcella. The great scholar Jerome, who translated the Bible into Latin (known as the Vulgate), did not hesitate to refer church leaders to Marcella for help in solving their hermeneutical problems.[4]

Women enjoyed great freedom of expression in the earliest days of the church. However, because various kinds of problems arose, the original freedom and liberty afforded them in the church's ministry were replaced by a more precisely defined code of conduct that was reactionary in nature. With each new and more detailed explanation of what was and was not acceptable, the role of women was restricted and diminished.[5]

Nevertheless, even through the Middle Ages there were women who were outstanding examples of spirituality and dedication. The Waldensians, a group beginning in the twelfth century that could be described as Protestants four hundred years before the Reformation, were charged with, among other things, allowing women to preach. Catherine of Siena (1347–1380) was a resolute servant to the poor, a doctor of the church, and a lover of God whose theology and piety were revered even by the Reformers.

One summer when Joan of Arc was about thirteen, she suddenly saw a bright light and heard voices while working in the fields. The voices, which Joan thought were either angels or saints, continued after that day, rode over three hundred miles across enemy territory to tell the dauphin Charles of her plans.

When Joan entered the large hall, the dauphin had disguised himself as one of those in the crowd. Joan walked right up to him and addressed him.

"I am not the dauphin," Charles replied.

Joan responded, "In God's name, gentle sire, you are."

Then she proceeded to reveal to him his private thoughts. The nineteen-year-old girl led the French forces and saved France, and Charles was restored to the throne. Mark Twain studied the life of Joan of Arc for twelve years and concluded that her life was "the most noble life that was ever born into this world save only One."[6]

Though it is impossible to discern between legend, facts, and spiritual anointing, Joan's prophetic experiences seem somewhat similar to others I know who have been called to the prophetic ministry.

Women have also played a significant role in the spread and development of Protestantism, particularly in the area of foreign missions. In the twentieth century, women began to emerge in ministry and leadership roles, first in the holiness churches and then with the Pentecostals. The examples are numerous, the two most notable being Aimee Semple McPherson, the founder of the International Church of the Foursquare Gospel, and Kathryn Kuhlman.

David Yonggi Cho has released women into ministry and leadership positions in the Yoido Full Gospel Church in Seoul, South Korea, and with their help has built the world's largest church with more than three quarters of a million members.

WOMEN'S MINISTRY AT THE IHOP MISSIONS BASE

We have had a number of women in our midst who have made profound, accurate, and edifying contributions to our prophetic ministry. While much of this has been behind-the-scenes service to our leadership team, we are enthusiastic about women moving in the prophetic arena. The limits and extent of a woman's function on the prophetic team are the same as those of a man. We do not give prophetic people a prominent public platform—men or women.

We have a growing number of women who are anointed to speak the Word publicly. They speak at our conferences, church services, and in our full-time Bible school as well as our music academy.

Our prophetic network consists of about two hundred fifty people who regularly receive dreams, visions, and prophetic words from the Lord. The oversight of this network is provided by our Prophetic Council. This council is made up of both men and women who help nurture the people in the network in their prophetic gifting as well as listening to their prophetic revelation to help us discern the interpretation and application. This prophetic network is designed to provide encouragement, training, and helpful correction to those who regularly receive prophetic information from God.

STEREOTYPICAL WOMEN

Stereotypes, prejudices, and unfair biases are commonly directed against women. This mind-set greatly hinders the work of God. Some of these deeply imbedded stereotypes in male-dominated cultures exist in the church as well. We need to clearly and boldly identify these false stereotypes so that we can renounce them.

However, more and more male leaders in the church can see the great impact that women are having in the kingdom of God. We highly esteem the ministry of a mother in the home. However, we believe that women are also called to function in public ministry outside their home.

There are also stereotypes about women and their psychological makeup. One common stereotype is that they are very intuitive but don't have the proper restraint to control the emotional side of their nature. I don't think this is a fair stereotype. I do believe that some women can be described that way, but some men are like that as well. I think it is too generalized a stereotype and should not be used to hinder women from ministry.

Both men and women are intuitive and emotional, just as both are intelligent and objective. Both can be controlling and manipulative as well as humble and passionate in their love for Jesus.

Dysfunctional relational skills among men and women cause problems in society and in the church. Some men have unfounded fears about women in ministry; for example, that women will lose their femininity if they lead and that women are more prone to deception (both of which are untrue). So they are afraid to allow women to prophesy or to preach. The problem is exacerbated by some of the radical feminist movements. Consequently, some men resist valid biblical expressions of women in ministry.

I believe that if men had honored women in the church throughout history, some of the radical feminist movement that we see in our society today might have been diffused. If the church had been leading the way by honoring women in the church, it might have had an impact on the entire society now. If there had been more women prominent in society because of the strength of affirmation by men in the church, the negative effects of the radical feminist movement could have been minimized.

This is one practical way that the church functions as a prophetic standard bearer to society—by honoring both women and children in a way befitting the grace of God (Mal. 4:6; 1 Pet. 3:7).

THE JEZEBEL SPIRIT

One of the most misunderstood issues relating to prophetic women in the church is the idea of a "Jezebel spirit," particularly when the term is defined as a controlling woman who dominates men. "Jezebel spirit" is not actually a biblical term. However, there is undeniably a powerfully negative Jezebel-type spirit or attitude in which some are clearly immersed.

To some people, whenever a woman stands up to a male leader, she is referred to as having a "Jezebel spirit." Some women definitely have a domineering spirit; however, some men also have it. Sometimes these women are wounded and even lack relational skills. Men also get wounded and also need improvement in their social skills. However, few men are referred to as "being a Jezebel."

There are many women today in the church with legitimate leadership gifts who are being falsely labeled as a "Jezebel" simply because they clash with insecure male leaders who have a controlling personality. Women should not allow insecure men to dominate and hinder their place of service in God's kingdom. Too many women are being hindered by unrighteous judgments against them because they simply spoke up and challenged a man who had a wrong spirit. This type of action does not make a woman a Jezebel.

It trips a wire in my own soul when I hear a woman quickly written off as a Jezebel. It can be a crushing emotional blow to a woman. It is usually an unfair judgment that can unjustly cause her to repress or neglect her ministry gift for years.

I believe that both domineering women and dominating men need to be confronted and offered a process of healing. We do not need to label either one of them as a "Jezebel." Some male leaders see a domineering man and wink at the problem, saying, "Well, you know he has such a strong personality, and that's just the way he is." But when a woman acts in the exact way, unjust criticisms are often brought against her. The prejudice toward women is often due to dysfunctional relational skills that exist with both men and women. In these negative situations, the pastors are sometimes called controlling by the women, and the women are sometimes called Jezebels by the pastors. This is all ridiculous. Both the men and the women need to be healed.

JEZEBEL—SEDUCTION TO IMMORALITY

I believe the idea of a Jezebel-type spirit *does* involve an element of domination and control. Between Queen Jezebel and King Ahab, Jezebel clearly seemed to be the more dominant (1 Kings 18). However, Jesus defined a Jezebel-type spirit very specifically in terms other than domination:

> You allow that woman Jezebel, who calls herself a prophetess, to teach and seduce My servants to commit sexual immorality.
> —Revelation 2:20

A Jezebel-type spirit, then, can be described as one who leads the people of God to allow and embrace immorality. It primarily refers to someone with a seducing spirit. When we talk about being seduced these days, we tend to think of it as something women do to men. But there are male leaders in the body of Christ today who regularly seduce women. They can have a strong sensual or emotional impact on women. Men are as skilled in seduction as women are. Consequently, many men can be likened to Jezebel.

I think the most seductive Jezebel-type spirit in the world today is found in certain aspects of the media industry, which is very effective in desensitizing and beguiling the nations to commit acts of immorality. They have promoted the prostitution racket and the X-rated—and worse—film industry.

These certain members of the entertainment industry are the ones who perpetuate the stereotype of the woman as the seductress, but it is really their love of money that pours the fuel on the fire of seduction in our society. They, more than anyone else, have the characteristics of Jezebel.

We need to esteem and make room for women with leadership gifts in the church. Some pastors need to be less defensive and insecure in their leadership style.

CHAPTER 7

SEVEN DIMENSIONS OF
THE PROPHETIC CHURCH

B EING PROPHETIC IS not simply just something that charismatics do. It is essential to the very nature and mission of the entire body of Christ on Earth. Those involved in prophetic ministry need to view what they do in the larger context of all the other dimensions of the church's calling as a prophetic servant community. The most common idea of the prophetic refers to those who function in the gift of prophecy. Every believer is called to earnestly desire to prophesy (1 Cor. 14:1). The New Testament church is to function as a prophetic servant community not only to proclaim the fulfillment of End Time events or to speak forth revelatory messages, but to do so in a much broader and multidimensional way.

People who receive dreams and visions do not comprise the prophetic ministry in its entirety, but are really only one expression of a community that is prophetic in at least seven dimensions. Some of these seven prophetic expressions overlap in the same way that some of the gifts of the Spirit do. The list of the nine gifts of the Spirit (1 Cor. 12:7–11) is simply a description of how the person of the Holy Spirit moves through individuals in the church. Sometimes it is hard to categorize and define certain manifestations. Was it a word of wisdom, a prophecy, or the discerning of spirits? In the same way, these seven dimensions of the church as a prophetic servant community may overlap in some aspects. The point is that prophetic ministry is not just something the church does, but something it *is* by its very nature.

1. The revelation of the testimony of God's heart

An angel told the apostle John that the testimony of Jesus is the spirit of prophecy (Rev. 19:10). The spirit or the purpose of prophecy is to reveal Jesus's testimony of what He has done and what is currently on His heart. The revelation of how He feels and what is burning on His heart is a foundational aspect of His testimony. In other words, prophetic ministry flows out of experiencing Jesus's heart. It is a ministry that *feels* and *reveals* God's heart. It has to do with experiencing a measure of different aspects of His heart ranging from His compassion, zeal, grief, affection, or even the joy that is in His heart. We prophesy each time we make known His passionate heart. Prophets in the Old Testament often prefaced their message by declaring, "The *burden* which the prophet Habakkuk saw" (Hab. 1:1, emphasis added). The word *burden* implies the emotional issues that weigh heavy on God's heart. So then, one prophetic dimension of the church's ministry is to proclaim and call to remembrance the things that burn on Jesus's heart. That includes His burning affection for His people. Of course, our affection for Jesus is the result of an ever-increasing revelation of His passion for us (1 John 4:19). John the Baptist expressed the testimony of Jesus's heart in a very special way. Jesus declared John the Baptist to be the greatest man born of a woman (Matt. 11:11). John described himself in his forerunner ministry as a "friend of the bridegroom" (John 3:29).

John went before Jesus's first coming to prepare a people to receive Him as the heavenly Bridegroom. As prophetic forerunners, we like John are to call the people to walk out the first commandment as wholehearted lovers of God. The Holy Spirit is raising up prophetic forerunners with this focus to prepare the church before Jesus's second coming. Jesus also described the apostles as "friends of the bridegroom" (Matt. 9:15). The "friends of the Bridegroom" reality is being emphasized by the Holy Spirit in this generation. It describes ministries that equip the church to live in her bridal identity with a wholehearted love for Jesus. As the Bridegroom's friends, we focus on preparing individuals to live in the intimate embrace of our heavenly Bridegroom rather than drawing the bride's affections to their prophetic ministry.

2. The proclamation of End Time prophecy

The church is a prophetic witness of Jesus's second coming. One aspect of being prophetic is to clearly understand and fearlessly proclaim God's End Time plan and events as declared in biblical prophecy. All that the church does to make herself ready—proclaiming prophetic scriptures, worshiping, celebrating Communion, witnessing, preaching the gospel, casting out demons, healing the sick, being peacemakers, and functioning as forerunners who prepare the church for His coming (Eph. 5:27; Rev. 19:7–8)—is a prophetic trumpet to the world of the relationship of Christ to His church and of the fact that Christ is coming again.

The apostle John was commanded to eat the scroll of End Time prophecy (Rev. 10:8–10; Ezek. 2:10–3:3) to prepare him to understand and feel God's heart related to the End Times. John was a prototype for the End Time prophetic messengers whom the Holy Spirit is even now raising up. These prophetic messengers will bring great strength in a time of revival, judgment, and adversity (Rev. 12–13).

3. The preservation and proclamation of the Word of God as His prophetic standard on the earth

One of the most dynamic prophetic realities that exist is the Scripture itself. It trumpets God's heart, purpose, and will. It is the transcript of God's holy and loving heart. How precious is the Word of God. The church preserves and proclaims God's unchangeable and immovable truths. The church proclaiming the Scripture is the pillar and ground of the truth in a fallen world (1 Tim. 3:15). We are most prophetic when we faithfully and regularly proclaim the Word of God. We recognize that the church's very presence is a continuing witness to biblical prophecies being fulfilled. Our primary task is to preserve and proclaim the good news of His death, resurrection, and coming again to judge the world. The church is a living testimony of prophecy fulfilled and a prophetic voice of what will come in the future. The next time you are sitting in a church service, remember that even though we are two thousand years removed from the first-century church, the very fact that you are gathering with others in His name is both a prophetic fulfillment and a prophetic statement to the world of what is to come.

4. The reception of prophetic direction

The fourth way that the church is prophetic is in discerning the current move of the Spirit. Just as the children of Israel followed the cloud through the wilderness, the church is to move when the Holy Spirit says to move (Deut. 1:33). The Spirit is continually doing a fresh work in each congregation. Israel moved whenever God moved as they followed the cloud of God's presence in the wilderness. Churches, ministries, or families "move" into different emphases given by the Holy Spirit at different seasons in their life together, yet always within the boundaries of God's unchangeable Word.

The leaders of new movements of the Holy Spirit are not necessarily those who focus on the gift of prophecy as mentioned in 1 Corinthians 12, but instead they are leaders who clearly sense the prophetic direction of where the cloud of God's presence is moving. They are like the sons of Issachar who "had understanding of the times, to know what Israel ought to do" (1 Chron. 12:32).

The prophetic church follows Jesus's prophetic leadership as we "follow the cloud" by embracing that which the Holy Spirit is currently emphasizing. Of course, He is always emphasizing the proclamation of the gospel and obedience to God. There are many examples in church history when the body of Christ embraced a specific direction of the Holy Spirit as relating to structure, strategy, or even particular truths. For example, in 1517, Martin Luther did this as the Holy Spirit brought reformation to the church in Europe by emphasizing justification by faith.

One purpose of the prophetic ministry is to alert the church to the "now-ness" of the Holy Spirit. It awakens us to the purpose of God in the *present*—what He specifically wants to do in us and through us *now*. In other words, it is the "now word" of the Lord. Of course, it must always go along with the written Word of the Lord. God wants to bring the Word and the Spirit together in the church. Someone has said, "If we have the Word without the Spirit, we dry up. If we have the Spirit without the Word, we blow up. But if we have the Word and the Spirit, we grow up." In this way we can walk together in the fresh move of the Holy Spirit.

5. Prophetic dreams and visions and the power of God

The demonstration of God's supernatural power and revelation through the church is a dimension of the prophetic ministry. The Spirit equips us with supernatural gifts, including prophetic dreams and visions and the ability to work miracles (1 Cor. 12:10–11). Miracles attest to the truth of God's Word. Miracles make people aware that God is actually present with them. They renew our awareness of His presence. They jolt our sensibilities and make us joyfully (or frightfully) aware of the fact the He is in our midst. A hundred sermons on God being with us may not awaken our hearts as much as a personal encounter with the manifestation of His power through the miraculous. This in no way diminishes the authority of the written Word. It simply means that in the miraculous, the living God of the written Word shows up in a powerfully personal, intimate, and tangible way. Through the miraculous, the church prophesies and proclaims that He is alive!

6. The prophetic outcry against social injustice

The church is to function as a "corporate prophet to the nation" concerning injustice, oppression, and unrighteousness. Such things provoke the judgment of God on a nation. Two stellar examples of this are seen in the prophetic outcry from William Wilberforce (1759–1833) working within the church and, prior to him, Lord Shaftesbury (1621–1683) crying out in the British House of Lords. These two men denounced injustice on two different fronts over two centuries. They are credited with the British Parliament outlawing the trading of slaves in England.

Many times prophets to the nation speak from a secular platform, not necessarily as those who represent the church. Joseph and Daniel were two biblical examples of people who represented God in a position of secular power. Abraham Lincoln and Martin Luther King Jr. prophetically stood for justice and righteousness in our social order. Today, men like Lou Engle and James Dobson speak in the church as prophetic oracles who continually cry against the injustice of abortion. God has raised up His prophetic servants in the church who take a prophetic stand against injustice in society by being actively involved in civil government at many levels.

7. The prophetic call to holiness

God has raised up leaders in the church throughout the generations who have functioned as prophets of God crying out against the sins of the people. John Wesley, for instance, turned England back to God when the people's personal unrighteousness and apathy brought them to the edge of societal chaos.

This outcry is similar to the prophetic cry against social injustice, but different in that it is specifically directed to the people in the church. It is less like Jonah prophesying against Nineveh and more like Isaiah and Jeremiah prophesying to Israel and Judah. Men like Charles Colson, John Piper, David Wilkerson, and A. W. Tozer stand out in my mind as prophetic voices who have cried out against unrighteousness in the church. Their words have been anointed by the Spirit to awaken many hearts to holiness and passion for Jesus. God uses such prophetic voices, just as He used John the Baptist, to prick the conscience of believers unto repentance.

SERVING IN THE PROPHETIC COMMUNITY

It is the nature of the church to be the prophetic expression of the kingdom of God on Earth, to represent, preserve, and proclaim the truth of God to this world. All the members who serve the church or function as a ministry of the church are themselves involved with the ongoing prophetic plan and purpose of God in the earth.

Those particularly gifted with dreams, visions, prophecies, and revelation need to be careful not to think of themselves too highly, as being *the* prophetic group. They serve only one dimension of the church's greater calling as a prophetic community.

My prayer and earnest expectation is that God will work mightily in our generation to help the church more and more to live up to and express its prophetic nature and calling among the nations of the earth. The proclamation and demonstration of the Word of God through a Spirit-filled church is the true hope for mankind. May the Holy Spirit come upon us in unprecedented measure for the glory of God and Christ Jesus.

EXPRESSIONS OF THE SPIRIT OF PROPHECY

- Prophetic oracles (Isa. 1:1–9; 15:1–9; 45:14–17; 48:17–19; 49:5–7; 50:1–3; Jer. 2:1–3; Ezek. 34:1–31; Acts 13:1–3)
- Prophetic exhortations (Isa. 12:1–6; 19:25; 29:22–24; 30:18; 35:1–10; 40:1–31; 41:1–4; 42:1–9; 54:1–3; 55:1–13; 56:1–8)

- Prophetic prayers (Ezra 9:6–15; Neh. 9:6–37; Isa. 25:1–12; 38:9–20; 64:1–12; Jer. 12:1–6; 20:7–18; Luke 1:67–69)
- Prophetic songs (Deut. 32:1–43; Isa. 5:1–30; 26:1–21; 27:1–11; 42:10–13; Ezek. 19:1–14; 27:1–36)
- Personal prophecies (2 Sam. 12:1–7; Isa. 37:21–35; 38:1–8; 45:1–7; Jer. 20:1–6; 21:1–14; 34:1–5; 45:1–5; Acts 21:10)
- Prophetic visions (Jer. 1:11–19; 24:1–10; Ezek. 1:1–28; 8:1–18; 9:1–11; 10:1–22; 11:1–13; 37:1–11; 40:1–49; 41:1–48:35; Dan. 2:19; 4:1–18; 7:1–28; 8:1–27; Acts 16:9–13; 10:1–33)
- Prophetic actions (Isa. 20:1–6; Jer. 13:1–11; 19:1–15; 27:1–22; Ezek. 14:1–17; 5:1–17; 12:1–16; 12:17–25; 24:1–27; 37:15–23; Hosea 1:1–11; 3:1–5; Acts 21:9–14)

OTHER SCRIPTURES ON THE PROPHETIC MINISTRY

- Genesis 5:29; 22:7–8; 27:28–29; 27:39–40; 48:13–20; 49:1–27
- Exodus 15:14–18; 16:6–7
- Leviticus 9:6
- Numbers 11:24–30; 13:30; 14:6–9; 23:7–10; 23:18–24; 24:1–9; 24:15–24
- Deuteronomy 32:1–47; 33:1–29
- Joshua 10:25; 24:1–14
- Judges 6:8–10
- 1 Samuel 2:1–10; 24:1–14
- 2 Samuel 3:18–19; 7:8–17; 23:1–7
- 2 Kings 3:15–18
- 1 Chronicles 17:4–15; 22:8–13; 22:17–19
- 2 Chronicles 15:2–7; 20:15–17
- Ezra 9:6–15
- Nehemiah 2:20; 9:6–37
- Psalm 89:19–37
- Isaiah 1:18–20; 12:1–6; 25:6–12; 26:1–21; 29:17–24; 35:1–10; 44:1–5; 44:6–8; 55:1–13; 56:1–8; 60:1–9; 60:10–14; 60:15–22
- Ezekiel 11:16; 11:17–20; 28:25–26; 34:11–16; 34:24–31
- Hosea 2:14–20; 6:1–3; 11:8–9; 14:1–7
- Joel 2:12–14; 3:18–21

- Amos 9:13–15
- Obadiah 17
- Micah 2:12–13; 4:1–5; 4:6–8; 7:18–20
- Nahum 2:2
- Habakkuk 2:14
- Zephaniah 2:7; 3:14–20
- Haggai 2:5–9; 2:23
- Zechariah 8:7–13; 8:14–17; 10:1; 10:6–12
- Malachi 1:11; 3:16–18; 4:1–6
- Mark 10:30; 14:8–9
- Luke 1:41–55, 67–80; 2:25–35; 22:31–32
- John 6:31–35
- Acts 1:4–8; 2:14–37; 11:28; 13:1–3; 15:30–35; 20:28–31; 21:10–11
- Revelation 2:1–29; 3:1–22

CHAPTER 8

THE COMING GREAT REVIVAL

T HE BODY OF Christ will participate in the greatest revival in all history in the generation in which the Lord returns. The greatest outpouring of the Spirit in history will be released just before Jesus's second coming. In this great revival, the Holy Spirit will release the miracles that were seen in the Book of Acts and the Book of Exodus combined and multiplied on a global scale, which will result in the following positive trends.

1. A victorious, unified, anointed church full of God's glory will emerge (Matt. 16:18; John 17:21–26; Eph. 4:13; 5:26–27; Rev. 7:9; 12:11; 15:2; 19:7–8).

2. The church will live in purity or without spot (compromise) as they walk out Sermon on the Mount lifestyles (Matt. 5–7). "That He might present her to Himself a glorious church, not having spot or wrinkle or any such thing, but that she should be holy and without blemish" (Eph. 5:27).

3. The great ingathering of souls from all nations will surely see over one billion new souls (Ps. 66:4; Amos 9:11–12; Zeph. 2:11; 3:8–10; Matt. 24:14; Rom. 11:12–15, 26; Rev. 5:9; 7:9; 14:6; 15:4).

"A great multitude…no one could number, of all nations…out of the great tribulation" (Rev. 7:9, 14).

4. The spirit of prophecy will operate in the church and rest on every believer (Mal. 4:6; Matt. 17:11; Acts 2:17; Rev. 11:3-6; 18:20). "I will send you Elijah the prophet before the coming of the great and dreadful day of the LORD" (Mal. 4:5).

5. The two witnesses will prophesy with great power for three and a half years during the tribulation: "I will give power to my two witnesses, and they will prophesy one thousand two hundred and sixty days.… These have power to shut heaven, so that no rain falls in the days of their prophecy; and they have power over waters to turn them to blood, and to strike the earth with all plagues, as often as they desire" (Rev. 11:3, 6).

6. There will be great demonstrations of power with unprecedented prophetic revelation and experiences.

In all this we must continually keep focused on our primary purpose to win the lost and build His church as a community that walks in the two great commandments focused on loving God and people (Matt. 22:37–40). Prophecy is a very significant tool used in building God's house, but it's not the house. When you construct a building, you don't call a hammer a *movement*. The hammer is just one of many significant tools. One reason God raises up the prophetic ministry is to inspire perseverance in intercession that releases the resources to build God's house in love by the power of the Holy Spirit. The Holy Spirit gives us prophetic words that are for many areas of our personal life and the life of the church. However, prophetic words are invitations not guarantees. They beckon us to cry out to God in faith. God speaks prophetically to invite us to more fully cooperate with the Holy Spirit in faith and obedience as we pray to release the manifestation of the things prophesied. In other words, the prophetic ministry provides fuel for the prayer meetings, and the prayer meetings release the things promised by the prophetic words. They are inseparable. It is not enough to just long for more prophetic activity without intending to use it to inspire more prayer. In other words, prophecy is not to be seen as an end in itself or as that which simply makes church meetings more exciting. It is the gas that fuels the tank of intercession, purity, and more effective outreach to others.

CHANGING THE FACE OF CHRISTIANITY
IN ONE GENERATION

For years I had read Jonathan Edwards, David Brainerd, Dr. Martyn Lloyd-Jones, and some of the Puritan writers, and I had adopted their theology of an unprecedented ingathering of souls at the end of the age.[1]

But it was years later in September 1982, in a dirty little motel room in Cairo, Egypt, that the belief in an End Times outpouring of the Holy Spirit became a personal issue to me. The eight-by-eight-foot room was equipped with a small bed, squeaky ceiling fan, stone-age plumbing, and an assortment of crawling things that periodically scampered across the concrete floor. It was primitive by Western standards. I was alone, so I set aside the evening to spend with the Lord in prayer. I knelt on the cement floor by the rickety bed for about thirty minutes when I had one of the most incredible encounters that I've ever had.

I didn't see a vision, and I wasn't caught up into heaven. I simply heard God speak to me. It wasn't what some people call the audible voice. I call it the internal audible voice. I heard it as clearly as I would have heard it with my physical ears, and, honestly, it was terrifying.

It came with such a feeling of cleanness, power, and authority. In some ways I felt I was being crushed by it. I wanted to leave, but I didn't want to leave. I wanted it to be over, but I didn't want it to be over.

I only heard a few sentences, and it only took a few moments, but every word had great meaning. The awe of God flooded my soul as I experienced a little bit of the terror of the Lord. I literally trembled and wept as God Himself communicated to me in a way I've never known before or since. The Lord simply said, *"I will change the understanding and expression of Christianity in the earth in one generation."* It was a simple, straightforward statement, but I felt God's power with each word as I received the Spirit's interpretation. God Himself will make drastic changes in Christianity across the whole world. This reformation revival will be by His sovereign initiative.

I knew by the Holy Spirit that the phrase "the understanding of Christianity" meant the way Christianity is perceived by unbelievers. In the early church, people were afraid to associate casually with believers partly because of the displays of supernatural power (Acts 5:13). However, today, most unbelievers consider the church to be irrelevant to them. God will change the way unbelievers view the church. They once again will witness God's wonderful yet terrifying power in the church. They will have a very different understanding of Christianity before God is finished with this generation.

I also knew by the Holy Spirit that the phrase "the expression of Christianity" meant the way the body of Christ expresses its life together. God is powerfully going to change the church so that it functions as a unified holy people in the power and love of God. What happens when we gather together will change dramatically. We will see unparalleled power, purity, and unity in the End Time church.

Christians' relationships with God and each other, the way we will be perceived by unbelievers, and even the structure and functioning of the church will be radically changed by God Himself across the whole earth. This change will take place—not in a month, a year, or a few years—but in one generation. That night in Cairo I understood this for the first time by a supernatural prophetic encounter with the Holy Spirit.

The understanding and expression of Christianity is going to be changed by a great outpouring of the Spirit that will cross all national, social, ethnic, and cultural barriers. It won't be just a Western-world revival or only a third-world revival. The Joel 2/Acts 2 prophecy says that in the last days God will pour out of His Spirit on "all flesh" (Acts 2:17).

A lot of things will change as a result of this progressive outpouring of the Spirit. It will have many multidimensional expressions so that it will not simply be seen as an evangelism movement, a healing movement, a prayer movement, a unity movement, or a prophetic movement. It will be all of those and more. Above all things, it will impart deep passion for Jesus through the Holy Spirit.

The Holy Spirit longs above all things to glorify Jesus in the human heart (John 16:14). He wants to impart holy affections for Jesus in the church as we understand our identity as the bride of Christ (Rev. 22:17). Speaking of this outpouring only in terms of a prophetic movement is a much too limited concept.

The increase of prophetic ministry in the local church involves more than verbal, inspirational prophecy. It will include angelic visitations, dreams, visions, and signs and wonders in the sky, as well as an increase in prophetic revelation, even the kind given through the subtle impressions of the Holy Spirit.

My experience in the Cairo hotel room lasted less than an hour, though it seemed like a couple of hours. I left the room and walked around the streets of downtown Cairo alone until about midnight, committing myself to the Lord and His End Time purpose. The awe of God lingered in my soul for hours. I woke up the next day still feeling its impact. This experience connected my heart in a deeply personal way to the End Time fulfillment of the Joel 2/Acts 2 prophecy on a global level in this generation. My approach to pastoring in the local church changed radically on that one evening in September 1982. Little did I know that I was about to be introduced to a new dimension of the prophetic—confirmation of prophetic words through the acts of God in nature.

THE ACTS 2 MODEL: WIND, FIRE, AND WINE

I believe that Acts 2 is a divine pattern of how God visits His church in power. In this passage we see how God launched His church on Earth on this historic Day of Pentecost. I will highlight three important manifestations of the Holy Spirit's power and presence. First, God sent the "wind" of the Spirit, then the "fire" of the Spirit, and then the "wine" of the Spirit. The wind of the Spirit speaks of the release of the miraculous that includes angelic activity. Hebrews 1:7 relates the ministry of angels to the wind. On the Day of Pentecost, those present heard the sound of a mighty rushing wind. In Acts 4, the building they prayed in shook, possibly by the direct activity of angels.

When God sends the wind of the Spirit, we can expect to see great signs and wonders such as the sound of rushing wind and the shaking of buildings as well as extraordinary healings—even raising the dead. A great harvest of souls will come as a result of this.

I know of several prophets who have had recurring visions of the great End Time revival, with large stadiums across the earth being filled with people who witness great signs and wonders leading up to countless multitudes being saved.

The fire of God came next in Acts 2. This baptism of fire will enlarge our hearts in the love of God. In this, we will receive a deeper understanding of God's love, which will result in a fiery, holy love seen as supernatural impartation of passion for Jesus and compassion for people. This new passion for God will cause the body of Christ to function in a dramatically different way. The focus will be on how to love Jesus with all our hearts and strength. Included in this particular aspect of the Spirit's ministry will be anointed intercession for the lost with a great harvest of new souls coming into the kingdom.

The wine of God is linked in the Book of Joel to the outpouring of the Holy Spirit. It is God's ministry through the Spirit of bringing joy inexpressible and refreshment to weary, burdened souls.

In April 1984, an amazing thing happened to Bob Jones and me. The Lord spoke audibly to us both at the same time yet in separate places. It was a Saturday morning when I heard the thunderous audible voice of God speaking to me. That very morning, Bob Jones also heard the Lord audibly. I will highlight only a part of what was happened. The Lord said, "In ten years I will *begin* to release the wine of My Spirit." I immediately had two questions. First, what is the wine of the Spirit? Second, how will I be able to wait for ten years? I was twenty-eight years old at the time, and ten years seemed like a millennium.

Now it seems more obvious what the wine of the Spirit is. One reason God sends His wine is to refresh and renew the hearts of His people in the midst of the weariness and despair. It was precisely ten years later, in 1994, that God began to release a wave of "His wine" that touched His church in many nations from a small church in Toronto under the leadership of John and Carol Arnott. That was only a beginning of the new wine that is yet to be poured out in its fullness.

In Acts 2, God first sent the wind, then the fire, then the wine. As God restores the church before Jesus's second coming, I believe the order will be reversed. First, He is sending the wine of the Spirit to refresh and heal the weary church. Then He will send the fire of the Spirit to enlarge our hearts in God's love and anointed prayer. Last, He will send the wind of the Spirit, which includes a manifestation of the ministry of angels. This demonstration of the Holy Spirit's power will bring countless numbers of new people to saving faith in Jesus Christ. The church truly has great things ahead. However, Satan will seek to challenge us like never before.

THE JOEL 2 OUTPOURING OF THE HOLY SPIRIT

We must learn to nurture and administrate the prophetic ministry in the local church in our expectation of an End Time outpouring of the Holy Spirit as foretold in Joel 2 and cited by Peter's first sermon on the Day of Pentecost.

> And it shall come to pass in the last days, says God, that I will pour out of My Spirit on all flesh.
>
> —Acts 2:17

Many Old Testament prophecies about God's kingdom will be fulfilled in two major ways. First, there was a partial local fulfillment that began in the church in the Book of Acts. Second, the total fulfillment will be released on a worldwide scale in the generation in which Jesus returns.

Jesus spoke of the kingdom not only as if the kingdom had fully come, but also as if it was still yet to come. As George E. Ladd puts it, the kingdom was both already and not yet.[2] The kingdom has come to Earth in part with the advent of Christ, but the complete manifestation of biblical prophecies concerning the kingdom of God will occur at the end of this age when Jesus Christ returns again.

For example, in the next to the last verse of the Old Testament, Malachi prophesied: "Behold, I will send you Elijah the prophet before the coming of the great and dreadful day of the LORD" (Mal. 4:5).

Jesus identified John as Elijah (Matt. 11:14) and later said of him: "Indeed, Elijah is coming first and will restore all things. But I say to you that Elijah has come already, and they did not know him but did to him whatever they wished" (Matt. 17:11–12).

We see an immediate local fulfillment of "Elijah's" coming in John the Baptist's ministry in Judea. However, we also see a future fulfillment when "Elijah" will come to restore all things at the end of the age.

In the same way, the Joel 2 prophecy concerning the outpouring of the Holy Spirit was partially fulfilled in Jerusalem on the Day of Pentecost. Peter quotes the prophecies and says, "These are not drunk, as you suppose, since it is only the third hour of the day. But this is what was spoken by the prophet Joel" (Acts 2:15–16).

But just because the outpouring at Pentecost was "what was spoken by the prophet Joel," it does not mean that it was *all* of that which was spoke of by Joel. The Spirit fell on one hundred twenty people in a small room in Jerusalem who touched three thousand people (Acts 2). But Joel spoke of more than that. He said, "I will pour out My Spirit on *all flesh*" (Joel 2:28, emphasis added). One of the unique things about the last great revival will be the signs and wonders described in Acts 2:19 that will be displayed in nature, both on the earth and in the sky.

> For you can all prophesy one by one, that all may learn and all
> may be encouraged.
> —1 Corinthians 14:31

At the time in which Joel spoke this prophecy, his ideas were new and strange to Old Testament Israel. The anointing of the Spirit had been given to just a few people in the Old Testament era, usually older Jewish men who were kings, judges, or prophets. However, Joel prophesied that the Spirit would be poured out on all flesh, Jew and Gentile, men and women, young and old. In other words, every believer on the planet will experience the anointing of the Spirit. Paul quoted Joel 2:32 and then applied it universally to all believers:

> There is no distinction between Jew and Greek, for the same
> Lord...is rich to all who call on Him. For "whoever calls on the
> name of the LORD shall be saved."
> —Romans 10:12–13

The only qualifier that Joel made to this all-inclusive promise to "all flesh" is the phrase, "my servants" (Joel 2:29, NIV). Thus, the "all flesh" are those who are servants of God. "My servants" does not speak of those who casually profess their faith, but of those who genuinely serve God.

THE SPIRIT OF PROPHECY

We must not separate Joel's prophecy of the outpouring of the Spirit of prophecy from its primary context in the End Times when the great ingathering of souls occurs and the deception of the Antichrist abounds. Some do not value the prophetic ministry. They see it as optional; thus, they write it off as not for them. How can a true believer not be into the prophetic? If we are into the End Time harvest, if we love people and want to bring courage to the fearful, then we need prophetic input from the Spirit. It is not possible to be ready for the good and the bad events in the End Times without operating in the prophetic anointing. It is nonnegotiable for us.

The prophecy in Joel 2:28–32 gives us great confidence for a global outpouring of the Spirit. This outpouring will be an issue of life and death in the pressures of the Great Tribulation. We will need to operate with a prophetic spirit in precise ways. This is the inheritance of the entire End Times church. We must contend for and earnestly seek it with sustained prayer with fasting. Paul exhorts us to seek the greater gifts, especially to prophesy (1 Cor. 12:31; 14:1). We seek to prophesy because the prophetic spirit is the key that opens us up to the other gifts of the Spirit. When we receive prophetic impressions from the Spirit, the other gifts flow forth. The promise that we will prophesy encompasses all that is involved in operating in the power and revelation of the Spirit. Prophecy reveals the testimony of what is in Jesus's heart and mind (Rev. 19:10). It involves receiving dreams, visions, and angelic visitations that impart the skill to understand End Times prophecy. Daniel received this type of anointing.

> O Daniel, I [Gabriel] have now come forth to give you skill to understand....I have come to tell you...therefore consider the matter, and understand the vision.
>
> —Daniel 9:22–23

We will operate in the spirit of Elijah as John the Baptist did, who spoke God's Word with power and authority to turn the hearts of people to God. Micah testified of experiencing prophetic power to preach God's Word.

> He [John the Baptist] will turn many of the children of Israel to the Lord their God. He will also go before Him in the spirit and

power of Elijah, "to turn the hearts of the fathers to the children," and the disobedient to the wisdom of the just, to make ready a people prepared for the Lord.

—Luke 1:16–17

But truly I am full of power by the Spirit of the LORD, and of justice and might, to declare to Jacob his transgression and to Israel his sin.

—Micah 3:8

The fullness of this Joel 2 prophecy is yet to be seen. It will have a worldwide scope to it where all flesh—that is, all believers, not just prophets—will have dreams and see visions. The greatest and fullest manifestation of the kingdom of God—the day of the Lord, the restoration of all things, and the outpouring of the Holy Spirit—is reserved for the consummation of all things initiated in the generation in which the Lord returns.

The prophetic anointing will be essential for survival. Some of these dreams and visions will be a source of direction when life and death decisions need to be made in the Great Tribulation. Jeremiah spoke of God giving prophetic direction that His people would find water for survival and to walk in a straight way instead of walking into calamity or the deceptions of the Antichrist.

They shall come with weeping, and with supplications I will lead them. I will cause them to walk by the rivers of waters, in a straight way in which they shall not stumble.

—Jeremiah 31:9

COSMIC SIGNS IN THE END TIMES

I will show wonders in the heavens and in the earth: blood and fire and pillars of smoke. The sun shall be turned into darkness, and the moon into blood, before the coming of the great and awesome day of the LORD.

—Joel 2:30–31

In describing the outpouring of the Spirit in the End Times, Joel gave three prophecies to Israel that the sun, moon, and stars would be dramatically altered as supernatural proof that the Messiah was in their midst (Joel 2:10, 30–31; 3:15). Joel also prophesied of signs on the earth. God will show "wonders in the earth," which will include manifestations of blood, fire, and pillars of smoke as well as great healings as Jesus did. Blood is listed as one of the major signs because blood will flow in unprecedented amounts. Blood is seen in the first three trumpets and the second and third bowl judgments (Rev. 8:7–10; 16:3–4). The two witnesses will have authority to turn water into blood. Entire rivers will be turned to blood like in the days of Moses. The blood of nations will flow because they shed the blood of the martyrs

> You are righteous, O Lord…because You have judged these things. For they have shed the blood of saints and prophets, and You have given them blood to drink.
>
> —Revelation 16:5–6

God has planned the most dramatic display of prophetic signs in His commitment to help the End Time church. These signs will be given at strategic times to signify significant messages to those who interpret them rightly. Prophetic signs will cause people to understand that they are living in the End Times. These marvels will warn unbelievers to no longer refuse God's Word. Joel connected these signs with prophetic dreams and visions and the pouring out of the Spirit. How astounding it will be when the whole world is watching as God's prophets proclaim a dream or vision ahead of time, giving exact details of when and where a comet or an earthquake will occur. The signs in the heavens and on Earth will not just appear in a vacuum, but at the precise timing that God determines as His servants declare them ahead of time.

The sun and moon will be affected by God's power in response to the intercession of the church and through prophetic decrees as in the days of Elijah. The miracles that Moses did had a great impact on Egypt and Israel. The river turned to blood at the moment he commanded it to. Such signs confirmed Moses's prophetic messages. The signs and wonders in the heavens and on Earth will also be used to bring in a great ingathering of souls. Some interpret the promise of signs in Joel 2:30–31 as being purely symbolic. In doing this, they see Joel's prophecy as being symbolically fulfilled in the past events of history. To the phrase, "the heavens tremble," some say that the heavens did not actually tremble because it is only meant to be understood as prophetic poetry. These cosmic signs are not to be dismissed as symbolic poetry. The biblical approach to these cosmic signs is to take them literally.

END TIME DELIVERANCE AND THE HARVEST

It shall come to pass that whoever calls on the name of the LORD shall be saved. For in Mount Zion and in Jerusalem there shall be deliverance, as the LORD has said, among the remnant whom the LORD calls.

—Joel 2:32

Joel prophesied that that whoever calls upon Jesus's name in the End Times will be saved. Being saved has several distinct dimensions to it in Scripture. First, we are saved in the initial sense of receiving forgiveness and being born again. Second, we are saved, delivered, or protected from physical death in relation to End Time disasters. Psalm 91 promises us physical protection in the End Times. Third, we are saved in the sense that God will provide the things necessary for life such as food and water. Israel experienced provision and protection in Goshen (Exod. 8:22–23; 9:4, 6, 26). Fourth, we are saved as we walk in God's saving power that we might enter into our full destiny. In other words, we are delivered from spiritual barrenness and powerlessness. Fifth, we are saved or protected from deception and from falling away from our faith (1 Tim. 4:1–2).

Get ready. An unprecedented revival is coming in which all believers will experience dreams, visions, and everything Joel prophesied.

CHAPTER 9

CONTENDING FOR THE FULLNESS OF THE PROPHETIC ANOINTING

S CRIPTURE PROMISES A global outpouring of the Holy Spirit in the End Times. This includes an unprecedented release of the spirit of prophecy on the church in the generation in which the Lord returns.

> And it shall come to pass in the last days, says God, that I will pour out of My Spirit on all flesh; your sons and your daughters shall prophesy, your young men shall see visions, your old men shall dream dreams. And on My menservants and on My maidservants I will pour out My Spirit in those days; and they shall prophesy. I will show wonders in heaven above and signs in the earth beneath: Blood and fire and vapor of smoke. The sun shall be turned into darkness, and the moon into blood, before the coming of the great and awesome day of the LORD. And it shall come to pass that whoever calls on the name of the LORD shall be saved.
>
> —Acts 2:14–21

The Holy Spirit will release grace to receive prophetic dreams and visions in the generation in which the Lord returns. It will be the common function of all of God's people. He will literally pour out the spirit of prophecy on the entire church, or on all flesh who believe in Jesus, not just on prophets. This includes all believing women, not just men, and all believing children, not just adults or mature believers. The word *all* refers not to all human beings without exception, but to all classes of human beings without distinction. This promise is spoken twice, emphasizing it as an absolute reality to occur. God desires, and has always desired, to personally encounter His people. From the beginning of creation, it was His desire to interact and fellowship with us in a very real way. This hasn't changed in any way at all, however, the method or the way in which He has chosen to manifest that desire.

He will release signs in nature both above in the heavens (sky, weather patterns) and below on the earth, including earthquakes. This will happen before the day of the Lord or the second coming of Jesus. What the Holy Spirit did on the Day of Pentecost was a down payment on this greater End Time outpouring.

Joel prophesied that when we turn to God with all our heart in prayer with fasting, the Lord would be zealous and compassionate and would pour out His Spirit on us (Joel 2:12, 18, 28).

Jesus promised that if His disciples tarried in prayer, the Spirit would endue them with power. "Behold, I send the Promise of My Father upon you; but tarry in the city of Jerusalem until you are endued with power from on high" (Luke 24:49).

In Acts 1–2, the disciples followed the pattern described by Joel as they sought the promise given by Jesus. Thus, they gathered to pray in the Upper Room. After ten days, on the Feast of Pentecost the Spirit came on them with power (Acts 1:14–2:4). It is possible that some of them expected the Joel 2:28 breakthrough of the Spirit at that time since Jesus had recently promised it (Luke 24:49). Peter explained this visitation of the Spirit as being that which was prophesied by Joel. These ten days of prayer occurred in a strategic, prophetic timing. It was preceded first by the death and resurrection of Jesus and by a dynamic prayer history that included Israel's greatest intercessors. Jesus and John the Baptist had prayed fervently for God's blessing to be released, as did Anna, who prayed for sixty years (Luke 2:37). In other words, the apostles stepped into a dynamic history of prayer that had been in place before that Feast of Pentecost had come.

They went up into the upper room where they were staying.... These all continued with one accord in prayer and supplication.... Now when the Day of Pentecost had fully come, they were all with one accord in one place. And suddenly there came a sound from heaven, as of a rushing mighty wind, and it filled the whole house where they were sitting. Then there appeared to them divided tongues, as of fire, and one sat upon each of them. And they were all filled with the Holy Spirit and began to speak with other tongues.

—Acts 1:13–14; 2:1–4

Peter said what happened in Jerusalem was spoken of by Joel. What did Joel speak of? Yes, he emphasized the fact that God would pour out the Spirit, but he also emphasized the conditions in which it would occur. Both are a part of the pattern seen in Joel 2. Peter was referring to the whole context of Joel 2, not just the end result of it. Thus, Peter was teaching us not only about the release of the Holy Spirit but also how we are to seek for it. The Joel 2:12–15 pattern of corporate prayer with fasting has been followed throughout church history, resulting in many great revivals. In our day, we must also follow the Joel 2:12–15 pattern. The greatest revival is yet to come, surpassing what the church experienced in the Book of Acts. The church today must see the importance of gathering in corporate intercessory worship until God releases the fullness of His blessing. We have a rich history of prayer behind us—one that has continued from Moses, David, Daniel, and then Jesus, Anna, and Paul, continuing through all church history. The bowls of intercession in heaven are surely filling up (Rev. 5:8).

God's promise to pour out His Spirit is the most well-known passage in the Book of Joel. Just prior to this point in his prophecy, Joel emphasized the agricultural blessings that God would release on Israel because of His zeal and pity or compassion (Joel 2:18–27). Now Joel speaks of the coming spiritual blessing to renew the people (Joel 2:28–32). The promise of the outpouring of the Spirit that Joel prophesied was not completely fulfilled in Peter's generation. This is evidenced by significant differences between Joel 2 and Acts 2. The fullness of what Joel prophesied has still not yet happened. Only a portion of it was fulfilled in Peter's day. Joel said that the sun and the moon would grow dark, and signs such as blood and smoke would be seen. The early church did not see these signs. Joel prophesied of a great outpouring of the Spirit on all flesh worldwide. The Spirit in Acts 2 only rested on one hundred twenty Jewish believers locally in Jerusalem, then on the three thousand who were saved that day. The fullness of Joel's prophecy requires a global dimension. Peter knew he only experienced the firstfruits of Joel's prophecy. The full expression of it would not happen until Jesus returned to Zion or in Jerusalem when He reigns (Joel 3:16–21).

THE TIMING OF JOEL'S PROPHESIED OUTPOURING OF THE SPIRIT

Peter said that the outpouring of the Spirit would happen in the last days (Acts 2:17). The New Testament writers used the phrase "in the last days" on five occasions and in two different ways. In Acts 2:17 and Hebrews 1:2, they refer to the last days as beginning in the generation of the Book of Acts. However, in 2 Timothy 3:1 and 2 Peter 3:3, they refer to the last days as the generation that the Lord returns. James 5:3 could be used in either way. We know that the last days began on the Day of Pentecost two thousand years ago and will culminate at the coming of Jesus. This narrows down the time frame of Joel's prophecy. At least we know it was not fulfilled in Joel's generation, but at a later time called the last days.

Joel prophesied of a great outpouring of the Spirit on all nations. When will the fullness of this take place? Joel tells us it will happen "afterward" (Joel 2:28). Of course, the question is: After what? It is after something specific. Some see the "afterward" of verse 28 as a reference to the Second Coming. This is not possible because Joel makes clear in verse 31 that the prophetic spirit and signs in the heavens occur before the day of the Lord or the second coming of Jesus.

> I will show wonders in the heavens.... The sun shall be turned into darkness, and the moon into blood, before the coming of the great and awesome day of the LORD.
>
> —Joel 2:30–31

In studying the options for what *afterward* refers to, it is best to understand it in the context of Joel's call to fasting and prayer (vv. 12–17). In other words, *after* the times of corporate wholeheartedness, God will pour out

His Spirit. It is as though Joel was saying, "When you cry out to the Lord with fasting and prayer, afterward He will bless you by releasing His Spirit." Some commentators link the word *afterward* to the passage just prior (vv. 21–27), when Joel prophesied of the agricultural blessings and the defeat of the northern enemy (v. 20) that God promised Israel in the millennium. It will be a time in which Israel is never put to shame again (vv. 26–27). This will only happen after Jesus returns. However, Joel said in verse 31 that the prophetic spirit with signs in the sky would occur before Jesus returns and the millennium starts.

Another timing indicator is given when Joel twice used the phrase, "in those days" (Joel 2:29; 3:1). This phrase ties together the events prophesied in Joel 2:28–32 into the same time frame as the events prophesied in Joel 3:1–21. The repeated use of this phrase makes clear that the themes in Joel 2 and Joel 3 go together and should not be separated. In other words, there should be no chapter division. Joel spoke of the outpouring as being at the time when Israel is surrounded by the Antichrist's armies and then is delivered from them.

Since Joel 2 and Joel 3, in the ultimate fulfillment of the prophecy, are in the same time frame, we know that the outpouring of the Spirit will happen in the *same time period* as when the Lord gathers the captives of Israel from all nations to bring them back to Jerusalem. It will also be in the same time frame in which the Lord assembles all nations to come against Jerusalem so that He might destroy them. In other words, these events occur in the generation the Lord returns.

In much of Christianity today, the vision of contending for the fullness of the prophetic anointing to rest upon the church remains ambiguous at best, or nonexistent at worst. Yet, all throughout the Scriptures, there is a promise that before the Lord returns, He is going to pour out His Spirit and raise up a church that will prophesy and walk in a power that the earth has not yet witnessed. Even Jesus, when He walked upon the earth, promised that "he who believes in Me, the works that I do he will do also; and greater works than these he will do" (John 14:12). While there are few moments in church history that excite and point to this reality, we have yet to see a sustained anointing of power rest upon the church that is greater than the ministry of power that Jesus walked in at His first coming. The church must not settle for anything less than the promise that we would walk as Jesus walked.

However, many in the church today are content to read and hear these prophetic promises and dismiss them as hyperbole or fulfilled by the apostles in the Book of Acts. Because of our lack of power, we try to relieve our barrenness by filling our time with more religious activities, programs, and gimmicks that give the perception we are living in the fullness of what God intended for us while falling far short of the reality of power. The apostle Jude's words in Jude 3 remain as relevant to us today as it was in his day as he challenged his disciples to "contend earnestly for the faith which was once for all delivered to the saints." If this exhortation was necessary for the early church in the first century, then how much more necessary is it now for us to rise up and fight to understand and experience the "faith" that the early apostles lived? Just as Jude addressed the early church for their dwindling vision to fight for the fullness of all that God had apportioned to them, it is incumbent upon the church today that we recover the "faith" that Jude encouraged the early church to contend for.

CONTENDING FOR THE APOSTOLIC FAITH

Typically, Christians in our day limit the meaning of "contending for the faith" to fighting for sound doctrine and sometimes including righteous living. While fighting for sound doctrine and living holy before the Lord are good pursuits, there is more to contending for apostolic faith that Jude describes than laboring only to have good theology and holy lifestyles. I can only imagine Jude's response to a believer in the twenty-first century telling Jude that he only wants sound doctrine and a godly lifestyle, but he doesn't want or need to heal the sick, cast out demons, and prophesy regularly. I am certain Jude would correct him and say, "If you only have right dogma and live righteously, but don't demonstrate the power of the doctrine and the outworking of righteousness, then you aren't fully contending for the faith." It is not enough to have good doctrine with a clean life. That's only part of the equation. We need to have the power to deliver the oppressed and the needy with a prophetic word. At the same time, it's not enough to experience power in ministry while living in secret sin or espousing false doctrine. We must contend for all three elements of true apostolic faith: biblical ideas, biblical lifestyles, and biblical experience.

This is the apostolic faith that was once for all delivered by Jesus and the apostles. This is the faith that we are contending for today.

Before I move onto explaining five ways that we can contend for the fullness of the prophetic anointing, I want to first address two subtle accusations that ofttimes come against people who desire to contend for the fullness of God's power.

False doctrine of God's sovereignty and grace

The first accusation that people contending for the fullness of God's prophetic anointing face is the inappropriate view of God's sovereignty and grace. In the church in the West, there is a false doctrine of grace and sovereignty that has become prevalent. This false doctrine teaches many to "trust" the sovereignty of God in an unbiblical way by "trusting" God to do what He has assigned us to do. This is gross negligence and presumption on our end. Though God may help us do our part, God will not do our part and we cannot do His part.

However, it is clear that we must contend for more because the Christian life is lived in cooperation with God's grace. God has given us a dynamic role in determining some of the measure of our quality of life that we experience in the natural and in the Spirit, including the gift of the prophetic anointing. James tells us in James 4:2, "You do not have because you do not ask." There are profound blessings that God has chosen to give us, but only if we will rise up to ask for them (Isa. 30:18–19; Ezek. 22:30).

Oftentimes, people tend to trust in the sovereignty of God in a way that He had not intended for us because such a false doctrine makes us feel more comfortable in our laziness and passivity. It allows for us to live in dulling compromise, selfishness, and laziness, believing that breakthrough will come in God's sovereign timing whether we contend for the breakthrough of power or not. This is an unbiblical and dangerous idea.

Because God has given us a dynamic role in determining some of the measure of our quality of life, if we seek Him more, He will give us more. If we seek Him less, He will give us less. This may make you feel uncomfortable, as it should, because too many of us are content sleeping in our compromise, all the while backing up such compromise with a false doctrine of grace and sovereignty, which allows for such hyperspiritualized carnality.

Seeking God's face and His hand

The second accusation that people contending for the fullness of God's prophetic anointing face is characterized by a familiar saying that seems to be growing more popular today that goes something like, "We should seek only God's face, but not His hand." Seeking His face generally refers to seeking intimacy with God, while seeking His hand refers to the blessings He has for us, including the release of His power in ministry. This saying sounds great, but it is not biblical. The Scriptures never instruct us to put intimacy with God in an adversarial relationship with God's power in ministry. Instead, they are active partners not opposed to one another. We seek God's power, including the gift of prophecy, to set people free so that they also might experience intimacy with Jesus.

The only truth within that phrase is that seeking God's face should be the priority and seeking power in ministry should be second, but we should resist any idea that contending for and seeking God's power is wrong. While it certainly is wrong to seek power as a higher priority than intimacy (Acts 8:18–22), it is likewise wrong to neglect seeking power at all. The apostle Paul clearly exhorted us to "earnestly desire the best gifts" (1 Cor. 12:31).

FIVE WAYS OF CONTENDING FOR THE FULLNESS OF THE PROPHETIC ANOINTING

While the power dimension of the faith that Jude describes includes much more than just prophecy, let's focus in on the five ways of how we can contend to walk in the fullness of the prophetic anointing.

1. Have a clear vision for the fullness of the Holy Spirit.

We contend for the fullness of the prophetic anointing by maintaining a clear vision for it. I find many in the body of Christ who do not have a vision for this. They have a vision for a "little bit more," but they do not want to contend for the quality of the prophetic anointing that the early apostles walked in. We must fight to have a vision to walk in everything that God will give the human spirit in this generation with a holy pain concerning our powerlessness and spiritual barrenness (Matt. 5:4).

Jesus tells us in Mark 4:24 to "take heed what you hear. With the same measure you use, it will be measured to you; and to you who hear, more will be given." In other words, we must be careful with what we hear or in what we believe is God's measure of fullness for our lives. We must be careful in determining what we will contend for in our experience in God, as most of us are too easily satisfied with bigger churches or better worship music or a few personal prophecies sprinkled throughout our services when the Lord desires to release so much more.

I believe the Lord has such a radically different vision for the fullness of the prophetic anointing than what we call the prophetic anointing in the church today. We must align our vision with His vision for the prophetic anointing instead of trying to manipulate Him into our meetings and values. I remember when one pastor was really frustrated and confused by this. He talked to me afterward and said, "I don't get this. I just don't understand what you're trying to say. It's as if you're expecting something dramatic to happen." I responded, "No. You do get it. You are listening. I really am expecting something dramatic to happen." He thought my response was weird, but I believe it was the biblical response.

The type of approach that God is looking for is to burn our boats, burn our bridges, and have the mentality that refuses to retreat under any circumstances. We must determine in our hearts to press in until we die and meet the Lord or until the Lord visits us with power and prophetic anointing.

2. Cultivate a spirit of gratefulness and faithfulness in smallness.

We contend for the fullness of the prophetic anointing by cultivating a spirit of gratefulness and faithfulness for all that the Lord has already released to us, no matter how small it may seem. While we must have a clear vision for the fullness, we must not despise the day of small beginnings. (See Zechariah 4:10.) We must contend for more because we see what we lack, yet we must give thanks for what we do have, no matter how little or insignificant it may feel. As we are faithful in the little, God will release more and more of the prophetic anointing on our lives (Luke 19:17).

3. Live a life of fasting and prayer.

We contend for the fullness of the prophetic anointing by pressing in with a lifestyle of fasting and prayer. We must determine to give ourselves in prayer and fasting in such a way that we refuse to back down in any way. We must press into God through prayer and fasting and settle the issue, "Why not me?" If you won't do it, who will? If it won't happen in our lifetime, then when?

Right now, the Lord is orchestrating a worldwide movement of prayer and fasting mingled with worship. Now, prayer and fasting do not earn us more blessings, but prayer and fasting position our hearts in such a way to more fully cooperate with Him in releasing His blessings to us and our cities. I believe that the Lord is calling us right now to shift out of the common mode of Christian ministry into a spiritually violent lifestyle of fasting and prayer (Matt. 11:12). To many in the church today, a lifestyle of prayer and fasting seems counterproductive to seeing the kingdom of God break into our cities. However, Scripture is clear that we enter into greater realms of prophetic anointing by the simple weakness of prayer, fasting, serving, and bearing up under persecution (2 Cor. 11–12).*

The message of voluntary weakness through prayer and fasting is an offensive message to the church. The problem is that when we begin to walk down the path of weakness, the power does not always break out immediately. The Lord tests our faith with a divine time delay. After a while of praying and fasting, but not seeing the immediate fruit of our prayers and fasting, we often want to draw back. At that point, we often give into the lie that the pathway to God is not really prayer and fasting and that we can skip that step and do it our own way.

Most ministries end up believing the lie that there is more power found by bypassing the weakness of prayer and fasting and engaging in frenetic activity rather than taking the road less traveled and pouring our time through prayer and fasting into the presence of God. Too often, they measure in the hear and now, but in the big picture of church history, it is clear that when people have persistently chosen to pray and fast, God has always proved true by releasing a greater dimension of His power. It may take years, sometimes even entire lifetimes, but it happens without exception.

---

* What do I mean by the "weakness" of prayer and fasting? Think of it this way. When you invest your time and energy in prayer, you are "forfeiting" valuable hours and energy you could be using to build your ministry, your business, or your lifestyle in some way. When you fast, you are giving away your physical strength.

4. Seek to fully obey God without compromise.

We contend for the fullness of the prophetic anointing by seeking to fully obey God without compromise. We must choose to walk out lives that reflect the Sermon on the Mount (Matt. 5–7), living free of any compromise by declaring war against all known sin in our lives.

Many times, people who desire to be free from all compromise grow discouraged because there are one or two or a few issues in their life that they do not feel they can get free from. The issue is not whether or not you still struggle with sin in your life, but that you are actively warring against it and seeking to be set free. I have never met a single person who is completely free from all the hidden sins and issues in his or her life, but I believe that if we seek to be free from compromise, we will find freedom in time.

I know of many people who jump into the prayer and worship movement and wear it as a badge of honor, thinking that they have joined some elite group that does not struggle with sin and compromise. They go to prayer meetings thinking they are free from compromise because they attend the prayer meetings, but their private lives do not correspond with what they are saying in the prayer meetings. Prayer and fasting can never serve as a substitute for a lifestyle of obedience in all the other areas of life. In order to receive the fullness of the prophetic anointing, it is imperative that we war against sin in order to live lives free of compromise and full of integrity.

5. Bear the reproach and stigma of the anointing.

Last but not least, we contend for the fullness of the prophetic anointing by bearing the reproach that comes with God's power. This is no small thing. Over the years, the Lord has allowed me to witness and even be a small part of a God-orchestrated stigma and reproach that accompanies the prophetic anointing. We have this false idea that when God releases the prophetic anointing and power, we will have dignity and honor and look "cool" in everyone's eyes. However, what I have noticed over the years is that when God releases His prophetic anointing on His vessels, they also become targets for both demons and men, sometimes even from good and godly men. This is not necessarily a judgment of God against them, but His mercy to keep them humble as He releases greater measures of His unusual supernatural manifestation of power.

Even the apostle Paul bore the stigma of the prophetic anointing. He made this clear in 2 Corinthians 12:7 by writing, "Lest I should be exalted above measure by the abundance of the revelations, a thorn in the flesh was given to me, a messenger of Satan to buffet me, lest I be exalted." This stigma can serve to keep us from pride and arrogance as God protects us by hedging us in with such reproach.

We must learn to take a stand and bear the approach before and after God releases His prophetic anointing. God will allow us to look foolish for our own sakes, so we must not wait around until it becomes popular to seek God with spiritual violence. Join in with those who are taking a stand, or be the first to stand now.

CONCLUSION

There are many scriptural promises of God releasing His prophetic anointing to the generation in which the Lord will return. I believe that we are living in that generation. We do not contend for the fullness of the prophetic anointing because it merely adds excitement to our meetings, but because the Lord promises that He will release His Spirit and we desire to cooperate and partner with Him in His purpose for this generation.

CHAPTER 10

FALSE EQUATIONS ABOUT PROPHETIC GIFTINGS

I T'S TOO BAD, Richard," I replied. "I'm sorry you feel that way." My friend Richard is a dedicated and godly Nazarene pastor with an earned seminary degree. He was shocked and offended at the idea that people with genuine prophetic ministries may be incorrect in some of their doctrines and have unsettled issues in their character. Some of them really do end up committing scandalous sins. Richard used a common but inaccurate equation to judge spiritual gifts. He thought that a person with a history of true prophecies also must be uniquely godly and biblically sound in all their doctrine. I strongly disagreed with him. He had no experience with prophetic people, yet he had his theories clearly worked out. When I first began to relate to prophetic ministries, I would have fully agreed with Richard. However, after years of experience with the prophetic ministry, I had to rethink many of my original theories. Yes, prophetic people must be clear about major doctrines like the person and work of Christ and the infallibility of the Scriptures. But on lesser points of doctrine, they might be misinformed or confused. It would be easier to just dismiss them as false prophets, but it is not quite that simple.

One of the things that surprises some pastors when they first begin to embrace the prophetic ministry is that the gifts of the Spirit really do operate in people who have some significant unresolved issues in their lives. Some think that only godly, mature people are used by God in demonstrations of power. This is simply not true, nor is it biblical. Of course, the first name who comes to mind is Samson. Some assume that a flaw in a person's doctrine or character is sufficient proof that the gifts functioning in their ministries must not be from God. Paul's first letter to the Corinthians gives us much insight to a carnal church that operated in the gifts of the Holy Spirit. They misused the gifts (1 Cor. 14), had wrong doctrines (1 Cor. 8–9), and lacked godly character (1 Cor. 3–5). There is no suggestion in 1 Corinthians that the misuse of the gifts makes them invalid.

GIFTS OF GRACE

The word used in the New Testament for spiritual gifts is *charisma*, or literally, "gifts of grace." In other words, these gifts are given freely and are not earned.

The sorcerer Simon misunderstood the gifts of the Holy Spirit, thinking they could be purchased (Acts 8:18–24). Peter severely rebuked him for seeking to buy the power of God. There is not much difference between earning gifts and buying them. Money is only a function of effort and labor. Contrary to some commonly held equations, the gifts of God are distributed at the will of the Holy Spirit, not by earning them even by godly character.

> But one and the same Spirit works all these things, distributing to each one individually as He wills.
>
> —1 Corinthians 12:11

They are not given as a token or a badge of God's approval of a person's level of spiritual maturity. Nor are they earned by our consecration. They are grace gifts.

Paul wrote to the Galatians who had difficulties understanding grace and kept putting law and works back into their spiritual equations: "O foolish Galatians! Who has bewitched you…? This only I want to learn from you: Did you receive the Spirit by the works of the law, or by the hearing of faith? Are you so foolish? Having begun in the Spirit, are you now being made perfect by the flesh?" (Gal. 3:1–3).

After the Galatians experienced the manifestations of spiritual gifts, some of them wanted to earn the gifts and perfect them by the spiritual accomplishments of the law or by the works of the flesh. Paul reminded them that being spiritually gifted is by grace just as justification is by faith (Eph. 2:8–9). Yes, just as we are saved by grace, not by works of merit, so we receive the gifts of the Spirit by grace, not works. Paul taught about receiving the gifts of the Spirit by faith and not works as analogous to receiving justification by faith and not works.

The lame man who begged for alms was commanded by Peter and John to walk in the name of Jesus. When Peter saw how amazed the people were about the healing, he said: "Men of Israel, why do you marvel at this? Or why look so intently at us, as though by our own power or godliness we had made this man walk?" (Acts 3:12).

Peter wanted to make that point clearly and quickly before there were any false assumptions. The manifestation of God's power was not a sign of his personal godliness. He went on to say: "And on the basis of faith in His name, it is the name of Jesus which has strengthened this man whom you see and know; and the faith which comes through Him has given him this perfect health in the presence of you all" (v. 16, NAS).

That passage contains many implications. But if it says anything, it is that the miracle was not about Peter's own spirituality. It had to do with God and His purposes and compassion to heal the man in need.

BECOMING THE GIFT

I am not suggesting an antinomian (lawless) approach to the use of spiritual gifts any more than those who preach justification by faith suggest living a lawless life. I'm desirous of strengthening our conviction to examine all things carefully even if they are from a famous prophetic vessel who is powerfully anointed as well as being open to receive from a vessel who is obviously broken. Also, when you are having a bad month, do not draw back from asking the Holy Spirit to use you to bless someone else by being a vessel used in prophecy to healing.

Paul writes, "But to each one of us grace was given according to the measure of Christ's gift" (Eph. 4:7, NAS). What Paul says in the following verses makes it clear that the *gift* he was referring to is a *ministry gift*: "And

He Himself gave some to be apostles, some prophets, some evangelists, and some pastors and teachers" (v. 11).

There is a common misconception about the anointed people referred to in this passage. Some assume that different ministries are given the gift of being a prophet, pastor, evangelist, and so forth. Paul saw it differently. Jesus gave some people to be apostles, prophets, evangelists, pastors, and teachers as His gift to the church. It was not an issue of the ministry ability being given as a gift for the benefit of the minister but rather for the benefit of the church. God's giftings are not about our promotions and esteem. They are distributed to people who become vessels and conduits of His mercy for the benefit of others. Thus, God anoints us for the good of others, not for us to gain some benefit from it. We cannot earn God's anointing.

The gifts of the Spirit in a person's life are not merit badges signifying their godliness. Yet, many see the gifts working through an individual as a symbol of God's approval of that person's life. They see that the more significant the giftings and power are, the more approval that ministry must have from God. However, if we understand that the manifestations of the Spirit are for the common good of the church and not for the good of the individual whom God uses, we would be less likely to stumble over the idea that God regularly uses imperfect, often immature people to bless the church in powerful ways.

There is a great difference between immature, unwise, and even carnal servants and those living in deliberate rebellion against God. We should not receive from people living in defiance of God no matter how powerful their prophecies or healing seem to be.

This whole idea of grace is contrary to our natural way of thinking. We naturally struggle with the idea that the gifts of the Holy Spirit are given on the basis of grace through faith without reference to our meritorious efforts. Paul taught about receiving the gifts of the Spirit by faith and not works as analogous to receiving justification by faith and not works (Gal. 3:1–5). Justification by faith alone makes sense when we realize that no amount of human effort could bridge the immeasurable gap between God and our sin. God's solution on the cross makes sense as we realize that the human effort equation is hopelessly flawed.

No amount of consecration can earn us the right to the gifts of the Spirit any more than they gain us forgiveness. When compared to the purity and holiness of God, the differences between the best of us and the worst of us are not as great as some of us might like to imagine.

In Scripture, God forgave and extended great mercy to people who, by our standards, did some pretty despicable things. Without diminishing the gravity of serious sins, Jesus showed everyone that God's opinion about things like pride, hypocrisy, treatment of the poor, unforgiveness, and self-righteousness was more serious to Him than we could have ever imagined. This violates some of our preconceived notions and our ranking of the "really bad sins." "Man looks at the outward appearance, but the Lord looks at the heart," the Bible says (1 Sam. 16:7). He is very patient and merciful with us.

We must not automatically judge the spiritual gifts in someone's ministry as invalid simply because of their spiritual deficiencies. God is sometimes more concerned about what He has set out to accomplish in the life of the prophetic vessel than about bringing full judgment on them in that season.

FALSE EQUATION #1: CHARACTER EQUALS ANOINTING

Equations work backward as well as forward, even misconceived equations. So, those who wrongly assume that spiritual giftings endorse character will also conclude that it is character that produces spiritual gifts. This encourages people in some circles to "fake it" so as not to appear "ungifted." It implies that the most spiritual, mature, and righteous people are those who have the most prolific power gifts.

This kind of thinking sets people up for condemnation, especially when everyone else seems to be prophesying, having prophetic dreams, and seeing visions. It puts much unnecessary pressure on people if they feel they are less spiritual than those with prophetic experiences.

I felt this way for a season, and the result was that I wrongly abdicated my leadership to those who had more powerful prophetic experiences than I did. The church was bruised and hurt by that wrong decision, which came out of my insecurity and false humility.

Remember, most prophetic people don't have the gift of leadership that is essential for a church to be healthy, balanced, and safe. A church led only by prophetic people will not be a safe environment for God's people.

One of the most important things to do in a church that wants to nurture and administrate prophetic ministry is to dial down the mysticism with its desire to look superspiritual.

This is not a spiritual beauty contest, but it can turn into one very quickly if people see gifts as merit badges rather than something to bless the church. It is not about the vessel. It's about loving the Lord and building up His church in love.

The fact is that God's power and revelation flowing through people is not necessarily a sign that God is pleased with them in other areas of their lives. Sometimes the prophetic gifts will continue to operate even when there is an inner crumbling taking place in their private lives.

People with high-profile prophetic gifts must constantly guard against high-mindedness. High-mindedness is simply considering that you are so important that you are judged more leniently. High-minded people are those who think that because they are doing such an important work for God and because His power is manifest through them, they are not accountable for things like integrity, honesty, and kindness—especially in the small and unseen matters of life.

It is this temptation to self-deception that plagues some people in positions of influence. It is a great deception because, in actuality, the opposite is true. To whom much is given, much will be required (Luke 12:48).

Every person through whom spiritual gifts operate are wise to remain acutely aware that a day of reckoning is surely coming. We will all stand before the judgment seat of Christ one day for a final evaluation of our lives and ministries (1 Cor. 3:11–15).

Some of God's servants who fall in sin are made an example of the truth that the Lord is patient with their sin and that His gifts are without repentance (Rom. 11:29). Others are made examples that God will openly discipline those He loves (Rev. 2:21–23). This results in many others trembling in the fear of God (1 Tim. 5:20–24).

Saul was a picture of both ways that God chooses to deal with His servants. Saul remained as king of Israel in his sin. God in great patience anointed him to win great battles. God partially blessed Israel under Saul even in the midst of his sinful failures. However, Saul eventually crossed the line with God and was removed.

God's gifts are freely given as a sign of His mercy and desire to bless His people, not as His approval. Don't invalidate all spiritual gifts that work in spiritually immature people. But also do not be fooled by God's grace and patience with prophetic vessels who remain anointed for a season as they continue in their sin. Eventually He will call us all to account as stewards of the gifts He has entrusted to us.

1. Accuracy of revelation does not equal godliness of character of lifestyle. This is a reality that offends our normal thinking. Why does God permit such a dichotomy? Ultimately, this is probably an "illegal" question, but we must soberly face its reality.

2. The story of Balaam is an Old Testament illustration of a man with a genuine prophetic anointing who led Israel into great sin. King Saul prophesied by the Spirit of the Lord but ended his life tormented by an evil spirit.

3. In the New Testament, we look to the church at Corinth for the most in-depth studies on both carnality and spiritual gifts. History reveals that those who continue in blatant sin while exercising supernatural gifts create an ever-widening gulf in their personalities, which results in spiritual, emotional, mental, physical, relational, and moral breakdowns.

FALSE EQUATION #2: ANOINTING EQUALS DIVINE ENDORSEMENT OF MINISTRY STYLE

The benefits that have come to our church as a result of the prophetic ministry have naturally been accompanied by some headaches. The greatest difficulties have had to do with ministry styles and methodologies.

In chapter 11, I will talk about some of the things God does that seem strange and unusual. He sometimes offends the mind to reveal the heart. The point here, however, is that the exhibitionist style that some prophetic people adopt is due to their pride and weaknesses.

I have had long and painful discussions about this with some prophetic people in our church. In the most problematic cases, some who are anointed by the Spirit have a ministry style that draws a lot of attention to them.

What often begins as slightly unusual in a ministry style turns into exaggeration and manipulation. In several cases I have simply had to say, "Please stop doing this."

Some prophetic people are tempted to think that their particular style is essential to the anointing working through their lives. They will sometimes say, "No, I have to do it this way or God will not manifest His power through me."

Methodology or ministry style does not produce power or anointing. That's a false equation that some fall prey to. Because you were standing in a certain place or doing a certain thing when God moved, it doesn't mean that the circumstances had anything to do with it.

Some will try to re-create the setting so they can see God's power again.

The Lord often used Bob Jones by having him lay his hands on people's hands. He would sometimes put his fingers against their fingers. In this way, God revealed things by the Holy Spirit to speak to that person. Bob was very accurate in using this method that God uniquely showed him. Before long others started imitating it. However, it did not work. Why? The discernment comes from the Holy Spirit, not from the methodology of Bob Jones.

I've seen many different people imitating methods because they think that the method is the key. But the person of the Holy Spirit is the key to operating in the power of God. Methodology does not release God's power.

We must not use the power of suggestion to get people to respond in the way we want. A leader succumbing to manipulation might speak to people in this manner: "Come up if you want to be touched by God. If you are sensitive to the Spirit, you will fall under the power of God."

If we subtly "suggest" that people fall down or speak in tongues, it is manipulation. I've seen a well-known minister rebuke people because they wouldn't fall down when he prayed for them. He told one woman, "Listen, just receive." The lady replied, "I am receiving."

But the minister said, "Don't tell me you are receiving. You're just standing there resisting."

They got into an argument, right on the spot. He wanted her to fall down as a sign that God was touching her or rather that the anointing was resting on him.

Ministers with power and prophetic giftings who are not in relationship with a balanced local church team often allow their method-as-power tendencies to dominate their ministry.

It is much more difficult to get away with manipulation and pretense when you relate closely to a local church of people who love genuineness and reality.

Some in ministry will push the person they are praying for until they fall down. To them it has become a personal mission because their public image is on the line each time they lead a ministry time. This is high-octane manipulation.

False equations about the need to use the methodology can often lead to hype. The methods themselves become a false prop. Nothing holy and supernatural is actually taking place. Thus, they feel they have to produce results. These ministers have started down a road of hype and institutionalized methodology. They are afraid to admit that God may not be moving in a particular ministry setting. They have too much vested in preserving their reputation in ministry as always being anointed. It is OK to admit it when not much is happening. To refuse to do this can result in the ministry time becoming a conspiracy of pretense.

God sometimes withholds His power in a ministry time to see if the leader will humbly trust Him instead of trying to appear anointed whether He is moving or not. On certain occasions He strategically does not manifest His power in order to win people's hearts away from the prophetic minister. Sometimes He will withdraw His Spirit's presence to keep from perpetuating our confidence in our methodologies.

When some hungry people get around a prophetically anointed person, they are so hopeful that God will speak to them that they cling to every word uttered. This makes both parties vulnerable to unique temptations.

I believe that it is wrong to utilize mystique to influence people. Unfortunately, this happens all too often. Many prophetic folks take themselves too seriously. They love the feeling of having such influence over others. They seek to make themselves more spiritual, holy, and sensitive than they really are.

It is easy to get one's identity from his or her prophetic ministry. I have seen prophetic people succumb to the expectations of the people who desperately want a word from God. They will prophesy whether God is saying anything or not!

Elijah poured water on the sacrifices on Mt. Carmel (1 Kings 18), instead of putting lighter fluid on them! This made it "harder" for God to set it on fire. Elijah was confident that the fire of God could consume even a wet sacrifice.

I challenge prophetic ministers to put some "water on the sacrifices" they prepare by trusting God to prove His power without them "helping" God out so much.

I encourage them to refuse to promote their prophetic mystique.

False Equation #3: Anointing Equals 100 Percent Doctrinal Accuracy

Throughout church history there have been many anointed ministries who held strange doctrines. A most notable example of this in recent history is William Branham.

Branham, poor and uneducated, began his ministry in 1933. He was a traveling Baptist evangelist, and his meetings were frequently attended by thousands of people. His ministry was characterized by amazing manifestations of healing and the word of knowledge.

When people approached him in a healing line, Branham could describe their diseases, give other facts and information about them, and sometimes even call them by their names. The gift, many people insisted, was 100 percent accurate.

An interpreter for Branham in Switzerland, who later became a historian, said, "I am not aware of any case in which he was mistaken in the often detailed statements he made."[1] The healings were also both numerous and astonishing.

However, Branham ended up preaching some doctrinal heresy, although never to the extent of denying Jesus Christ as Lord and Savior or doubting the authority of the Scriptures. He allowed himself to be spoken of as the "angel" to the seventh church referred to in Revelation 10. This caused great confusion among his followers. They reasoned that if God gave him so much true prophetic information about people's lives, then why didn't God in the same way give him sound doctrine? But the gift of prophecy doesn't ensure that one will have the gift of teaching or vice versa.

The problem is that some people with strong prophetic ministries often aren't satisfied with just being used by God in prophecy and miracles. They want to also be teachers.

I have seen prophetic people and evangelists become separate from the local church. When this happens, some are tempted to try to function as a teacher since they have a large number of people following them. However, if they do not have a teaching anointing, then they will end up promoting unbalanced doctrines. This happens when they teach the multitudes who gathered because of the gifts of the Spirit operating through them.

If they don't have a teaching gift that has been cultivated through proper training in the Scriptures, they are sure to teach unbalanced doctrine to their large number of followers.

FOR THE PROFIT OF ALL

The most important thing to remember is that "the manifestation of the Spirit is given to each one for the profit of all" (1 Cor. 12:7). Spiritual gifts are for the purpose of blessing the body of Christ, not exalting the person through whom they come. Paul appropriately said that we must be zealous of spiritual gifts as we seek to abound for the edification of the church (1 Cor. 14:12).

CHAPTER 11

GOD OFFENDS THE MIND
TO REVEAL THE HEART

M Y INTRODUCTION TO prophetic ministry was difficult because I
despised the weirdness of some of the people God used. I was
also bothered by some of their bizarre methods that were foreign
to everything in my evangelical background.

Some of what people claimed as the manifestations of the Spirit were
contrary to my sense of orderliness and respectability as well. Before I could
move forward, I had to deal with what offended me in these issues.

As Christians, some of us have wrong assumptions about how God deals
with us. He is a gentleman, we say, who will never barge in but who politely
stands at the door, quietly knocking and patiently waiting.

The Holy Spirit is often thought of as being shy or even skittish. If we
want the Holy Spirit to move, we get very quiet and still. If a baby cries, some
think, the Spirit might be quenched or perhaps scared off. Some operate
under notions such as these.

Paul instructed the Corinthians not to forbid tongues or prophecy, but to
"let all things be done decently and in order" (1 Cor. 14:40). Our leadership
team has worked hard at creating an atmosphere in which the free flow of
spiritual gifts can take place "decently and in order."

But Paul's instructions to bridle people who are operating in the flesh have been interpreted in such a way as to suggest that the Holy Spirit will operate only in ways that conform to our sense of order and respectability. That was not the case in the Old Testament, in the early church, or in revivals throughout history.

Two facts are clear. First, *the Holy Spirit does not appear to be overly concerned about our reputations.* The outpouring of the Spirit didn't do much to enhance the respectability of those in the Upper Room. "These [men] are not drunk, as you suppose," said Peter (Acts 2:15). Some seemed to be drunk as a result of being filled with the Holy Spirit. I can imagine Peter preaching his Acts 2 sermon while still feeling the effects of the holy hilarity of heaven. Peter preached to the Pharisees, who were deeply offended at what was happening with Peter and the apostles. Some of the devout Jews in Jerusalem that day scoffed at the apostles, "They are full of new wine" (v. 13). The disciples' behavior might have seemed out of order to these religious leaders, but it was, nevertheless, the work of the Holy Spirit.

A second fact about the Spirit's dealing with us is this: in contrast to the polite, shy, gentlemanly image we have of Him, sometimes *He intentionally offends people.*

God knew that many would be *offended* by the foolishness of the gospel message (1 Cor. 1:21–23). Paul warned the Galatians not to seek to remove the "offense of the cross" (Gal. 5:11). The fact is that the gospel is sometimes very offensive by God's design.

THE INTENTIONAL OFFENSE

Sometimes God intentionally offends people. A good example of this is what Jesus did in John 6. Jesus had fed five thousand people by multiplying the fish and loaves. Then they expected Him to prove Himself with greater signs, something even more dramatic than multiplying bread or healing people. They anticipated something comparable to the parting of the Red Sea or calling fire down from heaven. The people asked Jesus: "What sign will You perform then, that we may see it and believe You? What work will you do? Our fathers ate the manna in the desert" (vv. 30–31).

In other words, they were asking Jesus to do something like the manna-from-heaven miracle again. Jesus didn't give them their desired sign but responded by saying, "I am the living bread which came down from heaven....Most assuredly, I say to you, unless you eat the flesh of the Son of Man and drink His blood, you have no life in you. Whoever eats My flesh and drinks My blood has eternal life, and I will raise him up at the last day" (vv. 51–54).

Verses 60–61 state, "Many of His disciples, when they heard this, said, 'This is a hard saying; who can understand it?' When Jesus knew in Himself that His disciples complained about this, He said to them, 'Does this offend you?'" A few verses down, we find that "from that time many of His disciples went back and walked with Him no more" (v. 66).

Jesus offended them theologically by saying that He was the bread that came down from heaven. He offended their expectations by refusing to give them another great sign. He offended their sensibility and dignity by suggesting that they eat His flesh and drink His blood. They complained about Him and even "quarreled among themselves" (v. 52).

Throughout the Bible, God is revealed as One who offends and confounds those who think they have everything figured out. (See 1 Corinthians 1:23; 1 Peter 2:8.) Isaiah referred to Jesus as a stone of stumbling and a rock of offense (Isa. 8:14).

Jesus knew their hearts—He knew that those who followed Him did so with mixed motives. So He determined to *reveal their hearts by intentionally offending their minds.* By offending people's minds with His methods, God reveals the pride that lies hidden in their hearts.

Naaman, the commander of the Syrian army, was plagued with leprosy. With great desperation, he determined to see Elisha even though he was a Jewish prophet. Israel was a military enemy of Syria. Elisha didn't even bother to come out of his house to see Naaman, who had traveled so far, but rather he only sent a message to him, saying, "Go and wash in the Jordan seven times, and your flesh shall be restored to you" (2 Kings 5:10). Naaman, a prominent military leader in Syria, was so offended by the way Elisha treated him. He said, "'Are not...rivers of Damascus, better than all the waters of Israel? Could I not wash in them and be clean?' So he turned and went away in a rage" (v. 12).

I know some obnoxious individuals who make it a practice to offend people. God's offense, on the contrary, is redemptive. He offends people's minds in order to reveal their hearts. The Bible teaches that God gives grace to the humble but resists the proud (James 4:6, 1 Pet. 5:5–6). Dealing with Naaman's stumbling block of pride was the first step to his healing, which he received when he was humbly obedient to Elisha's words.

OFFENDED AT THE PEOPLE GOD USES

Paul wrote that God offends people not only by His message but also by His messengers.

> But God has chosen the foolish things of the world to put to shame the wise, and God has chosen the weak things of the world to put to shame the things which are mighty; and the base things of the world and the things which are despised God has chosen, and the things which are not, to bring to nothing the things that are, that no flesh should glory in His presence.
>
> —1 Corinthians 1:27–29

I understand that the context of this principle (God's intentional offense) relates to issues much broader than strange prophets and bizarre manifestations. But in these instances, the principle here can also be clearly applied.

While I was still pastoring in St. Louis, the principle that God offends the mind to reveal the heart became real to me. I preached on it several times. I thought God was preparing us for an outpouring of the Spirit that might include some unusual things. I had no experience with the prophetic ministry. Looking back, I see that the Lord was preparing me as He gave me these messages so that I would not stumble over the strangeness of the prophetic people I would meet in the months to come in Kansas City.

OFFENDED AT BIZARRE PROPHETIC METHODS

Some of the people whom God has called are different from you in their personality and culture. You may be naturally offended at the way they carry themselves simply because they are different. Others are led to do strange things by the nature of their prophetic call. Compared to the normal guy working down at the factory, some prophetic people are pretty eccentric.

It took me a while to get used to some of their idiosyncrasies that offended my mind at first. The truth is that some of their idiosyncrasies still irritate me, but I've learned to look past them for the sake of receiving God's blessings through them.

When I first met Bob Jones, I was convinced he was not of God. I did not desire to talk to him ever again. I had no experience with prophetic people and no thought-out theology on how to relate to them. Yet I somehow had a conviction that he was a false prophet.

I'm surprised now at how authoritative I was about things with which I had no experience. That is called pride. Looking back, I realized that one of the principal factors that influenced me was that Bob looked and acted so strangely.

He spoke in parables constantly. I knew God spoke to us in parables in the Word, but when Bob did it, it was *really* strange. Bob would tell me symbolic stories filled with parabolic word pictures for which I had no interpretation. Then he would claim that God told him those parables. I didn't have any paradigm on which to base his claim that God speaks in such abstract ways to people today.

His ministry style was like nothing I had ever seen before. He would talk about feeling the wind of the Spirit or about his hands getting hot during a ministry time. His language was that of an uneducated person. His appearance was such that no one could ever have accused him of vanity or of being too caught up in the fashions of the day. Occasionally his shirt and pants were too short. Sometimes his stomach showed slightly when he stood, and when he sat, his pants legs sometimes went three inches above his socks.

These things about Bob Jones somewhat offended me—his appearance, his language, his revelation, and his ministry style. Initially, I could not imagine that he was the "real thing" because he was not like me. However, after I had witnessed the accuracy of Bob's prophetic ministry over time, I finally begin to think his strange ministry style might be acceptable. His love for Jesus and the Scriptures was very apparent. Eventually, I found him endearing. Since becoming friends with Bob, the way I judge prophetic people has changed drastically.

Unbalanced people

Some unbalanced people are simply trying to be weird because of their misconceptions of prophetic ministry. They are excited about the idea of being some sort of mystical prophet; therefore, they intentionally act weird. They suppose their strangeness makes them more anointed. However, some such people are just eccentric, not anointed.

I don't believe the idea that because someone is prophetic they *should* be strange. People will try to get away with all kinds of things by claiming that nonprophetic people simply can't understand them. I don't buy that for a second.

Sometimes strange methods are just strange. It is not a case of God offending people's minds, but rather of the prophetic person having unusual styles and methods. Some things simply need to be changed so that the prophetic person can function more effectively in a public setting.

Unconventional ministry styles

Unconventional styles don't necessarily invalidate a prophet's message. Don't dismiss something simply because it's unconventional. There wasn't an Old Testament biblical precedent for Paul to send out handkerchiefs to sick people (Acts 19:12) or for Jesus to put mud on a blind person's eyes. Jesus said we were to judge the fruit of a prophet, not his methodology—unless, of course, his methods violate Scripture (Matt. 7:15–20).

If people have a track record of having accurate prophecies, then you can take them more seriously when their methodologies are a little unorthodox. It took some time for each member of our prophetic team to develop credibility with us.

Are prophetic people loners?

The Bible speaks of "schools" or "companies" of prophets (1 Sam. 10:10; 2 Kings 4:1; 5:22). This reminds us that there is a corporate dimension to developing prophetic gifting among believers. It is not always necessary for a prophetic person to hear from God alone and then deliver His word in public. Other more mature Christians can help those with less experience to sharpen their listening and discerning skills when prophetic ministry is developed among believers. At the IHOP Missions Base, we have hundreds of people on prophetic teams. Some of these people are mature in their prophetic calling, and others are just starting out. Together we can go further in God at a faster pace.

Public correction

Pastors have to be careful about correcting people too abruptly, especially in public meetings. We must deal with them in love; first, because they are valuable and important to God, and second, because if we don't correct them properly, others who are just starting out in prophetic ministry will not feel the confidence to step out in faith.

Over the years, I have developed a series of corrective steps to use if somebody continually prophesies in the flesh. First, if they prophesy something publicly that we discern is fleshly, we let it pass the first time or two unless it is clearly unbiblical or destructive in nature. People need to have room to make mistakes without the fear of being too quickly corrected.

If the problem happens again, then we talk with them privately in a gentle way suggesting that they need to be a little more restrained in their public prophesying. If they do it again, then we take it up a level by privately asking them to stop prophesying publicly. If they do it again, then we strongly warn them that we will publicly stop them the next time. If they do it again, we will confront the issue publicly. In twenty-five years of pastoring prophetic people, I have only had to publicly stop people about five times. Most people "get the message" somewhere in the process of the private discussions.

When correcting the person publicly, it is important to explain the entire process to the congregation in the very meeting in which the person was corrected. We tell the congregation that this person was instructed and warned repeatedly in private. This helps the people realize that the correction was not an abrupt and arbitrary correction. The others need to be assured that they will not suddenly be corrected publicly without prior private warnings. Most of God's people want to be a blessing and to do things in biblical order. Communicating the whole process publicly creates a safe environment that helps the congregation to not be afraid to step out in faith, and it also reinforces the fact that the leadership will deal directly with things that are out of God's order (1 Cor. 14:40).

OFFENDED AT THE OUTPOURING OF THE HOLY SPIRIT

People can be offended in several different ways by the Lord. Some are offended by the message of the cross itself. Some are offended by the type of people God uses. Others are offended by the way the Holy Spirit moves.

I was not prepared for unusual manifestations of the Spirit, but I was even less prepared for the unusual people whom God joined to our team.

When the power of the Holy Spirit is poured out, it is sometimes poured out in an unexpected way; consequently, it is ridiculed and rejected. In the first Great Awakening in America, as on the Day of Pentecost, a lot of strange things took place.

In October 1741, the Reverend Samuel Johnson, acting dean of Yale College, was suspicious of the revival then sweeping New England, which was led by the itinerant preacher George Whitefield. He wrote an anxious letter to a friend in England:

> But this new enthusiasm, in consequence of Whitefield's preaching through the country, has got great footing in the College [Yale]....Many scholars have been possessed of it, and two of this year's candidates were denied their degrees for their disorderly and restless endeavors to propagate it....We have now prevailing among us the most odd and unaccountable enthusiasm than perhaps obtained in any age or nation. For not only the minds of many people are at once struck with prodigious distresses upon their hearing the hideous outcries of our itinerant preachers, but even their bodies are frequently in a moment affected with the strangest convulsions and involuntary agitations and cramps, which also have sometimes happened to those who came as mere spectators.[1]

Jonathan Edwards's wife, Sarah, was deeply affected by the presence of the Holy Spirit. In her own words, she describes how for a period of time, lasting more than seventeen days, she was so overcome with the presence of God that all her strength would leave her and she would collapse. At other times she could would leap and shout for joy.[2]

Jonathan Edwards was a defender of the move of the Spirit, but the extreme manner in which people were affected was too much for the conservative Christian leaders of New England. Their respectability was offended, and thus, they condemned the movement for its excessive enthusiasm and unconventional manifestations of the Spirit.

Dr. Sam Storms obtained a ThM degree from Dallas Theological Seminary and a PhD in intellectual history from the University of Texas. Sam was somewhat skeptical about these spontaneous outbursts by people who were supposedly influenced by the Holy Spirit.

At the April 1994 Vineyard conference in Dallas, his skepticism was removed. Sam was at the back of the room when the power of the Holy Spirit fell on him. He first began to pray and weep as the Lord was ministering to some deeper needs in his heart. Shortly after this, he abruptly tumbled out of his chair laughing hysterically, even though he was trying desperately to control himself.

After the conference ended, he was still incapacitated by the presence of God. Finally his strength returned, and some of us helped Sam up and started for the car. But in the parking lot it happened to him again. Sam repeatedly fell down, thus running the risk of ruining his clothes. Twenty minutes later we got him to the restaurant, where God's power hit him again. We thought it was all over until we got up to our hotel room and realized Sam was missing. He was still in the stairwell, incapacitated by the Holy Spirit. The fruit of Sam's encounter with the Holy Spirit was renewed faith, greater reverence for the power of God, and what the apostle Peter described as "joy inexpressible and full of glory" (1 Pet. 1:8).

BLESSED IS HE WHO IS NOT OFFENDED

Both the Pharisees and the disciples misunderstood Jesus, and consequently, they were both offended. We usually think of Pharisees as the really bad guys. Actually, they were the conservative intellectuals who were the defenders of the faith, who held to orthodoxy against the corrupting influence of Greek culture. But their stumbling block was pride. This was especially manifest in their confidence that they were the only ones with an accurate interpretation of Scripture through the paradigm of the tradition of the elders. Adding to the problem of their pride was their contentment to be seen as orthodox without hungering for the presence of God Himself.

Throughout the Gospels, we see an underlying theme of the continued inability of Jesus's disciples to understand what He was doing. Many of Jesus's followers were offended as well. They turned away from following Him (John 6:60–66).

The most commonly used Greek word in the New Testament for "offend" is also translated "to stumble." The Greek word is *skandalizo*, from which our English word *scandal* is derived. What God does sometimes scandal-izes or offends the mind of His own people. By offending people's minds, He reveals the things hidden in their hearts. Their unperceived lack of hunger for God and lack of humility rises to the surface. Jesus is revealed in the Scripture as "the way, the truth, and the life" (John 14:6) as well as "a stone of stumbling and a rock of offense" (Isa. 8:14).

The biblical principles for functioning in prophetic ministry are very clear, but the application of them in each different contemporary context is not an exact science. Our control issues and religious codes will often be challenged as we embrace the prophetic ministry. This is part of God's design because true Christianity is a dynamic relationship with a living God that cannot be reduced to formulas and dry orthodoxy. We are called to embrace the mystery of God that will not allow us to neatly tie up every doctrinal or philosophical loose end. In humility before God, we should know that we do not have all the answers, at least not in this age (1 Cor. 3:18).

SELF-SATISFIED RELIGIOUS PRIDE

The Pharisees were deceived by equating their knowledge of Scripture and their association with the religious community with a personal knowledge of God that comes through encountering Him on an ongoing basis. Jesus directly addressed their problem as being rooted in religious pride:

> You search the Scriptures, for in them you think you have eternal life; and these are they which testify of Me. But you are not willing to come to Me that you may have life. I do not receive honor from men. But I know you, that you do not have the love of God in you.... How can you believe, who receive honor from one another, and do not seek the honor that comes from the only God?
>
> —John 5:39–44

The Lord challenged one of our staff pastors to embrace his prophetic calling by giving him a vivid spiritual dream. The Lord appeared to him and said, "You have been waiting to obey Me until you had comprehensive plans. I want you to obey Me without comprehensive plans." As he was kneeling before Jesus, a stack of transparencies came out of his belly and landed in his hands. He understood that these represented his own plans that the Lord could see right through. He felt sorrowful and began weeping and repenting. He was saying, "Lord, I don't want to be disobedient to You." After this, he looked up and Jesus was smiling at him.

To submit to this calling on his life, he went through some stiff dealings with God regarding his intellectualism and self-reliance in his approach to ministry. He humbled himself before God and the body through this process, which included acknowledging his errors both privately and publicly. If we become hungry for God with humility in our hearts, then the stumbling blocks in us will be used to become the stepping-stones that lead us forward in His purposes. Having said all this, I must also say that some prophetic people get off track when they become more focused on the unusual methods in giving their message rather than God's purpose in the message itself. The message is always more important than the method.

CHAPTER 12

PASTORS AND PROPHETS:
GETTING ALONG IN THE KINGDOM

T HE PROPHETIC MINISTRY in the local church functions in an "orderly freedom" only when the pastors, the prophetic people, and the congregation at large have a common understanding of how things should work from a biblical perspective. It is important that all understand how the prophetic ministry is meant to function in order to enjoy unity in the midst of the turbulence of the prophetic ministry. The principles for nurturing and administrating prophetic ministry need to be understood not only by pastors and prophets, but also by the majority of the congregation. One reason I wrote this book was to provide our ministry in Kansas City a unified, systematic teaching on the prophetic that would be available to all our people. Why? So that we could walk in a unified perspective together.

Each fresh wind of the Holy Spirit that blows across the nations comes with unusual and unexpected manifestations. Some who receive prayer fall to the ground as their bodies convulse as though electricity is going through them, or they see heavenly visions or hear the prophetic words from God as the Holy Spirit comes upon them to heal them or spiritually refresh them. We are just at the beginning of a wave of the Holy Spirit that will increase until Jesus Himself appears in the sky to usher in the age to come. The church needs wise and mature pastors who can lead, nurture, and administrate prophetic people in the midst of the increasing super-natural activity of the Holy Spirit.

God-ordained pastors are equipped to bring leaders to the church where God has placed them. They are in a strategic position to help the church succeed in becoming more prophetic if they wisely use their gift of leadership. God's desire is that pastors and prophetic people work together as a diversified team ministry. However, more often we see insecure pastors trying to lead rejected and pushy "prophets" in a team ministry that lacks diversity of gifting. There are real challenges in this, but they can be overcome with patience, humility, and careful attention to what the Scripture teaches about how prophetic people are to be led in relation to the larger church family.

NONPROPHET LEADERSHIP

I have had conversations with many good pastors who are frustrated because they do not move in spiritual gifts as freely as some of the people in their congregation. Sometimes they point out that some of the prophetic-type people in their church are spiritually immature in other ways that cause unnecessary division and disruption in the church. Some pastors may feel insecure, thinking that these prophetic folks are *apparently* more "in tune with the Spirit" than they are. Consequently they feel intimated about correcting prophetically gifted people.

In my personal ministry, when I have something prophetic to say, I usually share it within the context of my teaching ministry without mentioning that it is a prophetic word. I intentionally *tone down* drawing attention to my prophetic giftings.

When pastors realize that I am a teacher with limited prophetic giftings, their response is often something like this: "I do not know how you could have prophetic ministry happening in your church and survive as a pastor without being a prophetic person yourself." It doesn't take a prophet to nurture and administrate prophetic ministries in your church. It takes a leader with a vision for a multigifted, diverse team.

PASTOR AS PROPHET: THE FOX IN THE HENHOUSE

I will tell the story of one pastor who overused and misused the gift of prophecy in his leadership. He saw his prophetic ministry as an extension of his pastoral ministry. This is a good concept if it is done right. The fox was in the henhouse in the sense that there was not much restraint in how he used what he claimed were prophetic gifts. As time went on, his role as pastor began to be overshadowed by his role as "prophet." He was calling out people and giving them words in most services, which led to less and less teaching of the Word. He prefaced most of his private counsel to people as well as his decisions in the eldership with "thus saith the Lord." Some of the people were too intimidated to resist this counsel because, after all, it was coming directly from the Lord. This leadership style is guaranteed to bring strife and confusion to the congregation when they are all but mandated to receive most of what the pastor said as being from God. Over time, he wore himself out, as well as the people and his eldership. The church was a wreck, and finally, after a couple of years, the doors were closed.

A pastor with a strong prophetic gifting must understand the dynamics of administrating the prophetic ministry in his church. The prophetic giftings that he has, if not used with wisdom and restraint, can have a negative effect on his ability to pastor the church effectively.

I met some pastors who want to create a mystique about their gifting to perpetuate the image that they live on a higher spiritual plane. They are seeking to enhance people's confidence in their spiritual and pastoral leadership. This usually backfires.

Some pastors fall into a trap of showcasing their own prophetic gifting but drawing undue attention to it. In the end, this hinders the church from receiving the prophetic and causes some to lose their confidence in the pastor's wisdom and leadership abilities. In other words, he or she must not lead by claiming that most of their decisions come directly from their own prophetic words. Even when I do hear from the Lord on a decision, I usually just share the decision, knowing that if God is really in it, the leaders will eventually see it and come to unity without me pressuring them to receive most of my leadership directives as being from God.

Pastors who make most of their leadership decisions primarily through prophesying are making a mistake in their leadership style that will have a demobilizing effect on their leadership team and entire church. When I was senior pastor and now at IHOP, I am careful not to regularly add emphasis to what I say with "thus saith the Lord." I only rarely use that kind of language.

Another downside to a pastor who draws too much attention to his prophetic gifts is to end up with people being overly dependent on him instead of the people being dependent and connected more directly with Jesus. This is evident when too many people want to be with him, hear from him, and get a word from him. The insecure pastor enjoys this attention for a couple of years, but this style of leadership will eventually burn him out and leave his people spiritually shallow.

THE PAY IS THE SAME

We all have to learn to be secure in what God has called us to be and realize the value and importance of each person. Paul wrote about the different gifts and callings in the church when he wrote:

> From whom the whole body, joined and knit together by what every joint supplies, according to the effective working by which every part does its share, causes growth of the body for the edifying of itself in love.
>
> —Ephesians 4:16

Satan is a master at sowing into the people's hearts discontentment about who they are and what God has called them to do. This is a common problem that hurts the whole body of Christ worldwide. The grass often looks greener on the other side of the fence. I have met many prophetic people who desperately want to be teachers. They see all the pain associated with their prophetic gift, and they imagine that the teacher only enjoys success with respect and appreciation from the people. Others despise their God-ordained function of serving behind the scene because they so desperately want to be taken seriously as a prophetic person. We have created some of the problem by wrongly attaching status to different ministries and giftings. For example, some say prophets are ultraspiritual; apostles are super-ultra-spiritual; pastors and teachers are a little less; and so on down the line to deacons, ushers, and the person who prints the bulletins. The social status associated with different functions in the body of Christ causes people to do rather eccentric and unbalanced things, and in the end it affects the way the majority of the members of the body do their part to supply what is needed. We have a little saying that we have repeated often over the years. It goes like this: "Whether you are raising the dead or taking a nap, if you are doing God's will, the pay is the same when you stand before God."

Pastors, like everyone else, must be secure in their limited callings and spiritual giftings. If they are *at peace* within their limited sphere, then they are that much more prepared to appreciate, help, and support others with different giftings. Pastors are in a different role in needing to lead a team of people who often have gifts that are very different from theirs. They must not yield to the temptation to be intimidated by prophetic people who receive revelations more frequently and much more dramatically than they do. At first this was really hard for me.

In my late twenties, I was pastoring people like Bob Jones, who received profound and accurate prophetic words. I was very intimidated by this. My reluctance to confront prophetic people came to a head at nearly the two-year mark of the prophetic ministry in our church.

DUELING PROPHETS SUNDAY

During the second year of pastoring our new church plant in Kansas City, I noticed that five or six prophetic people regularly competed for the microphone during the Sunday morning services. I was becoming exasperated because it was clear to me that there was a lot of hype in what had been going on for the last few months. Some of the people were getting tired of feeling manipulated by these prophetic people and were starting to voice their feelings to me. I was definitely feeling the pressure from many of them to greatly reduce the amount of "prophetic" words that I was allowing to be shared in our Sunday services.

On one Sunday morning in December 1984, two of the main prophetic people got into a "prophetic duel" right in front of the church. One stood up and proclaimed something to this effect: "Thus says the Lord, 'A great thing is going to happen.'" Then the second guy stood up and said, "Thus says the Lord, 'Better things are going to happen.'" Then the first prophetic guy topped him. Not to be out-prophesied, the second prophet answered back by giving something even better. They went about three rounds each.

I was on the front row getting really angry. It was clear to me what was going on. These two guys were yielding to a common temptation to compete with others to be recognized as one of the "top prophets" in our church. It was scandalous, embarrassing, and ridiculous, and everybody could see it except these two prophetic people. This became known to our leadership team as "Dueling Prophets Sunday."

A dozen people came up to me afterward and asked how much longer I was going to let this sort of thing go on. Usually I tried to cover the prophetic people by encouraging people to be patient and reminding them of all the great things that had happened through the prophetic ministry in our midst.

But this time they had gone over the line. The emperor (or rather the prophets) had no clothes, and the only ones who didn't know it were these two prophetic people themselves.

I had to confront these prophetic people. This was a new experience for me at this time. Both of them were defensive and threatened that if I didn't accept their ministry style and what they had to say, the Holy Spirit's blessing would leave our church.

I was surprised that they resorted to such manipulation because they had the credibility as being the "real thing." In other words, they had both given prophetic words that had come to pass exactly as they had predicted. But when they issued this warning—to let them do what they wanted or the Holy Spirit's blessing would leave our church—it pushed a button in me. My eyes opened, and I saw the rank carnality in all of it. I was surprised that people with such depth of prophetic revelation could also be so carnal and manipulative. This was a new idea to me that anointed prophetic people could also be carnal and manipulative. I was provoked and offended by what they did in that Sunday morning service, so I rose up and told them both to stop carrying on in such a fleshly way or leave.

Both of them told me that they were finished with our church, and they assured me that God was canceling all the tremendous prophetic words spoken over the church and me personally. They assumed that God was going to leave because they were going to leave.

For a time, I was afraid that God's blessing was going to leave if they got their feelings hurt and left. Now I can assure you that God will not abandon you and lift His promised blessing from your life and ministry because the pride of a prophetic person is bruised. They may be used effectively by the Holy Spirit, but they are not the mediator between us and God. Only Jesus is. These two went from our confrontational meeting to complaining against me to some of the key people in the church. But these people called me up and congratulated me, saying, "Thank you, thank you!" They loved the prophetic vessels, but they realized that if the leadership did not stand up to set things in order, the prophetic people would hurt not only the church, but also their own ministries as well.

Ultimately, much of what happened on "Dueling Prophets Sunday" was my fault because I had not exercised my leadership responsibility earlier. Rather, I abdicated it by allowing these prophetic people to get us all into this difficult and embarrassing situation. Our leadership team was more gifted in leading the church than the prophetic people were.

Within two weeks both of those prophetic people repented of their manipulation. This gave me a new confidence to not abdicate my leadership to them. I determined that I was no longer going to dismiss my negative feelings when they were doing things that were not helpful to the church. I was initially intimidated by prophetic people who prophesied with real accuracy. I thought that if they heard from God on that level, who was I to tell them that they were missing God when they gave prophetic words on other occasions. I figured that if they heard God clearly enough to get the prophetic word, surely they could hear God clearly enough to know when to give and when not to. I found out the hard way that this logic is flawed.

One positive thing came out of "Dueling Prophets Sunday." Something became settled inside of me, and from that point on, I was no longer afraid to confront our prophetic team. I determined to provide real leadership in administrating the prophetic ministry in our midst.

Since that Sunday, I have decided that whenever I get a nervous feeling about what prophetic people are doing, I am not going to ignore it. To neglect the responsibility to lead the prophetically gifted people will usually result in harm to the church or ministry and to the prophetic people themselves. If they would have continued without restraints, they would have received a steady backlash of criticism from the people in the congregation. This is one of the main reasons that prophetic people just stop prophesying. The pain of feeling rejected eventually takes its toll. No doubt, some of the prophetic people would have only seen it as persecution instead of adjusting some of their ways that need correction. However, the end result would have been the same; they would have stopped prophesying. If pastors do not govern the prophetic ministry in their midst, the congregation eventually despises it and the prophetic people stop prophesying because of the feeling of being rejected by the congregation. If pastors do not lead, the prophetic ministry stops.

One of the greatest challenges in my ministry over the last twenty-five years has been in the necessity to govern the negative side of prophetic ministry by continually needing to restrain or change what prophetic individuals wanted to say publicly and to occasionally even need to strongly correct them without backing down.

Just to give a reality check, all was not forever fine after this one difficult Sunday morning. As I said, I warned them that if they did this again, I would publicly correct them. Soon after this Sunday, it actually happened again, and I did have to publicly correct one of them. It created no small stir. That was a disillusioning time for me. I was tempted to stop allowing prophetic ministry to be shared publicly in Sunday services. I'm glad now that I didn't give in to my anger and frustration because of the marvelous things that I saw God do in that church through the prophetic ministry.

The Motivation of Rejected Prophets

Most prophetic people get in touch with their giftings long before they cultivate the corresponding wisdom, humility, and character necessary to succeed in prophetic ministry. Some may appear arrogant or pushy in their zeal to be faithful to their prophetic gifting and calling. I believe that most of what appears as pushiness really comes from the wounding and fear of being rejected related to giving their prophetic insights.

Most prophetic people who have been around for a few years have been corrected plenty of times. Some of them have been dealt with in a harsh spirit and without being given the proper explanation as to what they were supposed to do differently. We cannot effectively correct anyone without them having some security in their relationship with church leadership. The average person who has been in the prophetic ministry for ten years is pretty beat up and bruised. By the time this person reaches forty or fifty, he or she is often very guarded and suspicious of authority figures. I really understand this. Some pastors are understandably reluctant to confront prophetic people. Why? Because the pastor has his own insecurities about how much he lacks prophetic experience along with the insecurity about how much division the prophetic people will stir up in the church against him.

When rejected prophets clash with insecure pastors in an uninformed congregation, then so many negatives occur. The combination of this causes churches to decide that it is just easier and better to avoid the prophetic ministry altogether. However, so much of this can be changed if we all work together. If the leadership will put forth clear guidelines for the prophetic *before* the prophetic people make their mistakes publicly, then much unnecessary trauma can be avoided. Add to this a clear plan that is in place for correcting and healing the prophetic with gentleness and love. Then we really can do it together long term.

Insecure Pastors and Leaders

Knowing where and how to draw the line with prophetic ministry minimizes the insecurity and fear a pastor may experience when first encountering such people. If a pastor understands how to deal with these people, he is less hesitant. Most pastors don't mind that things are a little messy if it is going to be profitable at the end of the day. But if they don't see the long-term benefit, they will not want to hassle with the problems. Pastors don't want their people becoming hurt, confused, and divided.

They sometimes get their eyes off God and yield to fear when things get beyond the comfort zone. They must learn to lead without fear, yet keep balanced in the area of risk-taking without sacrificing pastoral wisdom. Most pastors I know will let unusual, unprogrammed, and even strange-looking things happen as long as they know it is not hype or fake.

CHAPTER 13

ORIGINS OF THE PROPHETIC CALL

B
EING CALLED INTO the office of prophet is not a reward for our diligence in seeking to mature in prophecy. It is a matter of God's sovereign call. Yes, we must respond with diligence, but the calling starts with God. Paul wrote to the Corinthians: "But one and the same Spirit works all these things, distributing to each one individually *as He wills*" (1 Cor. 12:11, emphasis added).

We serve a personal God who has His own purposes for each individual. A Tibetan monk may go through exercises and disciplines, thinking these will help him become an ascended master. But the gifts and callings of God are not based on our striving, seeking, or searching; they are based on His sovereign choice and His grace. It is not a matter of our efforts to attain or develop spiritual skills. It is about God's sovereign calling and gracious giftings.

People sometimes ask how they can grow in the prophetic and receive more words from God. We can teach you to pay more attention to the impressions that the Holy Spirit gives you and even what to do with them once they come, but we cannot make the impressions come. That is the sovereign work of the Holy Spirit. We can only teach you how to cooperate with the activity of the Spirit, but not how to produce it.

In chapter 1, I told of the time when John Wimber asked me to pray for the gift of prophecy to be imparted to people at the 1989 Vineyard conference in Anaheim. Some people wanted me to pray for them to be called to the office of a prophet. Of course, there is no way I could do that. It is God's choice.

However, we have seen people who were prayed for in conference settings suddenly begin to receive an increase of Holy Spirit activity in the area of dreams, visions, and prophetic impressions. Many of them have continued to experience an increase of prophetic gifting from that time on. To some extent, this kind of gifting is transferable, but only to the degree that God sovereignly ordains. This is what Paul referred to when he urged Timothy not to neglect the spiritual gift that was imparted to him by the laying on of hands. (See 1 Timothy 4:14; 2 Timothy 1:6.)

There is a mysterious interplay between God's sovereign activity, human agency, and responsibility as we open our hearts before God, seek His will, and ask for what we desire. Then we let each individual's experience unfold without trying to explain fully the dynamics. The catalyst that releases the gift of God in a person is sometimes a divine encounter at salvation or even years later by a visitation of God without any human agency. Sometimes it happens suddenly in childhood, or it may be after someone has been a Christian for many years. With some, a growth of the prophetic anointing occurs slowly, while with others, the gift is imparted quickly through the laying on of hands (1 Tim. 4:14; 2 Tim. 1:6). There is a place for diligently seeking to grow in gifting, character, and maturity. But while diligence causes you to grow within your calling, it does not determine your calling.

VARIOUS WAY GOD CALLS PEOPLE
TO THE PROPHETIC

Indications while still a youth

Bob Jones, whom I have already mentioned numerous times in this book, is a man who has had a profound prophetic ministry. Bob had very little religious background and did not become a Christian until he was in his late thirties. Nevertheless, Bob had several angelic visitations and supernatural experiences as a boy that indicated he would have a prophetic ministry in his adult life. When Bob was thirteen, he heard an audible voice from heaven call his name. When he was fifteen, he saw himself in a vision being brought before the throne of God. These experiences terrified Bob. It took him several months to get over the vision. It never occurred to him until after his conversion that these things represented God's call on his life rather than God's judgment. Immediately after his conversion, to Bob's amazement, the prophetic gifts began to operate powerfully in his life. Bob is an example of how the gifts of grace and the calling of God were given as a result of God's grace, not his striving.

Sudden calling in one's adult life

Marty Streiker spent his whole adult life as a schoolteacher. In his early fifties, he heard the gospel and responded enthusiastically. Immediately after he was born again, he began to receive prophetic dreams and visions. However, he had no knowledge of the gifts of the Holy Spirit and, thus, no frame of reference for his experiences. The prophetic gifts that began with his conversion continued to increase over the years that followed.

Stirring up the gift

Michael Sullivant has been a pastor and teacher who for many years believed in the prophetic ministry. Yet Michael's function in the church was mostly in the areas of leadership and teaching. Several prophetic people told Michael that they sensed he would have a prophetic ministry someday, but that seemed unlikely since there was no notable sign in him of any prophetic gifting or calling. However, for thirty nights in a row, after one prophetic word was spoken over him, he had prophetic dreams. Since that time, Michael has grown much in the prophetic ministry.

John Wimber was teaching at Fuller Theological Seminary when he began to teach on healing. Soon after, healings started taking place. Before long the word of knowledge, which is a function of the prophetic call, began to operate in him in a mighty way. With John Wimber, there was no dramatic angelic visitation or voice from heaven. He simply began to regularly step out in faith by speaking the words of knowledge that God was giving him. In the process, the gifts of the Spirit began to operate through him more and more.

Phil Elston had recollections of "seeing" things as a boy and thinking that there was nothing unusual about this. He had several supernatural encounters with God. One of them led to his conversion to Jesus Christ. Phil did not have understanding about the prophetic gifting that manifested itself rather strongly in him after his conversion in 1976. He had many spiritual dreams and visions and heard God's voice. The most common way that this gift operates in him now is by receiving impressions from the Holy Spirit that allow him to know things he has no natural way of knowing. Now Phil travels internationally teaching and ministering prophetically.

These are just a few of the testimonies that could be offered in this book. The point of all this is that the prophetic calling on someone's life is a function of God's plan, issued before that person did anything to cultivate the gift. God has gifts and callings designed for your life. Bible training, discipline, fasting, and praying will not change your calling. However, these spiritual disciplines *will* enhance the release of the calling that has already been divinely determined. The goal is not to try to get God to call you as a prophet. It is usually a matter of stirring up the gifts and callings already determined for you by God.

The Pain of the Prophetic Calling

There is often a temptation to want something before we understand it. Then once we have it and experience the difficulties associated with it, our temptation is to want get to rid of it.

There is a lot of misunderstanding about prophetic ministry. Spectators don't realize how much prophetic people typically wrestle and struggle with the "down sides" of their own lives and ministries. If a person has a desire to be involved with prophetic ministry, it should not be because it seems exciting. The pain, the perplexities, and the attacks upon these people surely increase as their calling increases. To repeat Francis Frangipane again, "New levels bring new devils." In other words, new levels of the anointing inevitably bring new devils and intensifies spiritual warfare against us.

Some prophetic people I know complain with pain, asking the Lord to lift the prophetic call off their life. The "glory" of the prophetic ministry that some imagine when seeing a prophetic person minister in a conference setting is untypical of their everyday lifestyle.

We encourage prophetic people to find their joy in their spiritual identity as those who love Jesus and who know that He loves them. They should not think that having a "spectacular ministry" will make their life happy. I have never met a prophetic person whose life was made happy because of his or her prophetic gifting. Typically they experience increased demonic attack, opposition from godly people, and great perplexity in their own souls in the aftermath of their prophetic gifting.

I have noticed that prophetic people often have more disappointment with God than others. Why is this? It is because they see more clearly how things should be or how God plans for them to be in the future. But in seeing far ahead, they must wait with faith sometimes for many years for the release of what they know is on God's heart. Therefore, they are more prone to be heartsick because of enduring failed expectations. As Proverbs 13:12 says, "Hope deferred makes the heart sick."

Because their expectations are typically higher, they are more deeply disappointed. It's easier for those who are not so burdened with how things are supposed to be. Jeremiah complained that the Lord had tricked him. When Jeremiah prophesied of how God wanted to change things, he got in trouble with the leadership who were protecting their place in the status quo. He was ridiculed and rejected by so many. He wanted to quit. Nevertheless, the word of the Lord was like a fire burning within him; he could not hold it back, and so he continued to prophesy (Jer. 20:9). This resulted in even more rejection and pain for him.

An Important Reality Check

Through my years of pastoring, I have observed an agenda that operates in so many of us. It is subtle and hard to pin down. It is our commitment to avoid pain at almost any cost. Even as committed Christians, we seek to establish a painless environment for our lives. We will use the Bible, other people, and even spiritual gifts to achieve this end. Some imagine that if they could operate more in the prophetic gifting and thus more clearly discern the voice of God, then He would surely lead them into a more problem-free and satisfying life.

The problem is that when God speaks, He sometimes tells us to believe and do things that ultimately lead us into more testings, perplexities, and pain! Some of the most confusing and spiritually challenging experiences and seasons come upon prophetic people directly on the heels of being used by the Holy Spirit. Often they cry out for God to use them, and when He does, they complain about "feeling used"!

Paul describes three categories of experience in 2 Corinthians 6 that are characteristic of genuine apostolic Christianity. They are the negative pressures (vv. 4–5), the positive qualities (vv. 6–7) and the divine paradoxes (vv. 8–10) of ministry in the Spirit.

> But in all things we commend ourselves as ministers of God: in much patience, in tribulations, in needs, in distresses, in stripes, in imprisonments, in tumults, in labors, in sleeplessness, in fastings.
>
> [We commend ourselves as ministers of God] by purity, by knowledge, by longsuffering, by kindness, by the Holy Spirit, by sincere love, by the word of truth, by the power of God, by the armor of righteousness on the right hand and on the left.
>
> [We commend ourselves as ministers of God] by honor and dishonor, by evil report and good report; as deceivers, and yet true; as unknown, and yet well known; as dying, and behold we live; as chastened, and yet not killed; as sorrowful, yet always rejoicing; as poor, yet making many rich; as having nothing, and yet possessing all things.
>
> —2 Corinthians 6:4–10

If we minister in the power of the Spirit and seek to live according to God's Word, then all of these things will come our way in different measures from season to season.

We must understand that the opposing and perplexing aspects of life in the Spirit are as real as the positive and enjoyable aspects. If we are reconciled to this reality from the outset, then we are prepared to respond to them in a right spirit.

In praying for the power of God to be released in our ministry, I do not encourage anyone to look for trials or sufferings. We don't have to. They will automatically come our way because we live in a fallen world in which demons attack God's people. God intends to use these things to draw us into a deeper relationship with mature faith.

CHAPTER 14

EMBODYING THE PROPHETIC MESSAGE

E SSENTIAL TO PROPHETIC ministry are prophetic standards. The Lord
wants us to embody the message we preach; He will "wink" at our
carnality only for a season before disciplining us.

In this chapter I will discuss the fierce controversy that surrounded
Kansas City Fellowship beginning in 1990. We realize now that it was divine
discipline of our ministry, though most of what was said by our accusers was
inaccurate. They misrepresented our doctrines and practices and fabricated
many stories to validate their accusations. It was a difficult season of attack
and turmoil for our church. That does not change the fact that there were
several important issues in our midst that God was determined to address
and correct. He disciplines those He loves so that we grow up in the things
that are necessary to receiving our full inheritance (Heb. 12:5–11).

EMBODYING THE MESSAGE

The nature of prophetic ministry was revealed clearly to the apostle John
by an angel who told him, "The testimony of Jesus is the spirit of prophecy"
(Rev. 19:10). The revelation of the testimony of what is on Jesus's heart is the
focus of prophetic ministry. It involves more than simply communicating
His ideas; it also involves feeling and revealing the deep things of His heart.

God will often make the lives of His prophetic servants an illustration of the messages they are called to proclaim. He wants His messengers to feel some of what He feels. The prophet Hosea is an example of this. God instructed him to marry a harlot named Gomer. In doing so, Hosea demonstrated God's love and forbearance toward the harlot nation of Israel. This was a painful thing for Hosea because he didn't love Gomer. Hosea felt some of the anguish that God felt for Israel (Hosea 3).

God wants His servants not only to *say* what He is like, but also to *be* like Him; not only to *say* what He wants, but also to *do* His will; not only to *declare* His heart, but also to *feel* His heart.

The Lord spoke audibly to both Bob Jones and me on the same morning in April 1984. In essence, He said that He was going to bring a new emphasis on humility in the leadership in His church in the days to come. This speaks of much more than Him emphasizing the *doctrine* of humility. He will require that it be implemented in our everyday lifestyle.

God is going to dramatically confront the pride and selfish ambition of the leadership in the body of Christ worldwide. One way He will do this is by allowing us to be mistreated and then requiring that we bless our enemies. In this, we will see degrees of pride and selfish ambition in our hearts that we had never seen before.

He not only wants us to preach the doctrine of humility, but He also wants us to be a living demonstration of this message. If we are going to preach it, then we will have to live it. We haven't done a good job with this yet.

THORNS IN THE FLESH

When God communicates a purpose and message with dramatic supernatural manifestations (angelic visitations, audible voices, and signs in the heavens), then we know the Lord is urgent about making the message apply to our lives. He will challenge the areas in our lives that are inconsistent with the message He has given us to proclaim.

God sometimes sends a thorn in the flesh to those to whom He gives abundant revelation in order to protect their hearts from destructive pride. The apostle Paul said that he had been given a "thorn in the flesh" in order that he would not exalt himself. This was due to the fact that his ministry was blessed by an "abundance of the [prophetic] revelations" (2 Cor. 12:7).

God has determined to work humility in each of us. For some, the beauty of God's work in their heart is not put on a public stage where it is noticed by others.

Sometimes the Holy Spirit works in one's heart for almost a lifetime before that person is given the full platform to release the message. Some are given a platform early in their ministry as they preach beyond the maturing work of the Holy Spirit in their own lives. That has been our situation, to some degree. We were called to proclaim a message of humility that we ourselves did not yet possess in a mature way. If we really love God, He gives us the chance to respond voluntarily to the Spirit in this. Sometimes He allows the difficult circumstances of people attacking our character and ministry to help us grow in humility. The prophetic controversy we walked through in the early 1990s was meant to wake us up to see the unperceived pride in us. Of course, humility is a lifelong journey. God is very patient and gracious to us as He little by little reveals the unperceived pride that lies beneath the surface of our hearts. He is kind to us as He patiently waits for us to change: "Do you despise the riches of His goodness, forbearance, and longsuffering, not knowing that the goodness of God leads you to repentance?" (Rom. 2:4).

WATCHING THE WRONG GAUGES

In 1989, my ministry seemed to be going so well. It was growing very fast. As a young man, I was traveling with John Wimber and speaking regularly to crowds of thousands at international conferences. I enjoyed the attention and honor more than I realized. Because of John Wimber's prominence, I was meeting with high-profile Christian leaders from around the world. My pride was being stroked and strengthened in a way that I was not at all aware of. I was overwhelmed with the invitations to preach and requests for interviews for magazines and television. A dozen publishers wanted me to write books for them. Several companies sent proposals to distribute our tapes throughout the nation.

It was physically impossible to answer the multitudes of letters and phone calls that came monthly. We were overwhelmed and in over our heads. We complained about the pressures, but actually our team enjoyed the attention more than we cared to admit. We were out of touch with our pride, our limitations, and exactly what it was that God wanted to work in us during this season of our lives.

For a short season, whatever we touched seemed to prosper, so we figured God was excited about everything just as it was. But there were some warning signals going off. However, we were moving too fast to recognize them.

In our early stages of growth we didn't have enough spiritual maturity to discern some basic warnings about our pride. If someone would have said, "You have pride," we would have gone overboard repenting of pride. But that's not the same as actually seeing our pride from God's perspective.

WARNING SIGNS

One of the warning signs we missed was that we were "partying alone." We were so happy about the seemingly great things that were happening in our ministry that we didn't notice that some other ministries were not having such a great time. We were rejoicing in our increase, but we ignored the fact that others were having a difficult time.

Meanwhile, we partied on. We didn't see or feel their pain. We saw only our increase. If another church struggled or even disbanded, it was no real concern to us as long as we continued to grow.

We now lament over having been so self-absorbed. The older I get, the more aware I am of my natural tendency to pride. I am much more aware of the promises and struggles of other ministries in my city. I am no longer content to celebrate alone. When the Lord promises to visit us, we now ask, "But what about the other ministries in our city? Are you going to visit them too?" God told Moses that He would make from Moses's descendants a great nation after He first destroyed the nation of Israel. Moses pleaded with the Lord to forgive the sins of the children of Israel. Moses had no desire to see Israel destroyed and himself made the head of a new nation.

> "Therefore, let Me alone, that My wrath may burn hot against them and I may consume them. And I will make of you a great nation." Then Moses pleaded with the LORD his God, and said: "LORD, why does Your wrath burn hot against Your people whom You have brought out of Egypt with great power and with a mighty hand?... Turn from Your fierce wrath, and relent from this harm to Your people."... So the LORD relented.
>
> —Exodus 32:10–14

On another occasion, the spirit of prophecy was released on the seventy elders of Israel. Joshua was jealous for Moses's honor. He wanted Moses to be seen as the only one who prophesied. Moses corrected Joshua, saying, "Oh, that all the LORD's people were prophets" (Num. 11:29). Why would it be good if all God's people prophesied? Moses knew that God's purpose would be strengthened and His people would be blessed if more prophesied.

> The LORD came down in the cloud, and spoke to him, and took of the Spirit that was upon him, and placed the same upon the seventy elders; and it happened, when the Spirit rested upon them, that they prophesied.... And a young man ran and told Moses, and said, "Eldad and Medad are prophesying in the camp." So Joshua the son of Nun, Moses' assistant, one of his choice men, answered and said, "Moses my lord, forbid them!" Then Moses said to him, "Are you zealous for my sake? Oh, that all the LORD's people were prophets and that the LORD would put His Spirit upon them!"
>
> —Numbers 11:25–29

The Holy Spirit is raising up leaders today who have a heart like Moses, who are not content to have increased honor and blessing in ministry unless others are included.

A major warning sign we missed in those early days was that we did not think much about what other ministries in our area were going through. We were satisfied as long as our ministry was growing and we were being blessed. Looking back, I can see my inherent pride and self-centeredness that I was totally unaware of in those days.

The second warning sign was our lack of perception that we needed other ministries. A lot of people around the body of Christ had much to contribute to what we were doing, but we didn't realize our need for their insight and input. They could have showed us how to do a lot of things better, but we were too busy and too caught up in the euphoria of our seemingly early success to realize this.

THE TEMPTATIONS OF OPPOSITION

Things seemed to be going so well throughout 1989 because of the rapid increase of influence and honor that I received because of being associated with John Wimber's ministry. However, in January 1990, many things suddenly changed. It was as if we tripped a bomb wire when we stepped into the 1990s.

We were suddenly attacked by about ten different ministries who were misrepresenting our beliefs and practices and presenting us as a cult. They were passing on things about us that were greatly distorted. It was humiliating to our leadership team and confusing to our people. In the midst of this, we were faced with two temptations in regard to how we should respond to our accusers.

Temptation to retaliate

At first there was the temptation to retaliate. We had leaders from around America encouraging us to expose our attackers and set the record straight. They felt it was our responsibility to "defend the purpose of God." However, we were not comfortable attacking other Christians. Ironically, the prophetic ministry that was being attacked had earlier given us prophetic words that helped us to bless our accusers at this time. Several years earlier, from 1982 to 1984, the Lord gave several members of our prophetic team significant dreams that we would face this controversy. In September 1984, the Lord plainly revealed to us who one of the principal accusers would be and specifically when they would attack us. The Lord emphasized in these prophetic words that we were not to strike back.

Five years later, in December 1989, our leadership team discussed the fact that an attack against our ministry would probably be coming soon in light of the timing that God spoke to us back in September 1984. It did not surprise us when they started immediately after that in January 1990. Having this prophetic information for just over five years helped us to know that God was in control and how He required us to respond.

John Wimber's words of advice also helped us in our decision to not answer our enemies in a negative way. He used the illustration of Solomon and the two women claiming to be the mother of the same child. When Solomon pretended he was about to divide the child with a sword, the true mother gave up her rights to the baby and allowed the lying woman to have the child. By this, the true mother was revealed (1 Kings 3:16–28). John said that if we really cared about the bigger purpose of God, we would not retaliate. It would only create a destructive fury, and the purpose of God (the child) would be divided.

At that same time, I received a prophetic communication from the Lord. He said, "The measure of your anger toward these men is the measure of your unperceived ambition."

I reacted and said aloud, "No! It's not my unperceived ambition. Lord, I care about Your kingdom and Your name being defamed." Then the Lord asked me a question: "Why, then, aren't you this angry when My name is defamed when other ministries are attacked?" I had to be honest and admit that I was not mad when other Christian leaders were being criticized. It was the blow to my reputation that really bothered me. I saw with new clarity that my own agenda for honor was being hindered as the accusations against us persisted.

After struggling with it for a while, I realized that what the Lord said was very true: *the measure of my anger toward these men was the measure of my unperceived ambition.* We were monitoring the value of our ministry by the gauge of numerical and financial success.

But then I realized that there was an important indicator to which we had paid little attention—the fault line of selfish ambition hiding beneath our surface. Just as earthquakes expose the fault lines that lie deep below the surface of the earth, so also the current pressures on us were exposing our hidden fault lines of ambition and anger. We only had to be honest enough to admit it instead of lying against the truth.

> But if you have bitter envy and self-seeking in your hearts, do not boast and lie against the truth. This wisdom does not descend from above, but is earthly, sensual, demonic. For where envy and self-seeking exist, confusion and every evil thing are there. But the wisdom that is from above is first pure, then peaceable, gentle, willing to yield, full of mercy and good fruits, without partiality and without hypocrisy.
>
> —James 3:14–17

One of the primary ways that God disciplines us is by allowing us to experience injustices at the hands of others. He allows us to be tested, watching for a response of trust in Him and forgiveness toward our offenders. Proverbs states, "Reproofs of instruction are the way of life" (Prov. 6:23). The purpose of God's discipline is to equip our hearts with Christlikeness.

> For they indeed for a few days chastened us as seemed best to them, but He for our profit, that we may be partakers of His holiness.
>
> —Hebrews 12:10

The true gauges of successful ministry are those issues that pertain to our becoming Christlike. Were our hearts growing in tender affection for Jesus? Were we growing in our ability to endure hardship with love? Could we bless our enemies with humility? These are the issues that God wants the prophetic ministry to impart successfully. We discovered that we were not very successful by God's standards.

Temptation to blame the devil

Second, we faced the temptation to simply dismiss the accusations and attacks because they were sent by the devil. Scripture clearly teaches us to resist the devil and he will flee. (See James 4:7.)

However, notice it says we resist the devil as we are submitting to God and His Word. In retrospect, we see that God's hand was working in the midst of Satan's rage and the sin of our accusers. The Lord can easily overrule Satan's rage for our good (Rom. 8:28). Joseph understood that what his brothers meant for evil, God meant for good in his life. He said, "But as for you, you meant evil against me; but God meant it for good, in order to bring it about as it is this day, to save many people alive" (Gen. 50:20).

God was speaking to us about our errors and pride even through the voice of accusers who were speaking terrible lies. The issue was whether we would be focused on the lies against us or on the work that God wanted to do in us. Yes, the methods used by our accusers were often unrighteous. Were our critics totally misguided or partially right? Our conclusion now is that it was some of both. The lack of wisdom and humility in us provoked certain things in them. In addition to that, some of the things they were pointing out were true—especially regarding our pride.

In any case, the uproar that ensued forced us to confront some of our character problems and unwise practices. In that sense, we now see the redemptive hand of God in the whole mess.

The danger in only seeing an attack as the work of the devil is that in this mind-set, we are not as sensitive to what the Holy Spirit wants to say to us. Some prophetic people tend to have a persecution complex. They feel that the very nature of their calling means they are going to be persecuted. Consequently, whenever a genuine word of correction comes, some bristle and think to themselves, "Yes, we expected this because true prophets are always persecuted."

I am recalling a large Christian ministry that was being harshly criticized by a couple of "cult watchers" and "heresy hunters." The methods and information used against them were, in fact, questionable. This well-known ministry determined that since their critics were surely from the devil, what was happening was only about being persecuted. Because they perceived that their critics were solely the devil's instruments, they were not focused on receiving God's correction in the crisis they were facing. We do not want to "waste a good trial"; instead, why not receive insight into our pride and lack of wisdom from the Holy Spirit in times when we are being accused by others? The Holy Spirit has much to say to us in such times. Even if the methods used against us are as inappropriate, God can still give us life-giving correction in the midst. Remember, the Lord corrected Balaam even through a dumb donkey (Num. 22:22–35).

The Discipline of the Lord

The writer to the Hebrews points out two common wrong reactions to God's discipline:

> My son, do not despise the chastening of the LORD, nor be discouraged when you are rebuked by Him; for whom the LORD loves He chastens.
>
> —Hebrews 12:5–6

The first wrong response is to "despise" God's correction by denying our need for it. One way some despise His discipline is by only seeing their pressures as an attack of Satan without regarding the fact that God often wants to speak correction to us in them. Thus, we regard His discipline too lightly.

The second wrong reaction is to be "discouraged" by God's reproofs so that we feel overwhelmed. These are the ones who quit following hard after God in times of pressure.

We mustn't be either insensitive or hypersensitive when our heavenly Father points out our faults and errors. We need to learn to take our needed medicine or correction with a right attitude of grateful love for God.

God's overall goal for us is that we "be conformed to the image of His Son" (Rom. 8:29). God wants us to embody the prophetic message that He wants to speak through us. It is never enough to proclaim a message. We must seek to live the message we proclaim before we can genuinely claim to have a prophetic message and a prophetic ministry. God wants His Word to become flesh in our lives. Therefore, He sends various forms of redemptive discipline to help us see the unperceived weaknesses in our lives, those hidden fault lines beneath the surface. We can despise His discipline and decide to quit pursuing the Lord as fervently as we once did. We can become bitter at God for administering it.

Or we can respond in the only right way, which is to endure His redemptive discipline, knowing that it is for our good that we might share in His holiness (Heb. 12:7, 10).

LESSONS LEARNED THE HARD WAY

God used these events to bring correction to us in several ways. Let me share some of the lessons I learned.

1. Seeing our pride: We were caught up in the increase of our ministry far more than we were focused on increasing godliness and humility in our character.

2. Our need for other ministries: We grew to appreciate new parts of the body of Christ for whom we had no relationship

in our earlier days. John Wimber continually emphasized the need to "love the whole church," not just those who look and sound like us.

3. Understanding the prophetic process: We had such an immature and naïve view of the prophetic ministry. We saw manipulation in some of our prophetic team as they prophesied favorable things to gain favor from those who could open doors for them.

4. Becoming accountable: We saw our need for input from leaders outside of our local ministry who could speak correction to us. We believe every ministry should be in relationships with other ministries outside their staff. This provides the opportunity for godly leaders to see our blind spots.

5. A balanced ministry team: Every church needs balanced input from different types of personalities and ministries to maintain stability. Yes, we need the high-octane prophetic people with supernatural manifestations, but we also need trained teachers with theological depth, tender pastors with people skills, zealous evangelists as well as ministries with leadership and administrative giftings. Currently, on the IHOP Missions Base leadership team, we have four people with earned doctorates, eight with master's degrees, and five with law degrees. We integrate trained teachers with those who have prophetic giftings. This is not always easy, but it is worth the effort.

CHAPTER 15

COMMON ABUSES AND MISUSES
OF PROPHECY

I N THIS CHAPTER we address common misuses of simple prophecy. Keep in the mind the necessary distinction between "simple prophecy" and the office of a prophet. Simple prophecy is limited to edification, exhortation, and comfort (1 Cor. 14:3), whereas the office of a prophet has the authority to correct and/or give specific direction to a person, ministry, or nation. Everyone can function in simple prophecy. However, only people with a history of accurately prophesying future events can claim to function in the office of a prophet.

All prophecies must uphold and honor what is written in Scripture. By upholding this one guideline, we will save ourselves much pain and turmoil. We must not give or receive prophecies that violate the spirit and intention of what is written in Scripture.

Some who are inexperienced with prophecy are too quick to naïvely obey "prophetic" directives from those who boldly prophesy to them. Through the years, I have seen people receive "prophetic" directions that result in unnecessary pain and confusion. Much of this can be avoided by observing scriptural principles along with some basic common sense. When I was first exposed to personal prophecy, I was very open to receiving "prophetic" direction in areas of my personal domestic life. Thus, in 1986, I laid out several guidelines for receiving personal prophecy. I use those same guidelines today.

Misuse #1: Giving Direction in Domestic Areas

Simple prophecy is meant give encouragement and comfort, not give specific new direction to one's domestic life. Examples of domestic areas in which we should avoid giving or receiving prophetic direction include choosing a spouse, having babies, investing money, changing jobs, moving to a new city, buying or selling a house, going on ministry trips, joining a church, choosing a college, and so forth. We can give godly counsel to one another in the domestic areas of our life; however, I am strongly against giving it under the guise of prophecy. Many want prophecies about romance and finances. Others just want to be told what to do so they can end the indecision that plagues their life.

I have been given many prophesies over the years that have offered me direction in the domestic areas of my life. The vast majority of these "directive prophecies" have proved to be unhelpful and wrong. I am glad that I did not receive them. God never intended prophecy to be used this way. Instead, God wants people to relate directly to Him and hear from Him and employ the wisdom in their personal lives. God wants us to be responsible for the decisions we make.

Some are more willing to accept direction from prophetic words so that they can finally give away the responsibility and burden for decision making in their lives to others.

A young man told me of a lady about whom he received prophetic words to marry. The problem was that this young lady was already engaged to another godly man. However, he insisted that he had received prophetic words and dreams to marry her. I counseled him to let go of those "prophetic words." However, he continued to pursue this engaged woman. The fallout was disastrous as the young man put pressure on the lady by giving her multiple invitations to spend time with him. Of course, this angered the young lady's fiancé. When all was said and done, the young man ended up heartbroken because of his misuse of prophecy.

I have seen many believers make harmful and sometimes disastrous decisions because they followed a prophecy in the area of personal finance.

I have seen wise and successful business leaders throw away their wisdom as they naïvely received inaccurate "prophetic" words that end up causing them much unnecessary financial loss.

MISUSE #2: REDIRECTING THE ROLES OF PEOPLE IN THE CHURCH

We must not give specific prophetic words to people who indicate that they are to function in new positions in the ministry organization that they serve in. If the Lord gives you prophetic words about changes in someone's role, then give it to the leader who has authority to implement changes. Why? Prophetic words that point to a change in someone's role usually involve an element of promotion. The one receiving the positive prophecy naturally appreciates the one who prophesied. However, if the leader does not implement the promotion, then there is potential for resentment and division.

A friend of mine who pastors a megachurch invited a man with an international prophetic ministry to speak at his church. During one of the services, this prophetic minister called the pastoral staff to all come forward. He prophesied over each one. He told the youth pastor that God was about to promote him to be the executive pastor over the whole church. While this young pastor grew excited by the promotion, one of the other older pastors grew visibly agitated as it was clear that the prophetic word was indicating that the young pastor was about to take his position.

In fact, my friend, who was the senior pastor, was considering promoting the younger pastor to take over the position. However, what the older pastor who was growing angry did not realize was that my friend was preparing to promote him as well to become his successor to lead the church. Yet, when the visiting minister prophesied the role changes without first consulting the senior pastor, he created an unnecessary conflict. The angered pastor ended up leaving the church and taking many of the congregants with him to his new church. All this could have been avoided if the visiting minister had first submitted the prophetic word through the proper channels for the senior pastor to first review. Instead, the "fruit" of the prophetic word was an offended leader and a church split.

Just because you may receive a true prophetic word about a redirection of roles for people in the ministry organization does not mean it is beneficial to give the word publicly without first bringing it in an appropriate way to senior leadership.

MISUSE #2: GIVING CORRECTION TO PEOPLE

Simple prophecy is meant to encourage, comfort, and edify rather than to give correction that is confrontational and often embarrasses people. We must not embarrass people by revealing negative things about them in public gatherings. This sort of prophesying is neither helpful nor biblical. Scripture is very clear that negative words are to be spoken first to the person in private (Matt. 18:15–17).

A common example of correcting people publicly that I have seen throughout the years is in labeling people as having a Jezebel spirit. I have seen many men who are threatened by confident women in leadership use the "Jezebel spirit" label to correct them.

Another example of misusing prophecy is in publicly declaring that someone is rebellious or hardened of heart. I have seen this happen to several teenagers through my ministry when the prophet stood up and declared them as rebels when in reality they were immature but still sincere in their reach for God.

If the young person truly is rebellious, then using the "prophetic" to point it out publicly is actually detrimental instead of helpful.

It would be more effective for the prophetic person to counsel this young person and ask about the things he was discerning. However, it is damaging to the young person's heart and spiritual life if the prophetic person simply declares that God sees him or her as rebellious.

I have been in congregations where the prophetic minister called out people to accuse them of doubt and unbelief, rebuking them for lacking faith. The prophetic minister declares that if the individuals would just believe, they would see the work of God. The individuals feel shamed and demoralized instead of edified and comforted (1 Cor. 14:3).

I have seen people publicly called out and "prophetically described" as struggling with personal issues such as pornography or alcohol. This humiliated the person. Often the "prophetic word" ended up not being accurate. However, because of the stature of the "prophet," the congregation believed the negative report. It wrongly tagged the person in the minds of the congregation for years to come, causing much unnecessary pain. Even if the prophecy is accurate, such words should be given in a private setting with people whom the recipient trusts.

These kinds of words should rarely be given. However, when they are, they should be given in appropriate settings and without adding "thus says the Lord" to bolster the charge against the person.

If the prophetic word is accurate, then it should produce hope that there is a way out of the problem, and especially that God is revealing His great love for the person with desire to liberate him so as to bring him into a greater depth in relationship with Him.

Prophetic people should emphasize that Jesus is gracious, compassionate, and merciful (Exod. 34:6) to those who are sincere even if they are immature in their faith. Jesus is ready to forgive any who will run to Him and not away from Him. Remember, it is His kindness that leads us to repentance (Rom. 2:4).

Some Old Testament prophecies were directed to Israel at a time of great national rebellion. A prophetic person today must not apply prophetic words with the same tone to an individual who sincerely loves Jesus yet is struggling in an area of his life. They must remember that the Old Testament prophets were talking to a hardened nation, not to one who sincerely loved God. Even in the midst of those prophecies the Lord would again and again declare His kindness and His desire for His people to return to Him for forgiveness and full restoration. We must remember when prophesying to His bride that we are often talking to believers who sincerely love Him and who are seeking to walk in His ways.

Misuse #4: An Overreliance on Dreams

Many who are new to prophetic ministry at first overly rely on dreams for direction in the domestic issues of their lives. Without a doubt, the Bible teaches that God directs His people through prophetic dreams (Acts 2:17). However, most of our dreams are not meant to be understood as giving us prophetic direction. Dreams are not meant to be a substitute for gaining and applying wisdom in our life.

Dreams are most helpful when giving us confirmation of a decision that we are already beginning to sense. Some overly rely on dreams for their decisions because it absolves them from taking personal responsibility for decisions that turn out to be wrong ones. Over the years, I have seen people more confused by dreams rather than helped by them. This is because they did not take the time to weed out the dreams that were not meant to be understood as prophetic.

I receive several hundred prophetic dreams each year from people. I have found that only about 10 percent of them are helpful. For over twenty years, on a near weekly basis, I have received two to three dreams from people assuring me that God is pleased with me and my ministry and that great blessing is coming. At the very same time, I also receive two to three dreams per week that warn me that God is grieved with me and that disaster is soon coming to my life and ministry.

Solomon taught us that there is much vanity in the multitude of dreams and words that claim to be prophetic. He said in Ecclesiastes 5:3, 7, "For a dream comes through much activity, and a fool's voice is known by his many words.... For in the multitude of dreams and many words there is vanity. But fear God." In other words, we must use caution in receiving all words that claim to be directive prophecies.

Very sincere people often get thrown off by the details of their "prophetic dreams" as well as those given to them by others.

Some believers I know have an element of what I call "spiritual superstition." In other words, they have an inordinate zeal to follow the details of these "prophetic dreams" without regard to wisdom or even to what God has clearly put in their own hearts.

I knew a young man once who was desperate to hear God's voice concerning where he should live. He was married with small children but was restless and seeking God's voice for a move. He had several people in his life who were "dreamers." Every week he would get a dream from one of them telling him to move here or there or to just to stay put. Obviously, many of the "prophetic words" he received contradicted each other. This young man spent his days trying to dissect the details of each symbolic picture in each dream. He exhausted himself in the process and lost his focus on Jesus.

He lived in so much unnecessary confusion. He was frozen in fear of getting out of the will of God. The more dreams that he received, the more confused he became. He was listening to so many voices who were dreaming with their own agenda. They were interpreting the dreams they had through a lens of their own opinions while claiming that they were hearing from God. This confusion created chaos for him and his entire family. Yes, he was sincere before God and wanted to be in His will. However, the dreams created a fog in him that kept him from embracing God's wisdom and from hearing more clearly from the Lord. In other words, it had the very opposite effect than what God intended.

Misuse #5: Trivializing Prophetic Ministry

Another common way that people misuse prophecy is to trivialize it by seeking "prophetic" direction in such simple areas as which shoes to wear or parking space to use. While we want to be led by the Spirit, we recognize that using good "common sense" is also a part of operating in God's wisdom.

I have seen people do eccentric things in the name of following the Holy Spirit. For example, one lady in our midst refused to cooperate with the usher asking her to move from a seat reserved for another because "the Lord told her to sit there." One young man impulsively ran around the building in the middle of the service because "the Lord told him to do it."

I have seen some live in unnecessary indecisiveness for simple life decisions because they refuse to make a decision until "the Lord directed" them. They sit at the corner waiting for God to tell them which direction to turn, or they stand in front of their closet waiting for God to tell them what to wear. Yes, they do have a sincere desire to obey the Spirit. However, by relinquishing their responsibility to make simple decisions, they live paralyzed, and sometimes even stubbornly, as they wait for direction from the Holy Spirit. This trivializes the purpose of the prophetic gift. This type of eccentric behavior is not a part of operating in the prophetic anointing.

The Lord gives us a spirit of wisdom for the practical operation of life without needing to get a specific, direct word for every little decision. Yes, there are the rare occasions when the Spirit will direct you as you drive on the highway to suddenly change your plans and go somewhere you were not originally planning on going. Such divine appointments do happen, but they are rare. We are to walk in wisdom with an attentive ear to the Lord, being ready for Him to interrupt us yet without trivializing the prophetic anointing by waiting on it for every small decision that we make.

Some believers are impulsive in the name of following impressions they have as if they were all coming from the Holy Spirit. Such a mind-set can lead to bizarre, unstable activity. A man in our midst was convinced that the Lord told him to spin at each meeting for long periods of time. Impulses like this are not just a demonstration of a lack of wisdom; some are actually dangerous when acted on. I have seen people do erotic things in worship services, like taking off their clothes to show that they are humble and will obey anything God says, or like slamming themselves into walls, or lying in the middle of the floor as though frozen and refusing to move. Yielding to such impressions opens the door to more bizarre impressions and can progressively lead to more and more unstable and unsound activity. This opens a dangerous door to the spirit realm. Such people should repent of obeying these impressions and should not be encouraged to follow them. Some people are entertaining demons in walking out some of the impressions that come to their minds.

MISUSE #6: FLATTERY AND MANIPULATION

Sometimes, people will make up a prophetic word or add to a prophetic word to flatter or manipulate people with money or so that those in leadership will accept them. In 1 Corinthians 13, Paul talks about love in the context of spiritual gifts by emphasizing that love "does not seek its own" (v. 5). We must be vigilant to not prophesy in a way that flatters people to gain a personal advantage from them. Most human beings have enough pride to be vulnerable to being sucked into believing flatteries. This leads to self-deception.

People who use prophecy to flatter and manipulate others often seek to "prophesy" in secret so that others do not see what is happening. The reason they want to isolate the person they are "prophesying" to is so that others will not tip them off as to how foolish and nonsensical such prophecy is.

These people prophesy out of their own desires to motivate people to connect with them. They will use flattery and exaggeration to meet the desires of other people and then gain an upper hand over them.

James warns us that "if you have bitter envy and self-seeking in your hearts, do not boast and lie against the truth. This wisdom does not descend from above, but is earthly, sensual, demonic. For where envy and self-seeking exist, confusion and every evil thing are there. But the wisdom that is from above is first pure, then peaceable, gentle, willing to yield, full of mercy and good fruits, without partiality and without hypocrisy. Now the fruit of righteousness is sown in peace by those who make peace" (James 3:14–18).

Some are more vulnerable to flattery than others because they so long to hear prophecies about the bigness or uniqueness of their ministry calling.

I have seen several prophetic ministries who flatter those they want to join their staff as an assistant by prophesying that "their mantle" would be imparted to the potential assistant. Some prophetic ministries want assistants who blindly come under their authority.

Some young assistants are so eager to believe that they are uniquely called that they are willing to do just about anything to attain to that calling. Of course, manipulation like this creates much bitterness in the end, along with disdain for the prophetic ministry. I have seen some older "prophets" use this type of flattery over and over to gain the allegiance of young people.

MISUSE #7: PROPHESYING IN TOTAL PRIVACY

I encourage you to be cautious whenever someone wants to prophesy to you in total privacy without others witnessing what is being said. As a general rule, when someone insists that they have a prophetic word for you that he or she can only give to you in secret, know that something is probably wrong. Usually when prophetic people seek to draw others to a back room to prophesy, they do it so that those witnessing the prophetic word will not discern flattery or manipulation.

Those who walk in the light do not mind giving prophesying in the light or in a way in which they are fully accountable for what they say. It is best to only receive prophecies that are "in the light" with witnesses. I urge all prophetic teams to record the prophecies they give to others whenever possible.

I remember one incident where a visiting prophetic man asked to meet several young leaders in the church where I was speaking to give them personal prophetic words. He insisted that he could only give them words if in private. When all was revealed, this prophetic man was flattering these young leaders by telling each one how great they were and how the leadership of the church could not recognize their great leadership. He hinted to each one in different ways that they might have to leave their church and to help him form another church after he moved to the city. Most of these young men left their church to join him.

Again, beware of people who claim to be prophetic and want to go somewhere private to prophesy to you. Such people want to gain your confidence to be able to exert their influence over you so they can get your money or get you to help them.

Receiving a prophecy opens one's heart in a unique way. Let me explain. When a prophetic minister looks into the eyes of someone to proclaim aspects of their divine destiny, it moves the heart of the person listening. This can sometimes create a soul tie. Some prophetic ministers use this influence to seek to develop "close friendships" that eventually have sexual overtones.

Sometimes it is even more blatant then that. Once a man and his wife were visiting the IHOP Missions Base and saw a young woman singing. After she was finished, the man approached her to tell her he had a "prophetic word for her." He told her they needed to go outside so he could tell her the word, so she went with him and his wife outside. The man prophesied to the girl that the Lord wanted him to impart the "lover heart of God" to her. The girl was perplexed. Before she knew it, the man was embracing her and playing with her hair while his wife stood there praying in tongues! Once the girl realized what was happening, she pushed him away and fled for safety. I have heard numerous stories from those who have experienced this in one form or another. Usually the "prophetic person" takes them to a side room, looks them in the eye, flatters them, and tells them how awesome their destiny is. In the next meeting, they prophesy about how connected they are supposed to be in the spirit and how unique their connection is.

In these private "prophetic sessions," the deceptions develop into more and more. Then, over time, the "prophetic person" begins say that the Lord wants them to have physical relations to demonstrate what is happening in the spirit. Many have been caught in this as they blindly follow manipulative prophetic people who are, in essence, using the name of God in vain. The naïve are so desperate to reach their destiny that they are willing to do just about anything. Even if they are not at all attracted to the "prophet," some are willing to endure anything to attain their "destiny."

Common Abuses and Misuses of Prophecy

MISUSE #8: ASSUMPTIONS ABOUT TIMING

We must be careful to not give our assumptions to the timing of the fulfillment of prophetic words that we may give someone. Sometimes, prophetic people do this to "jazz up" a prophetic word. Sometimes they feel pressure from the person receiving the prophecy to add the element of timing to a prophetic word. This ends up bringing unnecessary confusion.

MISUSE #9: "I CANNOT HELP/STOP MYSELF"

Over the years, I have witnessed prophetic people being asked to stop speaking or behaving in a certain way. Some prophetic people claim that they are unable to stop because they are "overwhelmed" by the Holy Spirit. However, the Scriptures are clear that people operating in the power of the Holy Spirit are governed by love and self-control (Gal. 5:22–23). Paul said, "The spirits of the prophets are subject to the prophets" (1 Cor. 14:32). In other words, he was making it the responsibility of the prophetic person to keep his spirit under control. He would not let prophetic people in the New Testament church claim that they could not help what they were doing in a meeting. To repeat this, anyone claiming that they cannot control what they say or do because they are "overcome" by the Holy Spirit is naïve. There are certain types who want to be free of the responsibility for what they do and say by claiming that the Holy Spirit "made them" behave in such a way. Paul admonished and required each believer to contribute what he had in an orderly way by using self-control (1 Cor. 14:28–40).

Paul taught the prophetic people to be in control of themselves in such a way that they could pause while giving their prophecy long enough to allow another prophetic person to speak (v. 30).

One aspect of self-control is the ability to rule our spirits or to control our words and actions.

> He who rules his spirit [is mightier] than he who takes a city.
> —Proverbs 16:32

> Whoever has no rule over his own spirit is like a city broken down, without walls.
> —Proverbs 25:28

163

During one of our services, a woman shared a prophetic word for our congregation. When she shared the prophetic word with me, I bore witness to it being a true word. To my surprise, when she got up to share the prophetic word with the congregation, she began to flail her arms and legs around wildly while delivering the prophetic word. She was drawing much attention to herself and even hindering the congregation from hearing the prophetic word that she was giving. When I talked to the woman about her unnecessary and distracting behavior, she claimed that she could not control herself. When I told her that the "spirit of the prophet is subject to the prophet," she was upset with me and accused me of "quenching the Spirit."

Misuse #10: Drawing Attention to Ourselves

Paul said that we should seek the things that are excellent when ministering in the gifts of the Holy Spirit (1 Cor. 12:31; 14:12; Phil. 1:9–10). One of the ways that we show forth an excellent spirit when we prophesy is by drawing attention to Jesus and not to ourselves by our flamboyant ministry style. Some prophesy with a spirit of self-exhibition instead of being focused on Jesus and on what helps people receive from Jesus. In other words, they draw so much attention to themselves. They may get away with it in the sense that people do not rebuke them for it. However, this way is not the most excellent way to operate in prophetic ministry.

It is best to prophesy in a way that does not draw undue attention to ourselves. Some people who have a genuine prophetic word puff themselves up in the eyes of others as holier or more spiritual because they receive such accurate prophetic revelation.

I encourage prophetic people in our midst to dial down their emotions before giving a prophetic word and to only sparingly use "The Lord told me" or "Thus says the Lord." We can prophesy in a way that is "supernaturally natural" without always drawing attention to the fact that we are prophesying. We are encouraged to operate in the anointing of the Spirit in a spirit of excellence (1 Cor. 14:12).

MISUSE #11: NEGLECTING TO GIVE THE CONDITIONS FOR PROPHETIC WORDS

Most prophetic promises are conditional. They will only come to pass if certain conditions are met. For example, you might receive a prophetic promise that great blessing will come to you if you make more time to seek the Lord. But by neglecting to give the condition of the prophetic promise, prophetic ministers may cause individuals to miss the blessing that the Lord invited them to receive. Many prophetic words are not guarantees but invitations to cooperate with God. God requires faith and obedience as we work and pray in agreement with what He promises.

I have known people who received true prophetic words about their callings that were confirmed in unusual ways. The people understood the words as guarantees instead of invitations, and thus they failed to lay hold of the Lord in the way the Lord required them to enter into their new ministry.

I knew a young man once who was called out in a large congregation and given a prophetic word about his calling. It was confirmed supernaturally. However, the prophet didn't give the conditions that were necessary for this young man to walk out his calling. The prophetic word was an invitation, not a promise. This young man ended up with a false confidence in the prophetic word. He thought he could live any way he wanted, thinking that one day the prophetic word would just suddenly be fulfilled.

Because of the accuracy of the word and the supernatural confirmation of that word, this young man had a false understanding of the sovereignty of God working with his free will. He thought that when the word came it was a "done deal." However, the Lord was inviting him to live a life worthy of his calling by making changes that would usher him into what the Lord was offering him.

The prophetic word was intended to give this young man confidence that would empower him to make radical decisions to live differently in whole-hearted love for Jesus. The prophetic word was supposed to give him faith to make hard decisions and to stand firm in those decisions with endurance.

Instead of creating this kind of response, the young man just said, "What will be will be," and lived life in business as usual and missed what the Lord wanted to do with him. As I said earlier, prophetic words are invitations, not promises. If we receive a clear prophetic word that God supernaturally confirms, then we should tremble with a sense of awe so that we respond in a way that pleases the Lord. When giving these kinds of prophetic words, we must tell the people that their free will must work with the sovereignty of God.

MISUSE #12: GIVING NEGATIVE WORDS WITHOUT COMMUNICATING THAT THEY CAN BE AVERTED

There are times when it is appropriate to give someone a prophetic word that is negative in its implications. These negative words often give us insight into what Satan's intentions are in a person's life and can be God's mercy in revealing the enemy's plans. However, it is important that it is communicated that the fulfillment of these negative words can be averted by repentance, faith, and obedience. Neglecting to communicate that the negative fulfillment can be averted can lead to wrong responses, such as fear and anxiety, rather than the response God is looking for, which is repentance, wholehearted love for God, and obedience.

It saddens me and provokes me when I see this happen. People who believe the negative prophetic word is real and yet have no way out of the negative consequences end up in despair, thinking that there is no way out of the "judgment" they are under. I knew of a prophet who once told a young woman who confessed to being in a sinful relationship that she was going to "fall away" for seven years and then come back to the Lord. The woman was broken over her sin and had come to the prophet wanting to repent. She was asking God for mercy, but instead of telling her that God would forgive her and help her in His mercy, the prophet condemned her. The girl was in despair thinking she had no choice but to live "against God" for a seven years of darkness. She was terrified at the thought of being without God and desperately wanted to walk in the light, but she thought she had no choice. She thought the "prophetic word" was inevitable instead of seeing it as Satan's plan for her life that could be stopped. She took it as if the script were already written and finalized and, thus, couldn't be changed. It is against Scripture and God's heart to give negative words like this. Jesus provides a way of escape for those who repent and cry out to Him (1 Cor. 10:13).

MISUSE #13: SPEAKING WITHOUT CLARITY

I encourage people to give the meaning of their prophecies in a way that can be understood instead of speaking in a way that is overly mystical or cryptic. It is not very helpful to give a prophetic word that the people cannot decipher.

Some think that by speaking in strange and mystical ways with unsolvable riddles, they are somehow being more spiritual. That is nonsense because this leads to confusion and misunderstanding rather than edification. When giving a prophetic word, try to be as clear and simple as possible so that the people will be able to fully respond to it.

I have seen prophetic people give mystical words that bring such confusion because they are open to any interpretation and with many different possible meanings.

MISUSE #14: NOT ACKNOWLEDGING THE MISSED PROPHETIC WORDS WE GIVE

We must be accountable for the prophetic words that we give that end up not being true. At some point, we may miss it when giving someone a prophetic word. When we do, it is important that we take responsibility for missing it. Some people may fear that by being honest about missing a prophetic word, their credibility will be damaged. However, I believe the opposite is true.

When prophetic people are honest about when they miss it, a certain level of trust is established because they are honest not just when they are right, but also when they are wrong. Prophetic people who refuse to admit when they have missed it and continue to prophesy will only lose credibility, but those who miss it and own up to giving an untrue word gain trust.

I encourage all those who minister prophetically on our platform to be forthcoming with their inaccuracy.

CHAPTER 16

PRACTICAL WAYS TO GROW
IN THE PROPHETIC

G ROWING IN THE prophetic requires that we accept the foundational truth that everyone who is born again is able function in simple prophecy. It is the will of God for everyone who loves Jesus to prophesy. This really is the inheritance of every born-again believer.

> I wish you all spoke with tongues, but even more that you prophesied.
>
> —1 Corinthians 14:5

> For you can all prophesy.
>
> —1 Corinthians 14:31

The manifestation of the Spirit means a demonstration of God's power. First Corinthians 12:7 says, "The manifestation of the Spirit is given to each one for the profit of all."

I remind you again of the three purposes of simple prophecy. There are to bring edification, exhortation, and comfort to people: "He who prophesies speaks edification and exhortation and comfort to men" (1 Cor. 14:3).

The purpose of simple prophecy is to inspire people in their faith and love. It reminds people of God's care. It often emphasizes things that people are already familiar with or thinking about.

Edification speaks of spiritually building or edifying one's spirit in different ways, such as confirming their destiny or God's purpose for their life. A practical way to do this is by giving people a scripture. Often the scripture you give them will have been previously important to them. When this happens, it confirms that God is speaking to them. Edification includes assuring people that God will touch their heart or grant a breakthrough in a specific area of their life. It may simply declare that God is with them, or it may confirm a secret in their heart about a past event, dream, or something God previously told them. It may speak of a breakthrough in salvation or healing for their family.

Simple prophecy includes exhorting people to persevere instead of giving up on God's promises in hard times or giving in to sin during temptation. By the Holy Spirit we exhort them to persevere in their calling and in righteousness.

We also speak comfort by the inspiration of the Holy Spirit. This refers to giving them God's perspective in context to a disappointment or setback in their life. This provides confirmation or assurance that helps them stay focused and faithful to do God's will.

Simple prophecy includes words such as, "The Lord loves His people" or "The Holy Spirit is preparing us for a breakthrough." Small groups provide a good setting for people to release simple prophecy. It is usually a "safe" place for people to begin and grow in learning to prophesy. In an atmosphere of prayer and waiting on God in a small group, believers can speak out the impressions that come to them under the oversight of more seasoned prophetic leaders. Immediate feedback and evaluation can occur in this setting, and faith for prophetic ministry can gradually grow and mature.

How to Receive More Prophetic Impressions

A practical way to receive more prophetic impressions is by simply asking the Holy Spirit the question, "What are You saying or doing at this time that You want me to participate in?" There are aspects of His ministry in us that He will withhold until we actively ask for it. I seek to ask such questions several times throughout the day. Whether I am going to a ministry staff meeting, having a fellowship time, attending a recreational event, eating, or studying, I like to pause and ask the Holy Spirit, "Are You wanting to say anything to me or through me?" When sitting in the IHOP prayer room, I ask, "Holy Spirit, is there anything You want me to say to anybody? Here I am." When spending an evening with my wife or family, I ask, "Holy Spirit, do You want me to say anything?" Do not limit asking the Holy Spirit questions like this to only "spiritual" contexts. We ask for the Holy Spirit's involvement in small groups or large groups, at work or play, at school or social events, and so on. We can receive the Holy Spirit's prophetic impressions at a ball game with our children or with family friends. When you call to check in with a friend, ask the Spirit, "Are You wanting to say anything to me or through me in this phone call?"

It does not matter if you are talking to a believer or unbeliever. Remember, you do not have to say "thus says the Lord" when you prophesy. You can talk to an unbeliever without ever telling them that you are prophesying. I call it prophesying in a "supernaturally natural way."

Sometimes we will be aware that we are prophesying, and at other times we will not even realize it. I have given more "accidental prophecies" than intentional ones. In other words, I was not intending to speak to them from the Holy Spirit, but it happened suddenly in a "supernaturally natural way."

For example, when I am talking with someone, suddenly I say something that comes from the Holy Spirit. The person responds by telling me that their heart felt encouraged.

I want to prophesy in our board meetings. I want to prophesy in the coffee shop with a friend. I just want to prophesy to people. I want to do it without drawing attention to me or to it being prophetic. They will know when it moves their heart.

Jesus's Model for Prophesying

Jesus modeled how to walk in the Holy Spirit and move in the prophetic anointing. John 5:19 is a classic verse describing Jesus's relationship with the Father. Jesus did nothing until He saw the Father doing it.

Jesus answered and said to them, "...the Son can do nothing of Himself, but what He sees the Father do; for whatever He does, the Son also does in like manner."

—John 5:19

Throughout the day Jesus asked, "Father, show Me what You are doing today." The Father undoubtedly had many different levels of communication with Jesus. Sometimes He gave Jesus a prophetic impression revealing that He was going to heal a specific person in the meeting the next day. Sometimes Jesus received a prophetic dream about a healing that was soon to be released in His ministry. Sometimes the Father spoke to Jesus in more dramatic ways, such as sending an angel to Him. Jesus was continually paying attention to what the Father wanted to do. The question in His heart continually was, "Father, what are You doing?"

Jesus embraced the significant limitations of being human.

Therefore, in all things He had to be made like His brethren, that He might be a merciful and faithful High Priest.

—Hebrews 2:17

For we do not have a High Priest who cannot sympathize with our weaknesses, but was in all points tempted as we are, yet without sin.

—Hebrews 4:15

Although Jesus was never, ever less than God when He lived on the earth, He lived as though He was never, ever more than a man. In other words, as a man, Jesus had to wait and rely on the activity of the Holy Spirit before He could minister to people. What humility! Jesus is the uncreated God who created the heavens and the earth in Genesis 1. Yet He laid aside the right to use His power and lived as a man for thirty-three years in full dependence on the Spirit. Jesus waited and only spoke by faith according to what the Father spoke to Him. In doing this, He gave us a model for Christianity.

Four Ways We See What the Father Is Doing

There are several ways that we see what the Father is doing.

1. We may receive the prophetic whisper or impression from God. This can happen ahead of time, but the Spirit usually grants these in the moment that we are ministering to people. We pay attention to the Holy Spirit's impressions and promptings on our heart to walk in righteousness and avoid quenching the Spirit.

2. The Spirit may allow us to feel a physical sensation or pain that may correspond to how He wants to heal someone. The Spirit sometimes allows us to feel a physical sensation (fire, wind, and so on) or a physical pain (sympathetic pain) that corresponds with how He will touch others.

3. We may observe the Spirit's presence resting on someone as we see obvious outward manifestations such as their lips quivering, their face flushed, their body trembling, or simply their tears falling.

4. The Holy Spirit may show us what He is doing by giving us a prophetic dream or vision about a person before we minister to them.

Receiving the Whisper of God

The primary way that the Father will show us what He is doing is by speaking to us in the "still, small voice." The Father will also give us whispers or hints of what He is about to do. The "divine hint" may come as a subtle prophetic impression on our mind. Elijah saw the strong wind tear into the mountain and felt the earthquake and witnessed the fire, but the Lord was in the still, small voice or the whisper.

> Then He said, "Go out, and stand on the mountain before the LORD." And behold, the LORD passed by, and a great and strong wind tore into the mountains and broke the rocks in pieces before the LORD, but the LORD was not in the wind; and after the wind

an earthquake, but the LORD was not in the earthquake; and after the earthquake a fire, but the LORD was not in the fire; and after the fire a still small voice. So it was, when Elijah heard it, that he wrapped his face in his mantle and went out and stood in the entrance of the cave. Suddenly a voice came to him, and said, "What are you doing here, Elijah?"

—1 Kings 19:11–13

The Father will speak to us in the "still small voice" or, in other words, by faint, prophetic impressions. I call this receiving the "prophetic whisper of God." Often as I speak to a person, a Holy Spirit idea comes to my mind. I speak the ideas that come to me. I rarely mention to the person that the Holy Spirit is speaking to me. I figure that if it is the Lord speaking through me, the person will know it without me telling them.

Now, of course, I prefer to receive the thunder of God or an open vision. I have not had many of those types of experiences. I have heard the audible voice of the Lord only three times in thirty-five years of walking with the Lord. I have had several significant prophetic dreams along with a few other supernatural experiences, but 99 percent of the time I receive only God's whisper in my heart. God gives us impressions that communicate to us what He is willing to do (Eph. 1:17; Col. 1:9; Rev. 19:10). Do not feel pressure to come up with something.

The Lord will do more with the whisper than we realize if we will act on it by giving expression to it. We must give expressions to the impressions of the Holy Spirit. If we do not express them, then the power of God is not released in the same measure. When the Holy Spirit gives us a nudge in our hearts, we must not ignore it because it will go away and that person to whom you are called to minister may not get touched or healed.

For example, when praying for someone, I lay hands on them and wait for a moment on the Holy Spirit as I ask Him for a phrase or a Bible verse to come to my mind. When a scripture comes to us as a faint whisper of God, then we must speak it out over the person we are praying for. I have found that when I do this, it "grows." In other words, as we speak simple Bible verses that the Holy Spirit impresses on our mind at that moment, then more comes and the Spirit moves on that person's heart even more.

I compare functioning in the prophetic to putting up a sail in a boat on a lake during a calm day. A guy who is in the boat on the lake may see no wind. However, he puts the sail up, and suddenly the boat moves a little. We cannot always discern the slight blowing of the wind until we put the sail up. It is slight, but over time the little sailboat moves if we put the sail up.

We put up our spiritual sail by asking the Holy Spirit the question about what He is saying or doing. In other words, we get into a watchful mode.

When I am on the platform on Sunday, I may ask the Holy Spirit ten times for a prophetic impression. I ask to see an angel or to be used to heal a paralytic that day.

I urge our worship teams at the IHOP Missions Base to ask the question throughout the worship set that they lead. If they ask, they will receive fragments of prophetic information.

WATCHING: ATTENTIVENESS TO THE HOLY SPIRIT

We grow prophetically by what the Scripture calls "watching" (Matt. 24:42–43; 25:13; 26:38–41; 27:36; Mark 13:9, 33–38; Luke 12:38–39; 21:36; Acts 20:31; 1 Cor. 16:13; 1 Thess. 5:2–4, 6; Rev. 3:3; 16:15). First Peter 4:7 says, "Be serious and watchful in your prayers." And 1 Thessalonians 5:6 says, "Let us not sleep, as others do, but let us watch and be sober."

Watching in prayer includes cultivating a spirit of prayer and paying attention to what the Spirit is doing. We are attentive to the Holy Spirit's impressions and promptings on our heart. We posture our heart to receive faint prophetic impressions. In other words, we pay attention to the subtle breeze of the Holy Spirit that gives us a faint impression, or maybe a Bible verse will come to our mind. We ask the Holy Spirit what He is doing, and we calm down our soul to receive from Him.

> Surely I have calmed and quieted my soul, like a weaned child with his mother; like a weaned child is my soul within me.
> —Psalm 131:2

Paul asked the Galatian believers how they received the work of the Spirit.

> Did you receive the Spirit by the works of the law, or by the hearing of faith?
>
> —Galatians 3:2

Paul was teaching them that they receive the activity of the Holy Spirit by hearing with faith and confidence. In other words, it is by hearing or receiving prophetic impressions and having confidence in those impressions that we operate in the Holy Spirit. We do not earn prophetic impressions. However, we do have to listen for them and act on them with faith and confidence. Fasting and praying position our hearts to hear and receive more from the Holy Spirit. When I hear impressions and act on them, then the Spirit's power is released. Many stay in the passive mode by not asking for the Holy Spirit's activity on their heart. We must actively ask the question and value the impressions that He gives. This is called hearing with faith. We hear the faint impressions of the Holy Spirit.

WHY BELIEVERS NEGLECT TO PROPHESY

One reason that believers neglect to prophesy is because it takes love and spiritual vigor to prophesy on a regular basis. This includes sustaining attentiveness to the Holy Spirit to receive His small impressions. It requires energy to act on the impressions and demands that we take the risk of being wrong and then being unappreciated by those we minister to. It is easier to just draw back from this. To be attentive implies refusing the indulgence of anxiety and self-pity that cause so much emotional traffic in us. There is an intensity involved in being continually available to the Holy Spirit.

COOPERATING WITH THE GRACE OF GOD

The Christian life requires our cooperation with the grace of God. God will not do our part, and we cannot do His part. If we do not do our part, then God withholds a certain measure of blessing. Some think of grace as being on automatic pilot where everything good just sort of happens. There are many things that God wants to do that will not just happen because God will not violate the way He has chosen to partner with His people. Our part is to be faithful and to be watchful in our spirit. God's part is that He will give us prophetic impressions and release His power. However, we have to be watchful and faithful as we do our part. There are things we do not have in our life because we do not ask for them, and moving in the Spirit is at the very top of that list.

Some trust in the sovereignty of God in a way that is not biblical. This means they are trusting God to do the role that God assigned them to do. When we trust God to do our role, it is presumption. He will not do our role. We must stay open and feed ourselves. He will inspire us while we do that, and then He will move on us as we do so. However, He will not make us wait before Him or open our heart to the spirit of prophecy. Some mistakenly believe that if God wants something done, it will automatically be done. That is true sometimes in the broad strokes of His leadership over history. There are major events that God has determined to do, whether you or I cooperate or not. For example, the second coming of Jesus and His End Time judgments on the Antichrist will happen regardless of whether or not we obey God in a personal way. However, there are many things in our individual lives that affect the quality of our life in God. It is determined by things we do or do not do. Why? God is jealous for intimacy with us, so He will wait patiently until we seek Him before He answers us. He has chosen to give us a dynamic role in determining some of the quality of our life. There are things that God simply will not give us until we walk in faith and obedience. There are blessings that God has chosen to give us, but only if we ask for them. James says, "You do not have because you do not ask" (James 4:2).

THREE WAYS TO EARNESTLY DESIRE TO PROPHESY

We grow by earnestly desiring the best gifts (1 Cor. 12:31), by desiring spiritual gifts (1 Cor. 14:1), and by desiring them earnestly (v. 39). There are three ways in which we earnestly desire to prophesy. They are so simple that some trip over them.

1. We desire to prophesy by praying, "Holy Spirit, I want to prophesy." Ask the question, "Holy Spirit, what are You saying or doing?" (Take time to ask this.) I refer to the still, small voice as the "whisper of God" in my heart. Ask the Lord what He would do if you gave Him full room in your heart and mind. We have to intentionally make room for this in our hearts and minds by calming our hearts to ask the Holy Spirit for prophetic

impressions in the present tense. Some people say, "Lord, release Your power in me." Then when it comes time to pray for one another, they do not dial down and say, "Holy Spirit, release Your power in me *now*." Asking and expecting to receive prophetic impressions in the present tense is what it means to make room for them. We must quiet our hearts to better discern the Holy Spirit's impressions. Our spirit needs to be quiet. We need to dial down, not get stirred up in a fervor.

2. We have to give expression to the impressions that we receive. Verbalize them. We must give expression to the faint impressions of the Spirit. (Most prophesying will be in context to a few people rather than in the congregation.)

3. We must be grateful for the small things as we cultivate a lifestyle of watching and waiting. Value small demonstrations; be faithful in little things. (We do not despise smallness.) In our pride, we can easily despise the smallness of God's power in our midst. Some are only interested in God's prophetic anointing and the power of healing only when it is manifest in an unusual and dramatic measure. They will only be zealous to function in healing and the prophetic spirit when there is a significant measure of release. In other words, they want to walk in the prophetic on their terms. It takes humility to walk with God on His terms of being faithful and grateful in the days of smallness.

Do Not Despise the Day of Small Beginnings

We must be faithful and grateful for whatever small measure of power that God releases through us. We must not despise the day of small beginnings. "For who has *despised* the day of small things?" (Zech. 4:10, emphasis added). We have to be faithful to express the faint impressions. There is clearly a tension in being grateful for and faithful in the small measure of power while being desperate for a greater measure of manifest power in full revival. We are in a season of prerevival right now. I use the word *revival* according to standard of the Book of Acts. Now the Lord is surely moving in these days.

He is stirring things up and setting things in order for a soon-coming move of the Holy Spirit in the nations.

Some are waiting until God gives the unusual or dramatic measures of power before they start opening their heart to move in the prophetic. As I said earlier, they want to minister prophetically on their terms. However, the Lord wants us to serve Him on His terms. That is to be faithful in the day of small beginnings. We grow in the prophetic by being faithful in little. We must repent of despising the little acts of the Holy Spirit. We must honor anything that God does. If it is really little, we still honor it. In our pride, we can despise the smallness and only serve when the big things begin to happen.

Receiving a small impression of the Holy Spirit may not be as dynamic and dramatic as we want, but it is available to every believer right now. We must contend to walk in this.

Jesus promised that signs would follow everyone who believes. These signs include small measures of God's power to heal a headache. It is still God's power at work when a "small miracle" happens.

> These signs will follow those who believe: In My name they will cast out demons...they will lay hands on the sick, and they will recover.
>
> —Mark 16:17–18

Being used by the Spirit to touch others by prophecy or healing is an adventure in God. It changes our life. Every day is an opportunity where we might prophesy or release God's power to somebody. As we learn to open our heart with real expectancy, anything may happen at any time whether we are in the marketplace, a restaurant, a park, or while homeschooling our children. God wants us to be faithful in the day of small beginnings (Zech. 4:10). Many are ready to be used of God in big miracles. However, the Lord wants us faithful to move in healing when only headaches are being healed and in prophesying when we are only encouraging people in the simple things of God's love.

SEEK HIS FACE AND HIS HAND

We seek His face first; however, then we must seek His hand or the manifestation of His power. God will give us more revelation of His face and His hand if we hunger for it. We desire or seek the spiritual gifts by praying for them, making room for them, and then by using them in the day of small beginnings. I used to teach people to seek His face and not His hand. This sounds good, but it is not a biblical concept. The Bible teaches that we seek His face first without neglecting to seek His hand. We do not choose between His hand or His face. Our spiritual inheritance includes experiencing both. God wants to reveal His face in intimacy and His hand in power. Jesus does not make us choose between power and intimacy. He gives both of them to us. However, He wants them to have the proper priority in our heart. We are commanded by Scripture to earnestly desire to prophesy. Are you obeying this commandment? Are you earnestly seeking to prophesy? That is the only way that we will start prophesying. We must not wait on God in a nonbiblical way by waiting without asking the Holy Spirit for prophetic impression and not putting our spiritual sails up.

PRACTICAL POINTERS ABOUT GROWING IN THE PROPHETIC

- Understand that when we pray for people or events, our spirit will become sensitized to receive more of God's prophetic impressions for these people or events. Praying for people postures us to receive more. In this way, we are *intentional* about doing our part to receive the Spirit's prophetic leading in our worship gatherings, small groups, home groups, Bible studies, fellowship and social times, at the business meeting, in the marketplace, on phone calls, at the mall, during home-schooling, or at your children's soccer game. As we ask the Lord how to serve someone more effectively, we will receive prophetic impressions on practical ways to walk this out. Fasting and praying in the Spirit increases our capacity to receive prophetic impressions about people and events.

- I urge our worship teams to ask the Spirit what He is doing in preparation before they lead a worship service. The worship teams should pray this in the briefing before the service and then another five to ten times during the worship service.

- Appeal to people to operate in the prophetic in a "normal" way without taking themselves too seriously. Encourage them to be open to correction and adjustment, to offer their words in a humble style without melodrama, and to use language that all can understand and to do it without hype. This will make them more helpful to others.

- The leadership team must have the integrity and humility to "mop up" any messes that are caused by wrong prophecies or by their poor administration of the prophetic ministry. This helps ensure that the congregation's "corporate conscience" stays clear and good regarding the gift of prophecy.

- Let us all be encouraged to "preserve the unity of the Spirit" as we work together in love through the tensions and struggles of being good stewards of prophecy. Remember, to avoid swallowing camels, we're all going to have to eat a few gnats. Let us seek to evaluate all things in the light of God's value system in which justice, mercy, and faithfulness are given a preeminent place (Matt. 23:23–24).

- We encourage people to have an attitude of "open expectancy" related to the fulfillment of a prophecy. The exact way that God brings about a word in our lives is normally quite different than we envision when we first receive it. We also encourage people to "hold," "sit on," or "shelve" revelations that do not have a clear interpretation.

- Leadership must deal humbly and frankly with people whose prophesying is not edifying others in either its content or their presentation. Give them specific boundaries that you believe are appropriate for where they are in their prophetic "measure" of maturity.

- In our larger worship gatherings, we are limited by time restraints; therefore, at best, only a very few can give public prophecies in any given meeting (1 Cor. 14:29).

CHAPTER 17

THE PROPHETIC WORD
IN PUBLIC WORSHIP

T HE WAY WE handle prophetic words in public worship services has evolved over time. For the first two years, we allowed almost everything to happen spontaneously without the benefit of various guidelines that we have in place today. During those early years there were occasions when a prophetic word was spoken forth by someone in the congregation that resulted in a benefit to our church.

In January 1985, our seven-hundred-member congregation held its church services in a high school auditorium. On February 1, 1985, Augustine gave a public word that the Lord was going to provide a building for us by June 1. He went on to say that two men would make us an offer on a building that we could not refuse and that it would happen by June 1. Everyone cheered wildly at the word. We had four months until June 1. Three months passed, and by May 1 there was not any clear evidence that we would be getting a new building. To my surprise, on May 10 two men who owned an indoor soccer field asked me to lunch.

"We've heard about your ministry," they said. "We want you to have our indoor soccer building. It is a building that can seat two thousand people. The soccer schedule is over on May 28, and we would like you to take it immediately so that the building will not be empty and vulnerable to vandalism. We do not need a down payment or even a signed document. If you will give us your word that you will pay the agreed-upon price, we will let you have it." We were amazed.

On Saturday, June 1, they gave us the keys, and we had our first Sunday church service the next day on June 2. All this happened just as Augustine had prophesied it—two men made us an offer we could not refuse on a building that we would have by June 1. They offered it to us at a low price, loaned us the money without interest, and did not ask for a down payment. We were able to pay it off completely in three years. It was truly an offer too good to refuse, just as had been prophesied. I was overjoyed. This gave our congregation great confidence that we were in the right place at the right time with God's pleasure and favor on us. There would be some significant implications to knowing this, which would become evident in the years ahead.

"Anything Goes" Approach to Prophetic Ministry

Some who are new to the prophetic ministry are so afraid of quenching the Holy Spirit that they refuse the necessary process of administrating prophetic revelation. Therefore, they allow every word to be spoken publicly "just in case" it is from the Lord. The Holy Spirit is not as easily quenched as some imagine.

When I started out with the prophetic ministry, I was afraid that the Holy Spirit was like a skittish dove who might fly away at the slightest ruffle or mistake that I made. He's not that easily offended. He is very secure, patient, and kind. Consequently, in those first two years, except for some of really flaky stuff, I allowed too many "prophetic words" to be spoken publicly without any attempt to administrate them. I thought that administrating the flow of the prophetic was the same as standing in the way of what the Holy Spirit wanted to do.

We typically had three or four prophetic words each service, and sometimes as many as eight or ten. There were a couple of instances when people were so enthusiastically charged that the prophesying regretfully continued on long after God was finished.

Some wonderful things happened in those years, but there were plenty of negative things as well. The negative things could have easily been avoided if I would have had even a little bit of experience in giving leadership to the prophetic ministry. In those days, some prophecies were given that ended up being totally inaccurate, and some true words were misinterpreted and thus misapplied. A true prophetic word that is not rightly interpreted or applied can be as harmful as an inaccurate word of prophecy. For the most part, everyone was left to his own interpretation and application. This brings an unnecessary amount of chaos to a local body of believers.

Someone titled our church *Never a Dull Moment Fellowship*. However, I remember hours of meetings with discouraged people who ended up disillusioned and hurt by "prophetic words" that I did not administrate right. I was getting an education about my naïve approach to leadership that let almost anything to be said in public meetings.

LIBERTY AND STRUCTURE

I will mention eight basic components that are often seen in a worship service: (1) worship songs; (2) preaching the Word; (3) testimonies; (4) prayer for the sick, the hurting, and the lost; (5) prophetic ministry; (6) fellowship; (7) baptisms and Communion; and (8) church business (announcements, tithes, and so on).

Some people have the mistaken idea that liberty is simply changing the order of those eight elements. Just because someone decides to preach at the beginning and have worship second doesn't mean there is a freedom of the Spirit in the church.

Liberty consists of two things. First, it is consists of the assurance that we are forgiven and that the Lord is for us even in our weakness and immaturity. When we sense liberty before God without condemnation, then we are in position to grow in the Spirit.

Second, liberty is the willingness to allow the Spirit to interrupt what we have scheduled to do. If God wants to send a "Holy Spirit breeze" across the congregation in an unusual way, then we must allow it.

The church leadership has to be sensitive to the spontaneous wind or direction of the Spirit. If God does not indicate a change of direction, then be at peace with the normal format. Simply juggling the order of the service does not constitute liberty.

Some consider any kind of structure as a sign of a controlling spirit. Some have the idea that liberty is about reordering the eight components each week. It doesn't take much insight to see through this superficial definition of liberty.

At the IHOP Missions Base, we "put up our sail," and if the breeze of the Spirit comes across our gathering, then we go with it. We are not under the pressure to make sure that an unpredictable "breeze" breaks into every gathering. I have noticed that the "interrupting breeze" of the Spirit comes more in some seasons than others.

It is naïve to see structure and liberty as opposites. I know some who do not believe in any structure in their meeting. Thus, the people who attend are allowed to do anything they "feel led" to do with few boundaries. God put the gift of leadership into the church for a reason. It is not to restrict true liberty, but to facilitate, direct, and preserve the flow of the Spirit's life. Much of that flow can be enjoyed without changing the order of worship very week.

Giving a Prophetic Word Publicly

Some churches have a regular "programmed pause" to receive prophetic words in their services. The service begins with exuberant praise, slows down using tender worship songs, and finally slows down even more to a silent pause as the people wait for prophetic words to be given. We did this for years. Eventually, we stopped doing that because so many of the words were not weighty; the congregation became bored with most of the words that were given, and so they simply tuned them out.

Each week there are as many as twenty to thirty people in our spiritual family who receive prophetic dreams about the IHOP Missions Base. However, we seldom have spontaneous prophecies voiced from the congregation during our services. For several years, we put a microphone at the front row. The people came during the service to speak with a leader who would confirm their prophetic word, and then they gave it publicly.

In a large congregation there may be as many as fifty to one hundred people with a dream, vision, or prophetic word that they received in the worship service or throughout the previous week. Just because someone receives a revelation from God doesn't mean it is to be spoken from the platform on Sunday morning.

Our real issue is to understand what God is saying to us as a spiritual family and then to communicate it to the congregation in a way that is helpful and edifying.

I believe that most of the revelations that the Holy Spirit gives the people are not supposed to be shared publicly. The prophetic word is often given for the benefit of the individual who received it so he or she would pray or serve the congregation in a more effective way.

There are times when as many as ten people receive the same basic word. Nine of those words are not supposed to be spoken publicly but are given to confirm the word that only one person actually speaks publicly.

Currently, there are no programmed pauses in our worship services for spontaneous prophetic words to be given from the congregation. We have singers on the worship team who are gifted in singing the prophetic impressions they receive. They often sing forth what they receive from the Holy Spirit. They're on the platform with microphones in hand. In the course of the musical flow of worship, they sing out spontaneous prophetic prayers, encouragements, challenges, and longings. Sometimes a person from the congregation comes to a leader in our spiritual family to submit a prophetic message that he or she receives. If the leader feels it should be shared publicly, then we find a time for that. However, we usually wait until that prophetic word is confirmed.

When people give us prophetic words that correct or redirect the ministry, we wait for confirmation. We ask the Lord to confirm prophetic words by two or three other prophetic words that witness to the same truth.

> By the mouth of two or three witnesses every word shall be established.
>
> —2 Corinthians 13:1

> Let two or three prophets speak, and let the others judge.
>
> —1 Corinthians 14:29

CORRECTING UNANOINTED PROPHECIES

Occasionally, someone stands up in our meetings and shouts an unanointed or even an unbiblical word in the name of prophesying. It does not inspire or edify others. Paul said, "He who prophesies speaks edification and exhortation and comfort" (1 Cor. 14:3).

If words are unanointed, do not edify the body, and yet do not present doctrinal error, then we treat them as a less serious problem. We usually let them go the first time and probably the second. However, after two so-called prophetic words that do not edify the body, we will go to the person and gently *suggest* that they submit their word to a leader before giving their word publicly.

If it happens a third time, we then *require* them to submit their prophetic word to the leadership before speaking it out in a service. If the person does not heed this third private correction from the leadership, then we will stop them on the fourth time and correct them publicly.

This has happened only a few times. On each occasion we have taken time to explain to the congregation the whole process that evolved with that person. As I mentioned previously, if the whole process is not explained, then other prophetic people will fear being publicly corrected.

When the people understand the whole process, they have security that the leadership will not deal harshly with them if they make a mistake. They must not be afraid that they may be suddenly corrected before the church, or the prophetic ministry will diminish quickly.

INSTANT CORRECTION

There are two types of prophetic words that we publicly correct *immediately*—but again, as gently as possible. The first type is a prophetic word that rebukes or corrects the church without first going through the leadership team. I would never go to another church and give a prophetic word that was a correction or redirection without giving it first to their leadership. If the leadership of the church agrees with the word, I would ask them to present it to the church. It is usually more effective if the local leadership team speaks the corrective word instead of a visitor who is not well known by the local church.

The leadership team might ask me to share it with the church, but I would do so only after it was made clear to everyone I was speaking at their request.

If, in our private discussion, the leaders rejected the prophetic word, yet I was convinced that I had unmistakably heard from God, I might warn them in the pastor's office, "I think you guys are really in trouble." But I would never speak a corrective word publicly in a church outside their leadership and authority structure.

If a person gives a prophetic word that gives a new direction or a rebuke for our spiritual family without first submitting it to the leadership, I gently respond in this way:

> I appreciate the fact that you are trying to hear from God for this ministry and that you care about us. However, I would like you to take this word, share it with the leadership team, and let us discern it together. We invite you to be a part of this process if you wish, but for now we are not going to move in that direction. We will come back and give you a report later.

The other type of prophetic word we correct immediately is one that contains significant doctrinal error. Again, the correction must be done with kindness and gentleness because we are dealing with precious human beings. I would correct such errors on the spot. I would begin by saying, "I'm sure he meant well, but the word spoken calls into question a doctrine that we esteem as biblical." Then I would accurately state the doctrine that was called into question.

RECEIVING PROPHETIC DIRECTION IN OUR WORSHIP SETS

We ask for the Holy Spirit's prophetic leadership in the song selection during the worship set and in releasing prophetic oracles or singing the song of the Lord through the prophetic singers. In ministry time, we ask for words of knowledge in the following four basic categories of prophetic direction:

1. *Heart issues*: call to refocus on intimacy with Jesus and/or to receive prophetic revelation as well as receiving grace to overcome compromise, discouragement, and condemnation

2. *Personal circumstances*: favor for new doors to open in ministry or job opportunities or to help in crisis in their family, job, economics, being mistreated, need for direction, lawsuits, and so on

3. *Physical healing*: words of knowledge on specific needs or prayer for general healing

4. *Ministry impartation*: the anointing for prophetic spirit, evangelism, and intercession

CHAPTER 18

THE PROPHETIC SONG OF THE LORD

J ESUS LOVES MUSIC. Many people rarely think of God as loving to sing and as One who sings beautifully. Jesus is an excellent singer, songwriter, and musician. Zephaniah 3:17 tells us that our God is a singing God. Psalm 29 reveals that His voice is powerful and majestic. Revelation 15:3–4 tells us that He has His own special song called "the song of the Lamb." In fact, the Holy Spirit is such a good songwriter that He even has a whole book of songs in the Bible—the Book of Psalms. Clearly, music is in God's heart.

The Scriptures are clear that God is the author of all the anointed life-giving music that exists in both heaven and on Earth. Music existed within the angelic realm even before the creation of the earth (Job 38:7), and it powerfully reflects and expresses aspects of His personality. Anointed music has and always will be a means of communion and connection between God and His creatures above and below. It moves human affections in the deepest way.

Music is a providential gift that God has bestowed upon His creation. Music has been woven throughout all created order. Throughout the Scriptures creation is referenced and exhorted to give praise to God in song. Likewise, God's people are to sing "psalms and hymns and spiritual songs, singing and making melody in your heart to the Lord" (Eph. 5:19). For all of eternity, we will be singing songs to the Lord.

Satan has perverted music in his assault against God's kingdom. This is actually a testimony to its great value. Satan has used music to seduce people into darkness, including idolatry and sexual immorality throughout the ages.

The Westminster Catechism begins with the well-known statement: "The chief end of man is to glorify God and enjoy Him forever." So much for the Puritans being down on pleasure! Author John Piper has brilliantly changed this sentence to read, "The chief end of man is to glorify God by enjoying Him forever."[1]

One of the primary ways that we can enjoy God is by Spirit-inspired music that comes from God. Surely some of the pleasures that are at His right hand forevermore will be the heavenly music and songs that surround His throne (Ps. 16:11).

What Is the Prophetic Song?

The essence of the song of the Lord occurs when Jesus sings praise about the Father to the church. How does He do this? Jesus sings in the midst of the congregation by releasing His Spirit on singers in the church. Jesus is the head, and we are the body. In other words, we are the physical expression on Earth of what Jesus wants. We refer to this as prophetic singing, or the song of the Lord.

In Hebrews 2:12, Jesus is pictured as singing praise to the Father in the midst of and through the instrumentality of the congregation of the believing: "I will declare Your name to My brethren; in the midst of the assembly I will sing praise to You." This verse implies that the Holy Spirit gives the church a deeper revelation of the nature and personality of God in prophetic messages through song. It encourages us to declare the majesty and beauty of God through prophetic prayers that we can sing.

The risen Christ releases His songs in us by the anointing of the Holy Spirit that He might sing to God through us. This is foundational to what is sometimes called the "song of the Lord." This phrase, popularized by the Charismatic Renewal of recent decades, refers to the scriptural references of the Lord's song (Ps. 137:4), spiritual songs (Eph. 5:19), and singing a new song to the Lord (Ps. 33:3; 96:1; 98:1; 149:1; Isa. 42:10). The prophetic "new song" will be released in all nations, leading to Jesus's second coming. Isaiah

42:10–13 with Revelation 22:17 gives us the clearest picture of the End Time church praying in conjunction with prophetic singing to invite the second coming of Jesus. The End Time worship movement will be led by prophetic music and songs.

> Sing to the LORD a new song, and His praise from the ends of the earth, you who go down to the sea, and all that is in it, you coastlands and you inhabitants of them! Let the wilderness and its cities lift up their voice, the villages that Kedar inhabits. Let the inhabitants of Sela sing, let them shout from the top of the mountains. Let them give glory to the LORD, and declare His praise in the coastlands. The LORD shall go forth like a mighty man [Jesus's second coming]; He shall stir up His zeal like a man of war. He shall cry out, yes, shout aloud; He shall prevail against His enemies. "I have held My peace....I have been still and restrained Myself. Now I will cry like a woman in labor, I will pant and gasp at once. I will lay waste the mountains and hill [End Time judgments]..."
>
> —Isaiah 42:10–15

There will surely be an intensification of the Spirit's work in releasing His songs before the second coming of Jesus. God's treasury of heavenly music will be opened up and released to the body of Christ. This music will reflect a full range of the attributes of God, from His tender mercy to His terrible judgments.

Jesus has been releasing His songs through the church throughout the centuries. Some of these songs are spontaneous, as they are sung for the first and only time in worship services, prayer meetings, home groups, or in one's private devotional time. Others become well known as they are written down and sung by millions. These "prophetic songs" from heaven have been written down and sung as hymns by choirs across the earth.

The Holy Spirit is even now anointing and inspiring many prophetic musicians and singers to sing the intimate songs of God's heart along with the great war cry of the lion of Judah. In light of the nature and importance of music, it does not surprise us that God uses singers to inspire and activate the prophetic anointing (2 Kings 3:15).

David understood the reality of the Spirit manifesting His power through prophetic singing. David taught that when we sing praise, God inhabits or manifests His power in that context (Ps. 22:3). This is one reason that King David established a 24-7 tabernacle for prayer and worship.

David's revelation of heavenly worship as seen in the Book of Psalms is foundational to David's political throne, which was based on 24-7 worship and intercession. In other words, David's government flowed forth from prophetic worship (1 Chron. 23–25).

> Let the high praises of God be in their mouth…to execute vengeance [justice] on the nations, and punishments on the peoples; to bind their kings with chains…to execute on them the written judgment—this honor have all His saints.
>
> —Psalm 149:6–9

David had revelation of the spiritual impact of prophetic intercessory worship. He established 4,000 full-time paid musicians and 288 singers: "The number…instructed in the songs of the LORD…who were skillful, was two hundred and eighty-eight" (1 Chron. 25:7). "Four thousand were gatekeepers, and four thousand praised the LORD with musical instruments (1 Chron. 23:5).

When David played prophetic music before King Saul, demonic oppression lifted off him.

> Saul's servants said to him, "Surely, a distressing spirit…is troubling you. Let our master now command your servants…to seek out a man who is a skillful player on the harp; and it shall be that he will play it…when the distressing spirit…is upon you, and you shall be well."…And so it was, whenever the spirit…was upon Saul, that David would take a harp and play it….Then Saul would become refreshed and well, and the distressing spirit would depart from him.
>
> —1 Samuel 16:15–23

Elisha requested a musician to play when he was asked to prophesy to the king of Israel. Elisha, the prophet with a "double portion" of Elijah's prophetic spirit, needed a prophetic musician to inspire him to prophesy.

> Then Elisha said to the king of Israel, "What have I to do with you? Go to the prophets of your father....But now bring me a musician." Then it happened, when the musician played, that the hand of the LORD came upon him.
>
> —2 Kings 3:13–15

When King Jehoshaphat went into battle, he put the prophetic singers in front of the army because he understood that they would release God's power for warfare.

> Some came and told Jehoshaphat, saying, "A great multitude is coming against you...." And Jehoshaphat feared, and set himself to seek the LORD, and proclaimed a fast throughout all Judah....He [Jehoshaphat] appointed those who should sing to the LORD...as they went out before the army and were saying: "Praise the LORD, for His mercy endures forever." Now when they began to sing and to praise, the LORD set ambushes against the people of Ammon, Moab, and Mount Seir, who had come against Judah; and they were defeated.
>
> —2 Chronicles 20:2–3, 21–22

ANGELIC CHOIRS

It will become more common as we approach the time of Jesus's return that angelic choirs will be seen and heard by individuals as well as entire congregations. Each visitation of an angelic choir will probably emphasize a particular message that is on God's heart. Those who have had visionary encounters of heaven often report of the marvelous music they heard. I know of several people who have experienced the awesome music of angelic choirs.

I personally heard the angelic choirs one Saturday morning in the summer of 1990. I arrived at the church auditorium to attend a prayer meeting for revival. As I got out of my car and approached the door of the building,

I heard very loud music coming from the sanctuary. I thought that the sound team was playing something majestic like Handel's *Messiah* on the sound system at a very high volume. I rushed into the sanctuary because I was concerned that the volume being used was too loud and would hurt the sound system.

I continued to hear this awesome music up until the moment I opened the sanctuary door. The glorious music was instantly shut off, just as if someone had pushed the stop button on the stereo as soon as I opened the doors to the sanctuary. To my surprise, the sound system inside was not yet on, and only two guys in the building were up front, kneeling in prayer at the altar. They heard nothing. I was stunned as I realized that I had just had an encounter with the Holy Spirit.

I didn't tell anyone at the meeting what I had heard. In anticipation, I thought that surely the Lord was going to visit and especially bless this meeting in power. That must be why He let me hear the heavenly music. But to my surprise, it was just like most of the ordinary prayer meetings that we conduct each day—nothing spectacular; just some tired but sincere believers calling out to God for revival at an early morning hour.

Afterward I pondered the meaning of my experience. The Lord then made it clear to me that He is blessed by such "ordinary" daily prayer meetings that seem so weak and unanointed. The heavenly hosts regularly attend such prayer meetings, unseen and unperceived, to mingle our weak prayers and praises with their strong and glorious heavenly music, worship, and prayer. The angelic choirs are always functioning in the spirit realm in concert with our earthly prayer meetings. This experience built up my faith as I saw the significance God puts on "dry" intercession.

This story has encouraged other believers to persevere in dry prayer meetings, knowing that the Lord always adds the voices of His angelic choir to our intercession. We aren't responsible to make our prayers anointed; we're only responsible to continue in prayer and not give up!

The End Time Conflict: Two Global Worship Movements

The great conflict at the end of the age will be waged between two global worship movements. The Holy Spirit is raising up the most powerful worship and prayer movement that will contend against the Antichrist's worship movement and his persecutions. Even the Antichrist understands the value of music—Satan has been using music to seduce people into darkness throughout the ages. Satan has perverted music in his assault against God's kingdom, and he is influencing scores of people with false "prophetic" music.

I believe that the Scriptures are clear that the Antichrist will raise up a state-financed worldwide worship movement to hinder the Holy Spirit's worship movement (Rev. 13:4, 9, 12, 15). This worship movement will cause the people in the kingdom of darkness to have a deep heart connection with Satan. The music in this movement will move people emotionally and will be backed by demonic signs and wonders (v. 13).

However, paralleling the rise of the demonic worship movement will be the rise of a global worship movement that will be instrumental in the second coming of Jesus. As we approach His return to the earth, I believe there will be an intensification of the Spirit's work in releasing His songs through the redeemed as God's treasury of music will be opened up and released to the body of Christ.

The prophetic new song will originate at God's throne. It will be released in all nations and will be dynamically related to Jesus's return to the earth.

Now is the time for singers and musicians to begin to prepare and train themselves to receive and sing a new song to the Lord in the time of great revival and great judgment.

PRACTICAL WAYS TO INCREASE PROPHETIC SINGING

1. Sing directly to the Lord in your private devotions by singing straight from the Scriptures, along with singing their prayers. The Holy Spirit will use this to release prophetic songs in you. In private settings, your confidence can grow until you feel more comfortable singing such songs in public settings.

2. Singers may sing spontaneous prophetic songs before others in stages. Start in smaller group settings, such as the worship time in a home group or small prayer meeting. It is easier to start by singing songs *to God* rather than songs *from God* to the people. Stay steady on a worship team for many years.

3. Use the Bible itself to sing spontaneous songs back to God and to the congregation. The Psalms are an obvious place to look for inspirational material. I encourage our prophetic singers to sing straight out of the Psalms, opening their Bibles on the spot to provide the words to sing. If prophetic singers immerse themselves in meditation on Scripture, then their prophesying in song will become richer and fuller.

4. Singers should pay attention to particular themes that the Spirit anoints. They can discern this by watching to see if the congregation is especially engaged and blessed as a specific theme is being sung. If a singer notices a heightened involvement of the congregation on a theme, then he or she can simply sing that theme back to God in a spontaneous song. For example, a song with the theme of crying out for mercy, expressing gratitude, or celebrating God's goodness may grab the attention of the congregation in a special way. If, for instance, a song about receiving God's mercy is particularly anointed, as attested to by the congregation being moved by it, then the singer can respond by singing an "improvised" or prophetic song back to God that reflects that very theme. The song may include a divine response about how God's heart is moved by seeing the people believe in His mercy.

5. God can give prophetic songs to a singer weeks before the worship service in which he sings. Older well-known songs can have a prophetic edge on them when they are sung under the leadership of the Spirit.

6. Some misunderstand how the Spirit works with us. He does not force us to sing. Instead, He works within the framework of our personalities and the human dynamics of worship services (1 Cor. 14:32–33; Gal. 5:22–23). We can hold a prophetic song until it is the right time in a worship service. Be humble enough to allow others to judge or evaluate what you sang (1 Cor. 14:27–29).

7. The church leaders need to teach publicly on prophetic singing from time to time in order to place value on it and stir the faith and courage in the prophetic singers and musicians. Consider hosting a weekend seminar for the worship team to stir up the prophetic anointing on them. If necessary, bring in outside worship leaders who are experienced in prophetic music. Have these visiting prophetic worship leaders teach and model prophetic music. Then have them lay their hands on those who desire to be released in prophetic music. This gifting can be imparted from one believer to another by the Spirit (1 Tim. 4:14).

8. Worship leaders must make a little room for prophetic songs during worship services. If they simply pause a few times during the singing, the singers will have opportunity to sing out as the instruments continue. The worship team will quickly learn to flow together in this. Musical instruments can be used prophetically as they play spontaneously in a worship service. The worship leader allows times for the music to flow freely. There will be times the music swells in surprising ways.

9. We have found, as a rule of thumb, that a maximum of three to four prophetic songs is enough for most worship services that last less than an hour. There can be exceptions, especially for prolonged worship gatherings that continue for hours.

10. Prophetic songs should be limited to the boundaries of exhortation, encouragement, and comfort as described in 1 Corinthians 14:3. They shouldn't become a vehicle for bringing correction or direction to the body unless those with oversight over the church agree to it in advance.

11. The singers should avoid overly mystical and parabolic messages that are complicated. Avoid singing the picture or vision itself, but rather sing the truth behind the picture. When singing a prophetic song, sing ideas that are easy to understand and that help and edify others.

12. Discourage those who don't have the voice for it from singing their prophecies in public settings. They, like me, need to stick with speaking their prophecies! For those like me who are not called to sing publicly, I still sing in private. It edifies my spirit, and it is pleasurable to the Lord, even if it could only be called at best a "joyful noise"!

We must understand that God has called every believer to prophesy: "I wish you all spoke with tongues, but even more that you prophesied.... For you can all prophesy one by one, that all may learn and all may be encouraged" (1 Cor. 14:5, 31).

Singers must be eager and in faith that the Spirit wants to use them in prophetic singing. I encourage the singers to settle down or dial down in their emotions as they ask the Spirit what He is saying in any given worship service. They must pay attention to the small impressions or pictures that the Holy Spirit brings to their mind. They must value them enough to sing them.

We must understand that even the early beginnings for those who sing prophetically are important to God. Therefore, we must not despise them. Why is this so important? Because we can only grow in this one step at a time. We must not despise the days of small beginnings, but rather be faithful with the beginning stages of the song of the Lord. We must give expression to the small impressions of the Spirit instead of ignoring them. (See Zechariah 4:10; Matthew 25:21.)

CHAPTER 19

MANIFESTATIONS
OF THE HOLY SPIRIT

W
HEN GOD MANIFESTS His power through the church, it gives us the opportunity for spiritual growth as well as confusion and stumbling. Throughout church history, strange and even bizarre physical phenomena have accompanied outpourings of the Holy Spirit's power. In the early 1990s, testimonies began to circulate across the nations about people being blessed by manifestations of the Spirit that were accompanied with physical phenomena. The renewal in Toronto under the leadership of John Arnott and the work of the Holy Spirit associated with Rodney Howard-Browne brought new understanding and controversy to the church across the Western world.

Since that time, many believers have been spiritually refreshed and rejuvenated in their love for Jesus. However, other believers were skeptical and questioned if such manifestations represented a genuine work of God. What about the fleshly behavior that some people engaged in under the banner of being touched by the Holy Spirit? What shall we do with that stuff?

Some church leaders were perplexed about how they were to view these things and what they were to encourage or discourage in the midst of this genuine move of the Holy Spirit. It was a time in which many began to develop a biblical framework through which these manifestations and physical phenomena were to be interpreted.

THE MANIFEST PRESENCE OF GOD

Visitations of God's manifest presence upon individuals, movements, and geographic regions have often occurred in the history of Christianity. They have been disdained for various reasons. Sadly, they have most often been opposed by church leaders who were not humble enough to admit that there are spiritual experiences beyond their own with which God renews people. Such leaders feel that they have a firm grasp on what the Holy Spirit does and does not do. The Holy Spirit is much bigger than any of us.

We must always take the posture of being learners before the Lord as we acknowledge that we do not understand all that the Holy Spirit might do. No matter how mature an individual is in the Lord, we are all still only children and therefore must remain childlike in our relationship to Him as our Father. There is only one "know-it-all" in the kingdom!

Someone once asked the intriguing question, "Where does God live?" Another with a sharp wit answered, "Anywhere He wants to!" That is a good answer indeed. When Solomon dedicated the temple, he said, "Heaven and the highest heaven cannot contain Thee, how much less this house which I have built!" (1 Kings 8:27, NAS). There is mystery to the place where God chooses to manifest His presence. God is so close and yet so far. He is so predictable in His faithfulness yet so mysterious in His ways. Therefore, we are not naturally comfortable with all of His ways.

This is by His intentional design to humble us as we worship with awestruck wonder. God purposefully left the philosophical explanations for many of His attributes and ways unsatisfying to our finite intellect. How could it be otherwise when our finite minds try to comprehend infinity?

Human language falls short in fully conveying the personality and nature of God. We see the glory of God through a mirror, but only dimly (1 Cor. 13:12). We need to be reconciled to the fact of God's intentional mysterious ways if we are to enjoy our relationship with Him and to freely receive from Him. Deuteronomy 29:29 says, "The secret things belong to the LORD our God, but those things which are revealed belong to us and to our children forever."

So where does God really live? Where is His presence? First, He lives in heaven where He dwells in unapproachable light (1 Tim. 6:16). Second, He is omnipresent, and there is no place where He is not. Third, He has condescended to live within His "temples." In the Old Testament, it was first Moses's tabernacle in the wilderness and then in the temple in Jerusalem. In the New Testament, it is the church—the corporate body of Christ.

Fourth, He and His Word are one, and thus He is present in the Holy Scriptures. Fifth, He is present in the sacraments of the church. And finally, He periodically "visits" specific people and places by His "manifest presence." In other words, God "comes down" and interfaces with people in the natural realm in the revivals seen in the history of the church.

When God "draws near," the normal order of things can be disrupted. When the omnipotent, omniscient, omnipresent, infinite, holy, and loving God condescends to come down and touch weak, broken, and finite humans, what would we expect to happen to the normal order of things? It is only logical to expect something other than "business as usual."

We seek to honor the truth about God and His character and ways—we don't have to choose one aspect of His character above others or one truth at the expense of other truths about God. Following are four New Testament passages that refer to the biblical concept of the manifest presence of God.

Jesus promised to be "present" among us in a discernible way that is beyond the way He is with us at other times. Matthew 18:20 says:

> Where two or three are gathered together in My name, I am there in the midst of them.

Paul refers to the assembling of believers as the place in which Jesus's presence is manifest in a special way to bring discipline on unrepentant church members. The main point I am emphasizing in this passage is that the power of Jesus is present in a specialized way when believers gather together.

> In the name of our Lord Jesus Christ, when you are gathered together...with the power of our Lord Jesus Christ, deliver such a one to Satan for the destruction of the flesh, that his spirit may be saved in the day of the Lord Jesus.
> —1 Corinthians 5:4–5

There are occasions in which God's healing power is present in a greater measure than it usually is. The power of God flowed out of Jesus's body in a discernible way. The power of the Holy Spirit apparently did not manifest through Him continually at this measure. However, at specific times and in specific situations it did as God ordained.

> It happened on a certain day, as He was teaching…the power of the Lord was present to heal them.
>
> —Luke 5:17

> A great multitude of people from all Judea…came to hear Him and be healed of their diseases, as well as those who were tormented with unclean spirits. And they were healed. And the whole multitude sought to touch Him, for power went out from Him and healed them all.
>
> —Luke 6:17–19

BIBLICAL EXAMPLES OF GOD'S MANIFEST PRESENCE

Physical manifestations happen at the time when God's presence is manifest in the natural realm:

- Daniel fell, terrified by God's presence (Dan. 8:17; 10:7–10, 15–19).

- Fire came from heaven to consume sacrifices (Lev. 9:24; 1 Kings 18:38; 1 Chron. 21:26).

- The priests couldn't stand because of God's glory (1 Kings 8:10–11; 2 Chron. 7:1–3).

- King Saul and his men were overcome by the Spirit and prophesied as they drew near the camp of the prophets (1 Sam. 19:18–24).

- A bush burned but was not consumed (Exod. 3:2).

- There was thunder, smoke, shaking of the ground, sounds of trumpets, and voices upon Mount Sinai (Exod. 19:16).

- Moses saw the "glory of God" pass by him; Moses's face supernaturally shone (Exod. 34:30).

- Jesus and His garments were supernaturally made brilliant, and a supernatural cloud and Moses and Elijah visited Him (Matt. 17:2–8).

- The Holy Spirit descended in bodily form as a dove (John 1:32).

- Unbelieving guards were thrown to the ground (John 18:6).

- Peter and Paul fell into trances and saw and heard into the spirit world (Acts 10:10; 22:1).

- Saul of Tarsus saw a brilliant light, was thrown from his horse, heard Jesus audibly, and was temporarily struck blind (Acts 9:4).

- John fell as dead, had no bodily strength, and saw and heard into the spirit world (Rev. 1:17).

The record of church history is filled with testimonies of people who experienced the Spirit in many different ways. The Book of Joel uses the analogy of wine in relation to the outpouring of the Spirit. Peter prophetically interpreted what occurred on the Day of Pentecost as a partial fulfillment of Joel's End Time prophecy. On that day those observing the 120 who were filled with the Holy Spirit accused them of being drunk with wine.

They were probably overwhelmed by the manifest presence of Holy Spirit's joy! It is consistent with the nature of God to use something as simple and profound as joy, and its effects upon His people, to get the attention of burned-out, bored, and hardened unbelievers. The account in Acts 2 is not just a historical account of what happened in Jerusalem in the first century; it is a divine revelation of what occurs when the fullness of the Holy Spirit descends on a people. In Acts 2, there was the manifestation of the wind, the fire, and the wine of the Spirit. Before it's all over, there is going to be "blood, fire, and vapor of smoke." The fire of God convicts us of sin and releases passionate intercession and the fear of the Lord. The winds of God release angels with mighty miracles.

TESTING SPIRITUAL MANIFESTATIONS AND PHENOMENA

The Bible does not record all possible divine or legitimate supernatural activities and/or experiences that have occurred or may yet occur in the nations. Rather, it records examples of divine activity and legitimate supernatural experiences that fall into broader categories that are typical of how the Holy Spirit works. This concept is taught in John 21:25, in which John states that if all the wonderful works that Jesus did had been recorded, all the books in the world could not contain them.

The Bible nowhere teaches that God is bound to do only what He has done before. In fact, there are many prophecies of Scripture that speak of God doing things He has never done before. God is always and forever free to do unprecedented things that are consistent with His character as revealed in Scripture. He is God, and He can do anything He wants to.

The only thing the Bible says that it is impossible for God to do is lie. We must be very careful when suggesting that God would never do or could never do this thing or that. He does not ask our permission about anything He chooses to say or do. Let us remember how He confronted and dealt with Job when Job challenged the wisdom of God's ways. Western Christianity has too often been stripped of the supernatural side of faith and the sense of the mystery of God.

Sometimes people become overly zealous and/or possess deficient biblical hermeneutics and therefore twist and stretch Scripture passages in order to try to prove the validity of some spiritual manifestation or physical phenomenon that is not explicitly referred to in the Bible. For example, some attempt to defend the experience of uncontrollable laughing by this kind of "proof-texting," yet this phenomenon it is not specifically mentioned in Scripture.

However, a broader category of the Spirit's work, "joy inexpressible and full of glory," is referred to in 1 Peter 1:8. Why should it be a surprise to anyone that a person or whole groups of people might experience an aspect of this kind of joy that could lead to the experience of extended laughter?

Some sincere Christians panic when they hear of such reports and instantly conclude that a spiritual deception must be at work. But—just maybe—their view of God, His ways, and the Bible is too limiting. Ironically, it may be their deficient biblical hermeneutics that lead them to such biased conclusions. There is a vast difference between behaviors that violate scriptural principles about the nature of God's work among people and behaviors to which Scripture does not explicitly refer.

Unfortunately, some have a bias that nothing outside of their personal experience could possibly be from God—otherwise why hasn't God done it for them? Some church leaders feel the pressure, whether self-imposed or from their constituency, to have all the answers. It is easy to perceive the arrogance and presumption of this mentality. We must stay childlike before God as learners to enter and receive more of the work of the Holy Spirit.

To test the validity of spiritual manifestations, we look at a number of factors. First, we examine the overall belief system and lifestyles (and changes in them) of those affected by the manifestations. Second, we look at the overall beliefs and lifestyles of those being used as a vessel to release the Spirit's blessing. We should test the short- and long-term fruit of the experiences on individuals and churches. Finally, we need to evaluate overall glory given to Jesus in the context in which the phenomena are occurring.

Jonathan Edwards referred to five tests to determine if a particular manifestation was to be regarded as a true work of the Spirit. He stated that Satan cannot and would not, if he could, generate the following kinds of things in people.

If we can answer yes to one or more of these questions, then it is to be regarded as genuine despite any "little objections [criticisms], as many make from oddities, irregularities, errors in conduct, and the delusions and scandals of some professors [people who claim to be believers]."[1]

In other words, Edwards was saying that the presence of some human mixture does not, in general, invalidate the divine stamp upon any work within a true revival. Indeed, the presence of considerable human elements in and around a spiritual revival should be expected. Following are the five tests:[2]

- Does it bring honor to the person of Jesus Christ?
- Does it produce a greater hatred of sin and a greater love for righteousness?
- Does it produce a greater regard for Scripture?
- Does it lead people into truth?
- Does it produce a greater love for God and man?

HISTORICAL PRECEDENTS FOR
MANIFESTATIONS OF THE SPIRIT

Extraordinary physical phenomena caused by the operation of the Holy Spirit's presence upon people are fully documented and affirmed throughout the history of revivals in virtually every branch of the Christian church. Following are just several of hundreds of possible quotations substantiating this fact.

Jonathan Edwards is regarded as one of the greatest theologians of history and lived during the time of the Great Awakening in America in the 1730s and 1740s. Edwards provides the most thoughtful and comprehensive biblical evaluations, reflections, and writings about the manifestations of the Spirit.

> It was very wonderful to see how person's affections were sometimes moved when God did as it were suddenly open their eyes, and let into their minds a sense of the greatness of his grace.... Their joyful surprise has caused their hearts as it were to leap, so that they have been ready to break forth into laughter, tears often at the same time issuing like a flood, and intermingling a loud weeping. Sometimes they have not been able to forbear crying out with a loud voice, expressing their great admiration.[3]

> ...some persons having had such longing desires after Christ or which have risen to such degree, as to take away their natural strength. Some have been so overcome with a sense of the dying love of Christ to such poor, wretched, and unworthy creatures, as to weaken the body. Several persons have had so great a sense of the glory of God, and excellency of Christ, that nature and life seemed almost to sink under it; and in all probability, if God had showed them a little more of himself, it would have dissolved

their frame....And they have talked, when able to speak, of the glory of God's perfections.[4]

It was a very frequent thing to see an house full of outcries, faintings, convulsions and such like, both with distress, and also with admiration and joy.[5]

...many in their religious affections being raised far beyond what they ever had been before: and there were some instances of persons lying in a sort of trance, remaining for perhaps a whole 24 hours motionless, and with their senses locked up; but in the meantime under strong imagination, as though they went to heaven, and had there a vision of glorious and delightful objects.[6]

The following was the report of an atheist "free thinker" named James B. Finley, who attended the Cane Ridge, Kentucky, revival in 1801:

The noise was like the roar of Niagara. The vast sea of human beings seemed to be agitated as if by a storm....Some of the people were singing, others praying, some crying for mercy in the most piteous accents, while others were shouting vociferously. While witnessing these scenes, a peculiarly strange sensation, such as I had never felt before, came over me. My heart beat tumultuously, my knees trembled, my lip quivered, and I felt as though I must fall to the ground. A strange supernatural power seemed to pervade the entire mass of mind there collected....At one time I saw at least five hundred, swept down in a moment as if a battery of a thousand guns had been opened upon them, and then immediately followed shrieks and shouts that rent the very heavens....I fled for the woods a second time, and wished I had stayed at home.[7]

Teresa of Avila (1515–1582), on being rapt in ecstasy, wrote, "The subject rarely loses consciousness; I have sometimes lost it altogether, but only seldom and for but a short time. As a rule the consciousness is disturbed; and though incapable of action with respect to outward things, the subject can still hear and understand, but only dimly, as though from a long way off."[8]

A Catalog of Spiritual Manifestations and Phenomena

The Hebrew and biblical model of the unity of personality implies that the spirit affects the body. At times the human spirit can be so affected by the glory of God that the human body is not capable of containing the intensity of these spiritual encounters—and strange physical behavior may result.

Sometimes, though certainly not always, physical responses are simply human responses to the Spirit's activity and are not directly caused by the Holy Spirit.

At other times physical reactions may be caused by demonic powers being stirred up by the manifest presence of God. It seems to be common in New Testament narratives that demons would be forced to "blow their cover" when Jesus or the apostles came around (for example, the Gadarene demoniac and the fortune-teller at Philippi). Some of these strange experiences might be best considered as "revival phenomena" rather than "manifestations of the Spirit." However, this does not imply that they are therefore carnal and should be forbidden.

Following are phenomena and/or manifestations that have been observed in contemporary experience: shaking, jerking, loss of bodily strength, heavy breathing, eyes fluttering, lips trembling, oil on the body, changes in skin color, weeping, laughing, "drunkenness," staggering, travailing, dancing, falling, visions, hearing audibly into the spirit realm, inspired utterances (that is, prophecy), tongues, interpretation, angelic visitations and manifestations, jumping, violent rolling, screaming, wind, heat, electricity, coldness, nausea as discernment of evil, smelling or tasting good or evil presences, tingling, pain in the body as discernment of illnesses, feeling heavy weight or lightness, trances (altered physical state while seeing and hearing into the spirit world), inability to speak normally and disruption of the natural realm (for example, electrical circuits blown).

DIVINE PURPOSES FOR OUTWARD MANIFESTATIONS

God often offends the mind to test and reveal the heart. In the account of the outpouring of the Spirit at Pentecost in Acts 2:12–13, some people were amazed, some were perplexed, and some mocked. We continue to see these three responses to the work of the Spirit and some consequent events today. This "way of God" challenges our improper "control issues" and is intended to break down our unsanctified inhibitions and pride. Following are some of the reasons why God might choose to utilize strange and/or bizarre events to further His kingdom among men.

To demonstrate His power through signs and wonders

Signs are given to point beyond themselves to the God who is there. Wonders cause intrigue concerning the mystery of God's ways. Scripture validates the concept of transrational impartations of the grace, power, and wisdom of God. Sometimes, but certainly not always, God bypasses our minds when His Spirit moves on us. Some peoples' experience with renewal phenomena fit into this category.

To impart power to overcome inner bondages —fear, lust, pride, bitterness, and so on

One sister in Christ we know had an encounter with a release of joy and laughter one particular evening. She was rejoicing in the Lord as she went home that night. What surprised her was that as she walked into her dark house, she realized that a fear of the dark she had lived with and that had tormented her since childhood was absolutely gone. No one had prayed for her concerning this problem. Somehow it was trans rationally removed as a by-product of an encounter with the joy of the Spirit.

To impart love, peace, joy, fear of God, and the like

Sue recently fell to the floor under the power of the Holy Spirit. In the course of time, she saw a vision of Jesus healing her sense of "worthlessness" as the love of Jesus flooded her being with peace like she had never known in all her years as a believer.

To effect healings—physical and emotional

Jill had a remarkable physical healing. She recently received intensified prayer ministry that was attended by her falling to the ground under the Spirit's power a number of times. The only thing that she was aware was happening to her was that she felt great joy and peace.

However, she had been suffering from a severe eye disease as well as Parkinson's disease. The eye condition caused her body to be unable to produce tears normally. She had to take eyedrops hourly.

On the way home from the conference where these experiences occurred, she suddenly realized that she hadn't needed her eyedrops for four hours. Since that day she hasn't needed any eyedrops at all. In addition to this, she is able to walk and talk normally as the severe symptoms of Parkinson's disease are up to this point being alleviated.

To impart anointing for service

God took Scott through many trials and disappointments. He had gotten to the point where he was so spiritually "shell-shocked" that he lived with a constant fear that things would again fall apart in his life. The Holy Spirit gripped him in unusual and strange ways. He spent hours on the floor being moved upon by the Holy Spirit. Over the course of a year, Scott's heart was powerfully transformed and liberated by God's love. It's hard to question the genuineness and holy nature of Scott's strange encounters.

To release God's word—prophetic sensitizing and powerful preaching

JoAnn had several encounters with the Spirit. She has shaken and laughed and wept in God's presence. She asked the Lord, "What is all this 'unto'?" Then she received an anointing for prophetic revelation with a level of accuracy beyond any she had experienced before.

To enlarge and liberate spiritual capacities

Manifestations are given to refresh, encourage, and heal the hearts of God's people that they would mature as disciples of Jesus and be more powerful witnesses for Him.

Exposing False Equations About the Manifestations

False equation #1: If I were more devoted, then I would experience more manifestations of the Spirit.

Experiencing the manifestations of the Holy Spirit is not related to our spiritual passion and diligence, but they are the operation of God's free grace.

False equation #2: When many are visibly touched by the Spirit, then revival is here!

The classical definition of revival goes far beyond experiencing manifestations but includes vast numbers of conversions and deep transformation of lives across large geographic regions. The term *renewal* is a more appropriate description of what has occurred over the last ten to fifteen years in America. Hopefully renewal will lead to full revival.

False equation #3: The people God uses to impart His manifest presence are usually mature and sensitive to God.

People used in "power ministry" often unwittingly convey the notion that the power gifts are merit badges of their spirituality. This brings some dedicated and sincere believers into condemnation. The gifts and callings of God are free gifts of grace.

False equation #4: Just be open and sensitive to the Spirit, and you will receive physical manifestations of the Spirit.

It would be less perplexing if this were really the way it worked, but it isn't. It is true that some have mind-sets and emotional barriers that hinder the work of the Spirit. However, there are many who are skeptical and even cynical but who have been powerfully touched by God. Others who are very open and hungry for a touch are not powerfully affected in an outward way. We cannot judge who is "open" and who is "closed" to receiving from God.

There are barriers (for example, fear and pride) that can hinder us from receiving. Ask the Holy Spirit to reveal any barriers that may exist in you. He will be faithful, in His time, to answer such a request. In the meantime, do not assume that it must be a barrier that is keeping you from receiving from God.

False equation #5: If it is truly the Holy Spirit touching these people, then there will instant and lasting "fruit" in their lives.

God moves on many people who do not bring forth the fruit that He intended. There are no guarantees that "fruit" will result from these "divine invitations." People are free to respond fully, partially, or even ignore such gracious opportunities given them by the Holy Spirit.

False equation #6: If the power of the Holy Spirit touches people, then they should not have control over their responses.

The fact of Scripture is that it is very rare that a prophet would lose control when under the influence of the Holy Spirit. Paul emphasized this when he taught that the "spirit of the prophet" is subject to the prophet when he is under the anointing of the Spirit (1 Cor. 14:32). This passage teaches us that we are able to control our responses when the Lord is touching us. I agree that on rare occasions in Scripture, there are examples when a prophet had an "uncontrollable" response when seized by the Spirit. For example, Ezekiel was caught up by the Spirit and transported to Jerusalem from Babylon (Ezek. 8:3). Now, that surely qualifies as an "uncontrollable" response to the Spirit. There is a mysterious combination of divine and human elements surrounding the Spirit's work. Peter knew how to walk and had the power to do so when Jesus invited him out onto the water. The supernatural element was that he didn't sink as he walked. On the front end of welcoming the Spirit's manifest presence there is more control at our disposal to respond to His activity.

EXPOSING DANGERS REGARDING MANIFESTATIONS

We have mentioned the pitfalls of resisting the move of the Holy Spirit. However, at the other end of the spectrum some "over-respond." Love for God and one another must remain the preeminent value of our community. When the Holy Spirit is moving in power on a people and it results in physical manifestations, we must not "overrespond" in a way that violates Scripture. I will give a few examples of this.

- *Fanaticism.* In their enthusiasm, people can get carried away into excesses of behavior and be deluded into embracing strange and unbiblical ideas. This problem must be addressed as it arises. We should do this with compassion, both privately and publicly. This is a very delicate procedure, for the true fire of the Spirit will always be attended by a measure of "wild fire" introduced by the fleshly elements still resident within imperfect believers.

- *Neglect of the less exciting or less noticeable aspects of our faith.* This includes things such as daily devotions; humble service; helping the poor; showing mercy; loving our enemies; suffering patiently; honoring parents; restraining appetites; training children; working eight to five; running errands; paying tithes, bills, and taxes; and resolving relational conflicts.

- *Casting off all restraints in the name of "the liberty of the Spirit."* This tension between liberty and restraint must be embraced by the whole church. We will not always agree with how this tension should be stewarded. We must "swallow some gnats" to avoid "swallowing camels" (Matt. 23:24). We must try to not confuse the little issues (gnats) of various types of manifestations with the big issues (camels) of loving Jesus, people, and obeying Scripture.

- *Becoming distracted from focusing on Jesus and His primary purposes.* We must not get distracted from our passion for Jesus, evangelism, building the church, and so on by undue time and attention being given to the manifestations themselves.

- *Falling into pride of being sensitive to the Spirit.* We must avoid the subtle self-righteousness of being "more" blessed by the Spirit than others. God's grace is dispensed to magnify His love and mercy as it leads us into gratitude and humility.

- *Exalting outward manifestations above the work of the Spirit in people's hearts.* Progressive, internal transformation of the heart to walk in love and humility is the goal of the Spirit's work.

- *Exalting the human instruments that God is using in the work of the Spirit.* We must avoid any kind of "hero worship" in our hearts. We must stay focused on Jesus. However, the "facelessness" of God's army does not mean that there will not be any prominent members with public ministries. It refers to the attitude of humility that all must embrace.

POSTURING OURSELVES TO RECEIVE THE SPIRIT'S MINISTRY

So I say to you, ask, and it will be given to you; seek, and you will find; knock, and it will be opened to you. For everyone who asks receives, and he who seeks finds, and to him who knocks it will be opened. If a son asks for bread from any father among you, will he give him a stone? Or if he asks for a fish, will he give him a serpent instead of a fish? Or if he asks for an egg, will he offer him a scorpion? If you then, being evil, know how to give good gifts to your children, how much more will your heavenly Father give the Holy Spirit to those who ask Him!

—Luke 11:9–13

In this passage, Jesus is challenging His disciples to pray specifically. The verbs translated "ask," "seek," and "knock" are in a continuous tense in the Greek. This gives the phrases the sense that the desired blessings must be pursued with perseverance.

God wants us to really want what we desire and not be passive or nonchalant about it. God withholds the blessing for a short season to deepen our hunger for the thing we so ardently pray for.

The requests for the good things of His kingdom can be summarized by asking for the release of the ministry of the Spirit. God is a generous Father who wants to release the Spirit's ministry to us, but He wants us to earnestly desire it in all the fullness of His gifts, fruit, and wisdom. We desire to receive more of God, not just to receive outward manifestations.

Many report receiving more after "soaking" in the presence of God in renewal settings without having any outward manifestations. There is a chemistry experiment called a *titration*. In this experiment, there are two clear solutions in separate test tubes. Drop by drop, one solution is mingled with the other. There is no chemical reaction until the one solution becomes supersaturated with the other. The final drop that accomplishes this causes a dramatic chemical reaction that is strikingly visible. Some sit before God in prayer rooms and renewal meetings for hours with no apparent spiritual reaction taking place. Then, suddenly, they have a power encounter with the Spirit that radically impacts them. In retrospect, they come to believe that a spiritual "titration" was going on through the many hours of waiting on God and through soaking in the invisible and hidden ministry of the Holy Spirit. Whatever the case, it is not the outward effects of spiritual renewal that we must focus upon or draw attention to, but rather the inner transformation of our souls into the likeness of Jesus.

RECOMMENDATIONS FOR CONDUCTING RENEWAL MEETINGS

Dr. Martyn Lloyd-Jones said concerning the danger of being presumptuous about the mysterious work of the Holy Spirit, "Never say never and never say always concerning what the Holy Spirit might do or not do." The Lord, on purpose, doesn't submit to the boxes in which we try to confine Him!

- Plan on an extended and undistracted time of waiting on God with nothing else planned in case He doesn't "show up" in an unusual manifest way. Determine that it does not have to be a dry and uneventful time with God just because unusual things do not happen.

- Focus on the Lord Himself through worship and prayer-reading the Scripture.

- Only periodically give explanation about manifestations. It is better to explain them if and when they actually begin to happen in order to take away the accusation that the power of suggestion is operative. Having literature available that explains these things can be helpful.

- Give a Jesus-centered exhortation and be open to give invitations for people to receive salvation, as unbelievers come to renewal meetings.

- When testimonies are given, they should focus on how relationship with God and the fruit of the Spirit have been enhanced rather than drawing attention to phenomena.

- Discourage all exaggeration of the Spirit's work. The Holy Spirit does not need exaggeration to build faith in people for healing or to receive more of God. Do not allow testimonies to be shared that are not genuine and true, even if they seemingly "help promote faith."

- Avoid giving the impression that the Holy Spirit is under human control through a style of ministry. We humbly ask for His ministry as we boldly call for the release of His power. But we must not dishonor Him by pridefully commanding and demanding that He do this or that. He makes Himself available, but we must not take advantage of His divine humility by ordering Him around. If we abuse His presence and power long enough, He may withdraw His manifest presence. The history of divine visitations confirms this reality.

- If you draw attention to what is happening with an individual or a section of the congregation, do it for the specific intention to edify the whole group. Be sincere in your communication as a leader rather than being silly and fascinated with manifestations. Even when the Spirit imparts uncontrollable laughter, understand that a holy thing is occurring. Be sincere about the joy of the Lord even while enjoying it. After all, it is heavenly joy, and heavenly happenings are awesome by nature.

- Leave room for the Lord to touch people without direct human mediation. As this happens, faith builds, and fears of manipulation are quenched. Allow those gathered to soak in the presence of God for a while before prayer ministers are released to go and touch them.

- Give people gracious "outs" if they do not want to receive the laying on of hands. Tell them how to signal you or respond if they are interested in receiving personal prayer with coming up to the prayer line while giving them the option to commune with God alone.

- Worship teams should lead during the ministry times. At times simple background music is sufficient if a worship team is not available.

- Resist the pressure to make things happen. Seek to be supernaturally natural and naturally supernatural. Renewal is God's business. We trust Him to accomplish it. Receive the measure of power that God releases with a thankful heart. This is the atmosphere the Spirit honors.

- If renewal has not been occurring in your setting, consider inviting someone whom God has already been using as a catalyst for spiritual renewal into your fellowship to help impart the Spirit's ministry to a greater measure.

FORMING A PRAYER MINISTRY TEAM

To facilitate renewal ministry, it is important to equip a prayer team who will regularly pray for others. The qualifications should not be too stringent. It will be necessary to weed the few who will "prey" upon others rather than "pray" for others! Be clear on what qualifies and what disqualifies someone from the prayer team. This becomes a bigger issue as time goes on and those who have received "more" have a desire to "give it away." Following are characteristics for those who participate on a prayer ministry team:

- They should be happy and active members of the church.

- They should have a testimony of godly character and pursuit of spiritual growth.

- They should not be affected with glaring socially unacceptable behavior, appearance, speech, or habits.

- They should have completed a training course on personal prayer ministry.

- They should have a teachable spirit that receives correction without easily getting their "feelings hurt."

Members of the prayer ministry team should be those who value the fruit of the Spirit as listed in Galatians 5:22–23. The fruit of the Spirit is nothing less than the character of Jesus Christ being manifested in and through believers. Let's look at each fruit of the Spirit and consider how it might apply to prayer ministry.

- *Love.* Love is the overarching characteristic from which the other aspects of the fruit of the Spirit flow. As we pray for others, we must view ourselves as servants of love and not heroes of faith. The spirit of servanthood is the outstanding expression of love. As we pray for others, we are conscious that it's much more about them receiving from God, not about us "receiving credit" for moving in power as they are slain in the Spirit.

- *Joy.* We approach praying for others with the joyful awareness of the privilege we have been given. Even if we aren't emotionally "up," then we can draw on joy that resides within us as we put our personal pressures temporarily behind us.

- *Peace.* We seek to lead others into peace with God, themselves, and others as we minister to them with a peaceable spirit that rests in God's ability to work through us even in our weakness.

- *Patience.* Some need to slow down and take time as they pray for others. The Holy Spirit doesn't like to be pushed— He wants to do the leading. Usually, He takes His time in showing His power. In quietness of soul we are able to better receive the impressions of the Spirit.

- *Kindness.* We will often be praying for people whose lives have been wrecked by sin. Many haven't been taught social skills, and they have unlovely characteristics about them. Many have embraced wrong teachings and even are oppressed by demons. We must gracefully absorb some of their immaturity and deal kindly with their deception.

- *Goodness.* We care for the needs of others; therefore, we show that care to them in practical ways on the heels of praying for them. We may not have the resources ourselves, but maybe we know others who might to whom we can direct them. We refuse to take advantage of the sacred trust that others give us in making themselves vulnerable by allowing us to pray for them.

- *Faithfulness.* Prayer for others sometimes requires perseverance on our part. We often need to pray more than one time for the same people. We mustn't be intimidated by apparent failure. We commit ourselves to pray faithfully for people for the rest of our lives.

- *Gentleness (meekness).* We pray for others with the awareness that we don't have the answers for them, but we know Someone who does. This keeps us from presumption and platitudes. Our movements, both physical and verbal, need to be gentle rather than abrupt or harsh. If we can help set them at ease by knowing that they are safe in our presence, then they will be able to receive more easily from the Lord.

- *Self-control.* We encourage people to "dial down," both emotionally and physically, as they go to pray for others. If you are outwardly experiencing the manifest presence of the Spirit with "uncontrollable" laughing and twitching then shift over to a personal "receiving from God" mode instead of a "praying for others" mode. We do not want to unwittingly manipulate others by putting pressure on them to respond to us as we "manifest" while we pray for them. There are exceptions to this general rule. One is if a person specifically asks you to pray for them while you are in such a state. Another could be if the other person is a friend and you know that they would welcome such an experience. And there may be others. If we pray for others with these values in our hearts, we will be a blessing to the people we serve in the prayer lines. As individuals develop a track record for being exceptionally anointed in personal ministry, their leaders may give them more liberty to take bigger risks with prayer and/or prophetic ministry.

PROPER RESPONSES TO SPIRITUAL RENEWAL

- Take the posture of being "learners" rather than "experts" in the ministry of the Spirit. There aren't too many who have gone this way before. We must be like children before our heavenly Father. We are more confident in His ability to teach us than in our ability to learn. His commitment to us is stronger than ours is to Him.

- Be gracious, kind, and patient with differences in perspectives with other ministries in the body of Christ. We don't have to prove to anyone that something is of God if it really is!

- Give proper liberty and create sufficient opportunities for the Spirit to manifest Himself in settings that are specifically intended to welcome renewal ministry. God may break into any gathering with His manifest presence without human mediation. However, if only isolated individuals are being affected, then the leadership needs to make a judgment call if the course of any particular corporate meeting needs to be altered.

- Teach and model biblical restraints as we seek to be sensitive to each specific context. Ask, "What does love look like?" in each particular setting. Seek to submit to those in authority for the sake of unity. Mistakes in discernment will happen when the heightened fear of both "missing God" and "being deceived" are present.

- Study the history of revivals to gain wisdom and errors that past revivals embraced.

CHAPTER 20

GOD'S STRATEGY OF SILENCE

T REMENDOUS PRESSURES CAN weigh on those who are called to be prophets. They will end up with notoriety that will bring many pressures on their life, some because the people honor them and other pressures because the people hate them. Supernatural manifestations of power must be accompanied with spiritual maturity, or the pressures that come with it will cause one to stumble and fall.

THE PRESSURES OF SILENCE

One of the more difficult things to deal with as a prophetic person is coming face-to-face with people in great need, only to find God completely silent on the matter. God's heart and mind may have previously been revealed to the prophetic person with great clarity and astounding detail concerning a dozen other people in the same congregation. Then, when confronted with a person in a desperate situation who seemingly has more need for a word from God than anyone else, the same prophetic person may sense nothing from the Holy Spirit—complete silence.

This awkward situation, which will inevitably arise, presents a test of character and maturity for the prophetic person. If he or she says, "I have no word for you," people will be disappointed, if not angry, at this response.

That prophetic person's reputation will sometimes be on the line, along with future speaking invitations and honorariums.

The pressures of people's expectations and assumptions push many prophetic people into dangerous waters that can eventually shipwreck their integrity as well as their ministry.

In the pressure of the moment, the temptation is to give a word they don't have. It is the same temptation that provokes a Bible teacher to answer a question citing information of which he is not certain. But for some Bible teachers, it's just too hard to say, "I don't know." In the same way, for some prophetic people, it's just too hard to say, "I don't have anything." The same immaturity and pride that cause the teacher to think his credibility is based on his ability to know it all is also what prevents the prophetic person from saying in a needy situation, "I have no word for you."

Notwithstanding the pressure of people's expectations or his own desire to help a person in need, a prophetic person must remain silent when God is silent. Manufacturing a word in his own mind, whether it is out of compassion or the pressure to establish his own credibility, can work directly against the purpose of God in the life of a church or an individual. Such lack of integrity never builds people's faith over the long haul, even though the people may be excited for the moment over a man-made prophetic word.

Sometimes prophetic people add to what God says because they are trying to be more loving than God by quickly answering people's questioning hearts and giving them a word even when God is silent. I call this a "hamburger-helper" prophecy—giving in to the temptation to add filler. They give in to pressure to embellish a "prophetic word" out of their own heart and mind so that others are not disappointed in them.

People are constantly thrust into ordeals in which they agonize over the question, "Why would God allow a certain person to continue in suffering?" In order to "bail out" God and His reputation, some prophetic people rush in to provide the answer. Maturity as it relates to prophetic ministry is not only the willingness to speak a difficult word when God gives it, but also the willingness to be silent, even when offering a prophetic word might seem appropriate. Some prophetic people find the circumstances of people in crisis so acute that they feel they *have* to give a prophetic word to them.

When God is silent at a time when *we* desperately want Him to speak, it tests the spiritual maturity of both the people and the prophet. Each believer must trust God when He is silent. It's an inescapable part of spiritual growth, and a prophetic person must submit to God even when He is being silent about a situation. If he does not, then he will end up manufacturing words for people when God's purpose was for him to say nothing. Regardless of his well-intentioned efforts to make God *look good*, he becomes a stumbling block for those whom he seeks to help.

WALKING CONFIDENTLY IN DARKNESS

Isaiah describes the person who walks in the fear of the Lord as one who trusts God even when they are in the times of darkness, which refers to times of crisis when we do not have the word of the Lord.

> Who among you fears the LORD? Who obeys the voice of His Servant? Who walks in darkness and has no light? Let him trust in the name of the LORD and rely upon his God.
> —Isaiah 50:10

Walking in darkness as it is used in this context doesn't refer to moral darkness that comes from sin or demonic oppression. It means walking in unknown territory without clear light in a time of great need. Isaiah continues in the next verse:

> Look, all you who kindle a fire, who encircle yourselves with sparks: walk in the light of your fire and in the sparks you have kindled—this you shall have from My hand: you shall lie down in torment.
> —Isaiah 50:11

This verse highlights the peril of those who refuse to wait for God's light; instead, they create their own fire in an attempt to manufacture some light. This fire speaks of a man-made counterfeit fire that can never be a substitute for God's light. People who resort to this counterfeit will lie down in turmoil instead of peace. This is a strong warning to avoid manufactured prophetic words!

Isaiah warns the person who fears the Lord not to kindle his own flame.

Do not manufacture an artificial light out of your frustration with the darkness. Or, as it relates to the prophetic ministry, do not manufacture the "prophetic light" for someone in need.

God's silence forces us to grow in trusting Him while we walk through the darkness, lacking a sense of direction. We eventually realize He was nearby all along. In this way, we develop our own personal history with God.

MISUNDERSTOOD SILENCE

Jesus often did not answer people in the way we would have expected Him to. When we think He should have answered, He was silent. At times when we suppose that He should have intervened, He was inactive. Therefore, we must be careful not to presume to know what Jesus would say or do in needy situations.

As Jesus passed through the region of Tyre and Sidon, He was confronted by a Canaanite woman who was crying out for deliverance for her demon-possessed daughter. Jesus's answers were totally unpredictable in this crisis situation.

> A woman of Canaan came from that region and cried out to Him, saying, "Have mercy on me, O Lord, Son of David! My daughter is severely demon-possessed." But He answered her not a word. And His disciples came and urged Him, saying, "Send her away, for she cries after us." But He answered and said, "I was not sent except to the lost sheep of the house of Israel." Then she came and worshiped Him, saying, "Lord, help me!" But He answered and said, "It is not good to take the children's bread and throw it to the little dogs." And she said, "Yes, Lord, yet even the little dogs eat the crumbs which fall from their masters' table." Then Jesus answered and said to her, "O woman, great is your faith! Let it be to you as you desire." And her daughter was healed from that very hour.
>
> —Matthew 15:22–28

At first, Jesus *seemingly ignored* her by not initially answering her even with one word. As she continued to cry out, He *apparently refused* her, saying, "I was not sent except to the lost sheep of the house of Israel." She still pursued Him, then Jesus *seemingly insulted* her: "It is not good to take the children's bread and throw it to the little dogs." The woman would not be denied. Jesus finally *rewarded* her and said, "O woman, great is your faith! Let it be to you as you desire."

We would have been astounded if we had witnessed this encounter. Jesus's initial lack of response, then even His seemingly "rude" answer certainly does not fit in with the model of how we believe the God of love should act. But from our perspective today, we see that Jesus was probing her and testing her to draw out her faith.

Because of our preconceived notions, we sometimes draw wrong conclusions from God's silence or His presumable lack of intervention on our behalf. We may conclude that God's love has waned or perhaps that we are being punished for something. But that was certainly not the case with this woman and her demon-possessed daughter, who was eventually healed. The same was true when Lazarus was sick until he died. Jesus clearly loved Lazarus and his sisters, Mary and Martha. However, His delay in coming to heal Lazarus was strategic.

> Now Jesus loved Martha and her sister and Lazarus. So, when
> He heard that he was sick, He stayed two more days in the place
> where He was.
>
> —John 11:5–6

Jesus's seeming lack of response had nothing to do with lack of love, but it had to do with fulfilling the redemptive purpose of God. In this situation, Lazarus, Martha, and Mary learned to trust Jesus, even when they had to walk in darkness beyond the edge of their understanding.

John the Baptist was a great man, yet Jesus did nothing to prevent him from being beheaded by King Herod. Jesus's inaction was neither from lack of love for John nor lack of worthiness in John himself.

> Assuredly, I say to you, among those born of women there has
> not risen one greater than John the Baptist.
>
> —Matthew 11:11

It is obvious that God had appointed John to experience the honor of a martyr's death and that this would bring the most glory to God and His kingdom in the bigger picture. We stumble over the fact that God doesn't speak or act the way we think He should. But from Isaiah we learn not to manufacture our own light when we walk in darkness. From the Gospels we learn that God's silence does not mean we are rejected or unloved; it must be understood in the light of God's redemptive purposes. A prophetic person must understand that often people desperately want the prophetic word that God Himself refuses to give. They ask for information about circumstances, and God gives information about their relationship with Him. They want peace and assurance, but God has a different way for them to receive peace. If God is not answering, sometimes we are asking the wrong questions.

A Famine of the Word of the Lord

There can be a variety of reasons known only to God for His silence. Perhaps He is teaching us faith, or even sometimes He is judging those who have deliberately rejected His words in the past and have not yet repented. Amos prophesied of a famine in hearing the prophetic word because rebellious Israel had refused to obey previous prophetic words from God:

> "Behold, the days are coming," says the Lord God, "that I will send a famine on the land, not a famine of bread, nor a thirst for water, but of hearing the words of the Lord. They shall wander from sea to sea, and from north to east; they shall run to and fro, seeking the word of the Lord, but shall not find it."
>
> —Amos 8:11–12

It seems strange to us that God would withhold His prophetic word from Israel when they seemed to be searching so hard to find it. What actually happened was that Israel had regularly rejected God's prophetic word that had previously been spoken to them. They wanted God to speak prophetically; however, they didn't want to hear what God had to say. So they sought for a new prophetic word. What happened to Israel as a nation takes place in the lives of stubborn individuals.

For example, to a man who has been hurt, God's specific word to him is that he should fully forgive. But having rejected that simple answer, he begins a process of running to and fro, seeking prophetic words that answer his growing problem. Even though he is apparently seeking diligently, a famine of the word of the Lord has resulted because he rejected what God already said clearly. God's word was simply too unpleasant for him to receive.

On the other hand, God is silent not due to one's rebellion but because He is setting up the situation that will bring more blessing to the person at a later time. In this case, some sincere, though immature, believers are confused by thinking that the silence of God is a sure sign of His displeasure and abandonment. Because some people experience long periods of silence from heaven, they wrongly conclude that God has withdrawn from them or that they must have sinned grievously in some way. They fall prey to accusation, condemnation, and rejection.

BE SILENT WITH REVEALED KNOWLEDGE

A vital test of a prophet is in his willingness to speak a hard word from God, then his willingness to accept the persecution. This is a test of surrender and consecration to God.

Another vital test is being able to remain silent when God has not spoken, regardless of the apparent need of the moment. This is a test of honesty and integrity before God.

A third vital test is the willingness to remain silent about something God has clearly revealed to you, yet requires your silence on. This is a test of maturity and security in God. Some speak everything they receive from God because they are desperate to receive credit in the eyes of man for having received revelation from God. Sometimes they're like children who know a secret and just can't stand it; they have to tell it to someone.

CAUTION WITH CORRECTIVE WORDS

We also encourage prophetic people to be very careful about giving prophecies that correct people in public. Such prophecies have the potential of causing shame, pain, and confusion. If someone receives prophetic correction for someone, we must follow the process that Jesus taught us when we see a brother in sin in Matthew 18:15–18. These principles instruct us to go to a person privately about his sin before going to him publicly. It takes a seasoned prophetic minister to be silent at times when God has shared something that is for his ears only.

PROPHESYING OUT OF THE IMAGINATION

Another common problem in context of the prophetic ministry is related to those who manufacture a positive word when the Lord is actually speaking a negative one. Jeremiah taught against those who prophesied out of their own imagination and who spoke a vision that they devised in their own heart.

> Do not listen to the words of the prophets who prophesy to you....They speak a vision of their own heart, not from the mouth of the LORD. They continually say to those who despise Me, "The LORD has said, 'You shall have peace'"; and to everyone who walks according to the dictates of his own heart, they say, "No evil shall come upon you."
>
> —Jeremiah 23:16–17

In Jeremiah 23, we see the warning directed to "prophets" who ignored God's judgment over Israel's national rebellion. They disregarded God's warning of judgments to them and fabricated a prophecy proclaiming only wonderful things, assuring the Jewish people that God would protect their nation from judgment. God threatens judgment on such "prophets" who opposed God's discipline that could lead to healing of an entire rebellious nation.

NOTES

CHAPTER 2
CONFIRMING PROPHECIES THROUGH
THE ACTS OF GOD IN NATURE

1. Marquis Shepherd, "Gentlest of Winter Goes Out With a Blast of Snow, Cold," *Kansas City Times*, March 21, 1983.

2. "Comet's Path to Give Close View," *The Examiner* (Independence, MS), May 7, 1983.

CHAPTER 4
OVERVIEW OF THE PROPHETIC MINISTRY

1. Wayne Grudem, *The Gift of Prophecy in the New Testament Today* (Eastbourne, England: Kingsway Publications, 1988).

2. Ibid., 14.

3. Ibid., 198–209.

CHAPTER 5
THE DIFFERENCE BETWEEN THE GIFT OF
PROPHECY AND BEING A PROPHET

1. Grudem, *The Gift of Prophecy*, 20–22.

CHAPTER 6
WOMEN OPERATING IN PROPHETIC MINISTRY

1. Catherine Kroeger, "The Neglected History of Women in the Early Church," *Christian History*, Winter 1980, 7.

2. Ibid., 14.

3. Ibid., 8.

4. Ibid., 6.

5. Ibid., 20–24.

6. Mark Twain, *Personal Recollections of Joan of Arc*, viewed at Fordham University, http://www.fordham.edu/halsall/basis/conte -joanofarc.html (accessed June 27, 2008).

Chapter 8
The Coming Great Revival

1. I highly recommend Iain H. Murray's book called *The Puritan Hope* (Carlisle, PA: Banner of Truth, 1979).

2. George E. Ladd, *The Presence of the Future* (Grand Rapids, MI: William B. Eerdmans, 1974). Ladd was for many years professor of New Testament at Fuller Theological Seminary in Pasadena, California.

Chapter 10
False Equations About Prophetic Giftings

1. David Edwin Harrell Jr., *All Things Are Possible* (Bloomington, IN: Indiana University Press, 1975), 38.

Chapter 11
God Offends the Mind to Reveal the Heart

1. "Samuel Johnson to George Berkeley, 3 October 1741," *The Great Awakening at Yale College*, ed. Stephen Nissenbaum (Belmont, CA: Wadsworth Publishing Co., 1972), 57–58.

2. Jonathan Edwards, *The Works of Jonathan Edwards,* vol. 1 (Carlisle, PA: The Banner of Truth, 1979), 62–70.

Chapter 18
The Prophetic Song of the Lord

1. John Piper, *Desiring God* (Portland, OR: Multnomah Press, 1986), 14.

CHAPTER 19
MANIFESTATIONS OF THE HOLY SPIRIT

1. Jonathan Edwards, *The Works of Jonathan Edwards*, vol. 2, "An Humble Attempt to Promote Explicit Agreement and Visible Union of God's People in Extraordinary Prayer, for the Revival of Religion and the Advancement of Christ's Kingdom on Earth," Christian Classics Ethereal Library, http://www.ccel.org/ccel/edwards/works2 .vii.ii.ii.html?bcb=0 (accessed July 9, 2008).

2. Jonathan Edwards, "A Treatise Concerning Religious Affections, in Three Parts," Christian Classics Ethereal Library, http://www .ccel.org/ccel/edwards/affections.txt (accessed July 9, 2008).

3. Jonathan Edwards, *The Works of Edwards*, "A Narrative of Surprising Conversions and the Great Awakening," (1736; reprint, Carlisle, PA: Banner of Truth, 1991), 37–38.

4. Ibid., 45.

5. Ibid., 547.

6. Ibid., 550.

7. John White, *When the Spirit Comes With Power* (Downers Grove, IL: InterVarsity Press, 1988), 70.

8. Francis MacNutt, *Overcome by the Spirit* (Old Tappan, NJ: Chosen Books, 1990), 35.

WHAT IS THE IHOP-KC MISSIONS BASE?

It is an international missions organization committed to prayer (intercession, worship, healing, prophesying, etc.), fasting (covering 365 days a year), and the Great Commission (proclaiming Jesus to all nations with power as the way to establish His justice in the earth). Our work includes equipping and sending missionaries as dedicated intercessors and anointed messengers working to see revival in the church and a great harvest among the lost.

IHOP-KC MISSIONS VISION STATEMENT

To call forth, train, and mobilize worshiping intercessors who operate in the forerunner spirit as End Time prophetic messengers. To establish a 24-hour-a-day prayer room in Kansas City as a perpetual solemn assembly that "keeps the sanctuary" by gathering corporately to fast and pray in the spirit of the Tabernacle of David as God's primary method of establishing justice (full revival unto the great harvest). To send out teams to plant Houses of Prayer in the nations after God grants a breakthrough of His power in Kansas City. The forerunner spirit operates in God's grace in context to the fasted lifestyle (Matt. 6) and prepares others to live in wholehearted love by proclaiming the beauty of Jesus as Bridegroom, King, and Judge.

VISITING IHOP ON WEEKENDS

Encounter God Services: Weekends at IHOP-KC—renewal, conviction, refreshing, impartation, and equipping are what we pray to be released in these weekend meetings at IHOP-KC. On Friday nights, Mike Bickle teaches on themes related to intimacy with God. On Saturday nights, he teaches on themes related to the End Times. On Sundays, join the IHOP-KC staff for worship and teaching. Childcare is available. One-day seminars are taught on Saturdays.

See www.IHOP.org for details, visitor's accommodations, and more information on joining our staff or attending our internships or Bible school.

Visit IHOP-KC at www.IHOP.org

The International House of Prayer Missions Base Web site has been designed for ease of browsing. We have incorporated the following branches of our community into one cohesive site:

- *IHOP*
- *Onething*
- *Children's Equipping Center*
- *Forerunner School of Ministry*
- *Forerunner Music Academy*
- *Joseph Company*
- *Events & Conferences*
- *Internships & Training Programs*
- *Omega Course*

It's all located at our easy-to-remember address: *www.IHOP.org*. Whether you are interested in visiting IHOP, receiving the Missions Base podcast, browsing the bookstore, watching live Webcasts, or enrolling in FSM's online eSchool, the Web site delivers the information you need and offers many opportunities to feed your heart. With login capabilities that expose you to even more comprehensive IHOP materials, we hope our site will become an ongoing resource for many years to come. Some of the Web site features include:

- *Podcasting*
- *MP3 Downloads*
- *Forums*
- *Free & Subscription-based Webcasts*
- *Sermon & Teaching Notes*
- *eSchool Distance Learning*
- *Internship Applications*
- *Prayer Room Blogs*
- *Online Bookstore*
- *And More!*

Visit us soon at www.IHOP.org!

IHOP INTERNSHIP PROGRAMS

IHOP offers a variety of three-month and six-month internships for all ages. Each internship has the same basic components, including prayer meeting attendance, classroom instruction, practical ministry experience, community fellowship and team building, conference participation, practical service, and Bible study. Internship attendees regularly participate in prayer meetings—between fifteen and twenty-five hours a week—in the prayer room, which can include worship team involvement, intercession for revival, personal devotional time, and study of the Word. Education and instruction cover a wide range of topics, including Christian foundations, prayer, worship, intimacy with God, the Bridal Paradigm of the Kingdom of God, the prophetic and healing ministries, serving the poor, and many others.

Intro to IHOP is a three-month internship for people of all ages, married or single, who want to learn and experience all that IHOP represents—prayer, worship, intimacy, etc.

Simeon Company is a three-month training program for people ages fifty and older who refuse to retire in their desire to radically serve Jesus through prayer, fasting, and worship.

Onething Internship is a six-month daytime internship for young adults between the ages of eighteen and twenty-five who are singers, musicians, intercessors, or evangelists. This program includes housing and eighteen meals a week.

Fire in the Night is a three-month nighttime internship for those between the ages of eighteen and thirty who want to worship and minister to the Lord through the night, midnight to 6:00 a.m. This program includes housing and eighteen meals a week.

Summer Teen Internship is a three-week summer program to equip teens in prophetic worship, intercession, and intimacy with Jesus. Housing is provided with IHOP-KC families.

Please visit *www.IHOP.org* for more information.

FORERUNNER SCHOOL OF MINISTRY

*Redefining Theological Education
Through Night and Day Prayer*

FOUR PROGRAMS:
- Apostolic Preaching Program
  Four-Year Program
- Worship and Prayer Program
  Four-Year Program
- Healing and Prophecy Program
  Two-Year Program
- Biblical Studies Program
  Four-Year Program

ONE ACADEMY:
- Forerunner Music Academy (see below)
  Three-Year Program

THREE INSTITUTES:
- Joseph Company
- Apostolic Missions Institute
- Evangelist Institute

CTEE:
- eSchool – offering access to
  Video/Audio/Class Notes

FORERUNNER MUSIC ACADEMY (FMA)

FMA is a full-time music school that trains musicians and singers to play skillfully and to operate in the prophetic anointing. FMA offers a comprehensive course of high-quality musical training in the context of IHOP's night-and-day prayer and worship. King David understood that prophetic music and songs would release the power of God. He paid 4,000 full-time musicians and hundreds of prophetic singers to gaze night and day upon God as they sang the prayers of Zion. This was their primary occupation in life. They were employed in the Tabernacle of David, which combined worship with intercession that never ceased as it continued 24/7.

CONTACT US:
12444 Grandview Road
Grandview, Missouri 64030
Phone: 816.763.0243
Fax: 816.763.0439
E-mail: FSM@ihop.org
www.IHOP.org

OTHER RESOURCES BY MIKE BICKLE

AFTER GOD'S OWN HEART

This book gives in-depth insight with many practical examples of how to sustain a life of intimacy with God. King David's relationship with God is used as a model of how we can live a radical lifestyle filled with confidence before God while acknowledging our profound weakness.

THE SEVEN LONGINGS OF THE HUMAN HEART

God has placed deep longings in the heart of every human being. We all long for beauty, for greatness, for fascination, for intimacy. We all long to be enjoyed, to be whole-hearted, to make a lasting impact. Only God can fulfill the longings He has given us. When we realize our longings are godly and God wants to fulfill them, we find freedom and joy.

THE REWARDS OF FASTING

Fasting is a gift from God that goes way beyond not eating. Jesus promised we would be rewarded for fasting. Done in the right spirit, fasting increases our receptivity to God's voice and His Word and allows us to encounter God more deeply than we otherwise would. This book explores all the rewards and delights that come to those who fast.

THE PLEASURES OF LOVING GOD

This book invites you on a most unique treasure hunt, a journey of discovery into intimacy with a Bridegroom God that loves, even likes, you and wants your friendship. Dimensions of the forerunner ministry and the House of Prayer are also examined.

PASSION FOR JESUS

This is a book about the powerful, concrete connection between knowing the truth about how God feels about you as the way to experience passion for Him. When the Holy Spirit wants to awaken love in you for Jesus, He reveals Jesus's affection to you.

ENCOUNTERING JESUS AUDIO SERIES

"A Prophetic History & Perspectives About the End Times." Over the last twenty years, Mike Bickle has taken time to share bits and pieces of this prophetic history but never as comprehensively as he did in these twelve one-hour sessions! These experiences explain the prophetic history of this ministry in Kansas City as well as establish convictions about the generation that the Lord returns. Although Scripture is our highest standard and guardian of truth, on occasion, the Lord also releases prophetic experiences to encourage our understanding and perseverance.

SONG OF SOLOMON AUDIO SERIES

Mike's completely revised and updated course on Song of Songs, this is his most comprehensive and powerful presentation on this glorious book to date. The CD version includes the Study Guide in PDF format.

STUDIES IN JOEL AUDIO SERIES

As we approach the great and terrible day of the Lord, we will be facing a flood of horrors far greater than in the days of Noah. In his brilliant verse-by-verse teachings from the book of Joel, Mike blows the trumpet and sounds the alarm, offering us a road map of the End Times.

RESOURCES FROM FORERUNNER MUSIC

ALWAYS ON HIS MIND — Misty Edwards

"Diving deep into intercession, into the Word, into the passionate heart of God." From IHOP-KC, *Always on His Mind* is a live recording that captures Misty Edwards and her team leading worship, intercession, and songs born out of prayer.

CONSTANT — IHOP-KC

Constant is an album that is steady and lyrically inspiring! This collection of songs is thematic of the faithfulness of God. His greatness and our great need for Him are sustained throughout. All the music on this album was written and performed by the International House of Prayer worship leaders.

MERCHANT BAND — Merchant Band

With sounds of Brit pop meets American rock, Merchant Band's self-titled debut album has woven a modern sound with the IHOP messages of intimacy and urgency. Packed with original material that is both fresh and powerful.

ETERNITY — Misty Edwards

This best-selling CD captures the heart of the extravagant worshiper. Misty Edwards is one of the International House of Prayer's most beloved worship leaders. Her unique gifting draws your heart before the Lord, our Majesty, into a deep realm of intimacy with Him.

LIMITED EDITION — IHOP-KC
Connect to the Prayer Room Through Limited Edition

Through IHOP's *Limited Edition* CD subscription club, Forerunner Music now offers you an ongoing glimpse into the International House of Prayer's prayer meetings. We record the worship and intercession that goes on night and day at IHOP. Then we take the best recordings from a two-month period, compile them, and make them available to you. Join IHOP's worship leaders and prayer leaders as they keep the prayer fire burning 24/7.

As the name suggests, these CDs are "limited editions," meaning once we've sold out, no more are available. And the CDs are only available to subscribers. Join the *Limited Edition* CD club, and every other month you will receive the latest CD, as well as other news from the prayer room and regular email updates.

Each *Limited Edition* CD is packed with live worship and prayer. You will find your heart connecting to Scripture and with IHOP's current prayer burdens. We invite you to join us as we seek after the fullness of God. Enter into fiery, passionate intercession with recordings from our corporate intercession sets or sit at the Lord's feet through a Worship With the Word or Devotional set recording. Our desire is that the *Limited Edition* CDs will equip and bless you as you draw nearer to the One you love.

For more information about resources from Mike Bickle and the International House of Prayer or for a free catalog, please call 1-800-552-2449 from 8:30 am–5:30 pm Monday–Friday. Also, visit our Web site and Web store at www.IHOP.org.